Jane
Austen's
Cults and
Cultures

Jane Austen's Cults and Cultures

CLAUDIA L. JOHNSON

THE UNIVERSITY OF CHICAGO PRESS *Chicago & London*

Claudia L. Johnson is the Murray Professor of English Literature at Princeton University. She is the author or editor of several books, including Jane Austen: Women, Politics, and the Novel *and* Equivocal Beings: Politics, Gender, and Sentimentality in the 1790s, *both published by the University of Chicago Press.*

The University of Chicago Press, Chicago 60637
The University of Chicago Press, Ltd., London
© 2012 by The University of Chicago
All rights reserved. Published 2012.
Printed in the United States of America

21 20 19 18 17 16 15 14 13 12   1 2 3 4 5

ISBN-13: 978-0-226-40203-1 (cloth)
ISBN-10: 0-226-40203-7 (cloth)

Library of Congress Cataloging-in-Publication Data
Johnson, Claudia L.
Jane Austen's cults and cultures / Claudia L. Johnson.
pages : illustrations ; cm
Includes bibliographical references and index.
ISBN-13: 978-0-226-40203-1 (cloth: alkaline paper)
ISBN-10: 0-226-40203-7 (cloth: alkaline paper)
1. Austen, Jane, 1775–1817. 2. Austen, Jane, 1775–1817—
Appreciation. 3. Women authors, English—19th century.
I. Title.
PR4036.J57 2012
823'.7—dc23

2011046240

♾ This paper meets the requirements of ANSI/NISO
Z39.48-1992 (Permanence of Paper).

Contents

Figures

Abbreviations

The following abbreviations have been used in the text and notes. All references to Austen's writings are based on the nine-volume Cambridge edition of the *Works of Jane Austen* (Cambridge: Cambridge University Press, 2005).

BN   "Biographical Notice of the Author," Henry Austen, in *A Memoir of Jane Austen: And Other Family Recollections*, ed. Kathryn Sutherland (Oxford: Oxford University Press, 2002)

CH1   *Jane Austen: The Critical Heritage*, vol. 1, 1811–1870, ed. B. C. Southam (London: Routledge, 1979)

CH2   *Jane Austen: The Critical Heritage*, vol. 2, 1870–1940, ed. B. C. Southam (London: Routledge and Kegan Paul, 1987)

DC   *Debits and Credits*, Rudyard Kipling (Garden City, NY: Doubleday, Page, 1926)

E   *Emma*

J   *Juvenilia*

JAFP   *Jane Austen: Facts and Problems*, R. W. Chapman (Oxford: Clarendon Press, 1948)

L   *Jane Austen's Letters*, ed. Deirdre Le Faye (Oxford: Oxford University Press, 1995)

Letters 1   *Letters of Jane Austen*, vol. 1, ed. Lord Brabourne (London: Richard Bentley and Son, 1884)

Letters 2   *Letters of Jane Austen*, vol. 2, ed. Lord Brabourne (London: Richard Bentley and Son, 1884)

Memoir   *A Memoir of Jane Austen: And Other Family Recollections*, James Edward Austen-Leigh, ed. Kathryn Sutherland (Oxford: Oxford University Press, 2002)

MP   *Mansfield Park*

NA   *Northanger Abbey*

QF   *Queer Folk: Seven Stories*, Edward Hugessen Knatchbull-Hugessen [Lord Brabourne], 4th ed. (London: Macmillan, 1874), v

P   *Persuasion*

PP   *Pride and Prejudice*

PS   *The Portrait of a Scholar and Other Essays Written in Macedonia, 1916–1918*, R. W. Chapman (London: Oxford University Press, 1920)

RF   Reginald Farrer, "Jane Austen, *ob*. July 18, 1817," *Quarterly Review* 452 (July 1917): 1–30

RH   "Regulated Hatred: An Aspect of the Work of Jane Austen," D. W. Harding, in *Regulated Hatred and Other Essays on Jane Austen*, ed. Monica Lawlor (London: Athlone Press, 1998), 5–26

SS   *Sense and Sensibility*

VW   *The Void of War: Letters from Three Fronts*, Reginald Farrer (Boston: Houghton Mifflin, 1918)

Acknowledgments

Over the many years I have taken to complete this book, I have accumulated a vast list of people and institutions to thank for their encouragement, their enthusiasm, and their support. Despite my nagging fear that I might inadvertently miss someone, it is a pleasure to recollect the names of those whose conversation has been so helpful. But recollection brings sorrow as well, because some very important people have passed away. I will never be able to tell Joan Pawelski, Brian C. Southam, Brian Stewart, and Henry Rice how grateful I am for their company and their research.

I could not have sustained work on this book without the assistance of the Guggenheim Foundation, the National Endowment for the Humanities, the Burke-Austen Scholar-in-Residence Program at Goucher College, and Princeton University, all of which provided me with resources and time for research and writing.

Tom Carpenter was marvelously generous in showing me the archives of Jane Austen's House Museum at Chawton, and Louise West and Isabel Snowden patiently helped me with images and permissions. John Hardacre, Jo Bartholomew, Gill Rushton, and John Crook of Winchester Cathedral abetted my projects, as did the staff of the Hampshire Record Office. Nancy Magnuson provided me with valuable insights into the making of Henry and Alberta Hirschheimer Burke's extraordinary collection of Austen material at Goucher College's Julia Rogers Library. Anne Rice, Robin Roberts, and Brian Rice proved exhaustless repositories of information about Austen family history, and Allan Soedring supplied me with important images.

As an editor, Alan Thomas of the University of Chicago Press has both inspired and steadied me with his wisdom about books and their making, and it has been joy to share my career with him. My copyeditor, Kathy Swain, has preserved me from error and infelicity, as have Elizabeth Melly and (especially) Jacqueline Shin, both of Princeton University, who assisted me in the final stages of manuscript preparation.

I have presented parts of this book as lectures over the years, and countless folks—scholars and "common readers" (not that there is anything common about dedicated readers of Jane Austen)—have challenged and spurred me. The Jane Austen Society of North America—especially the regional chapters in Chicago and eastern Pennsylvania—provided me with exemplary Austenian companionship. But I am most indebted to the people who have read and commented on the manuscript in progress and shaken me up with their suggestions. In addition to the readers for the University of Chicago Press, Marilyn Butler, Margaret A. Doody, Sophie Gee, Susan Greenfield, U. C. Knoepflmacher, Jessica Richard, Susan Wolfson, Michael Wood, and my dear sister, Leslie A. Johnson, each gave me—and often repeatedly—the benefit of their searching and truly collegial support when I needed it the most. Sarah M. Anderson has fostered this study since its inception with the subtlety and precision of a true scholar. Clara Tuite has been the ideal Austenian interlocutor, and without the searing intelligence of Jeff Nunokawa's and Emily Bartels's conversation, this work and my life would be poor things.

Introduction
Jane Austen's Afterlives

his book is about Jane Austen's afterlives, and so I begin it with a ghost story. The setting could not have been
less spooky. It was not a dark and stormy night. It was
a brilliant summer morning, and the sun was gleaming
through the leaded gothic windows in my office at Princeton University. At the time, quite a while ago now, I was
working on the text of *Mansfield Park*, to be published later as a Norton
Critical Edition. The particular species of intensely close—the benighted
have said intensely dull—scholarship in which I was engaging was textual criticism. For the benefit of the uninitiated, this branch of philology is concerned with the identification and removal or containment of
errors from manuscripts or (in my case) printed texts, with the object
of producing an edited text that the editor believes comes as close as
possible to a lost or purely notional original that either existed or was
intended to exist in the past.

There are texts for which the stakes of this work are conspicuously
high—the Bible, for instance—and the tasks immeasurably complex:
where texts have come down to us in scores of versions, copied by different hands in different places, each introducing variants and errors, and
where the relation of each to some notional "original" is difficult to determine. Closer to home, there is the ever-looming example of Shakespeare,
a figure repeatedly invoked from Macaulay on during the nineteenth century, and in the early twentieth century by scholars such as A. C. Bradley
and Caroline Spurgeon, who worshipped at the altars of Austen as well
as the Bard. Shakespeare's plays, like Austen's six major novels (excepting
the canceled chapter of *Persuasion*), come to us solely through printed
editions. We have only to consider a couple of famous cruxes—does
Hamlet lament this too too *sallied* flesh, *sullied* flesh, or *solid* flesh? does
Othello compare himself to an *Indian* or to a *Judean* who has thrown

away a precious pearl?—in order to realize how the painstaking collation and adjudication of witnesses to Shakespeare's plays present us with momentous questions, and thus to appreciate how rewarding—if ultimately impossible—the work of a textual scholar can be.

Shakespeare and Austen are the preeminent instances in the English literary tradition of beloved but fundamentally absent authors about whom quite little is actually known, and the nonexistence of manuscripts in their own hands makes them seem distinctively more remote. In the case of Austen's major novels, textual matters, though very important, are at once simpler and more frustrating. The stakes must be ratcheted down to the point of virtual evanescence, which, as we shall see, is itself significant. Once again, with only printed editions to consult, and very few at that, much of what we do is correct typesetters' errors (inverted letters, missing quotation marks, and the like). Two of the six novels, however, went into second editions over which Austen had some oversight, and these do give us something substantive to do. *Sense and Sensibility* is one of these. The other is *Mansfield Park*, published by Thomas Egerton in 1814 and by John Murray in 1816.

A simple-seeming but a profoundly difficult, superbly self-conscious writer, Austen is one whom generations of readers have pored over closely and repeatedly, squeezing nuances out of sentences we have come to regard as chiseled. You would think a collation of two printed editions prepared under her eyes might give us intimate and infinitely rewarding access to how she revised and perfected her work. But this turns out not to be the case. Austen playfully (and, now, famously) described herself as a miniaturist working on a "little bit (two Inches wide) of Ivory . . . with a fine Brush" (*L*, 323, 16 December 1816),[1] which perhaps might imply a passion for minute detail, but by comparing these two editions we can fairly deduce that she was not a compulsive reviser, fretting over every particle, every word, every line, in the manner of (say) Henry James. Her letters show that she corrected proofs and cared about accuracy and the clear and correct assignment of dialogue, but she also seems to have known when her work was done, forbearing stylistic revisions. Accordingly, most of the changes between the two editions of *Mansfield Park* are localized and pointed. Between the publication of the first and second editions, she clearly consulted with her sailor brothers about nautical terms confined to a single passage, changing phrases such as *just astern of* to *close to*; or *alert*, a term about naval readiness, to *sharp*, for example.

This kind of accuracy was worth revising considerably to attain. But as for the other 477 pages, her revisions are sparing, and the differences discovered on collating the two texts—particularly with respect to punctuation—may well be the work of editors or, just as likely, by typesetters, rather than Austen.[2] In any case, Austen's riff on Scott's *Marmion*—

> I do not write for such dull Elves
> As have not a great deal of Ingenuity themselves

—is sometimes adduced in reference to weighty matters of interpretative practice, particularly with respect to her notoriously dangerous irony, and Austen has on this account been imagined to have divided her audience into two groups, the dull and the ingenious, with the latter alone being able to grasp her subtlety. But Austen's remark actually refers to "Typical errors" (i.e., errors made by typesetters), and it suggests that she was confident that clever readers would not be confounded or impeded by them (*L*, 202, 29 January 1813).[3]

So: there I sat, that fateful summer morning in my office, wrapped in silent concentration, pondering small discrepancies between the two editions of *Mansfield Park*, trying to tell the difference between changes so subtle that they are virtually invisible on the one hand, and changes that might not really be there at all, that might be entirely chimerical or unintended on the other. One case—the second sentence of the eighth chapter—seemed particularly vexing, a difference in comma placement, in the first edition *before* the adverb "especially" and in the second edition *after* the adverb "especially":

> Mr. Rushworth arrived, escorting his mother, who came to be civil, and to shew her civility, especially in urging the execution of the plan to visit Sotherton. . . . 1814

> Mr. Rushworth arrived, escorting his mother, who came to be civil, and to shew her civility especially, in urging the execution of the plan to visit Sotherton. . . . 1816

The distinction here is slight, but substantive. In the first case *especially* modifies the verb *urge* (Mrs. Rushworth intends to show her civility in a number of ways, the most demonstrative of which is her "urging" the visit to Sotherton as the acme of civility). In the second case the adverb *especially* modifies the verb *show* (Mrs. Rushworth is making a special performance of her civility, and the stress is on her parade of good manners, not on the invitation).

Clearly, though these two readings are distinct, the difference is subtle and at times elusive. Struck by the minuteness of the stakes, I could well imagine people not seeing it or not caring one way or the other. But it was my job to make a decision as to which text to follow and which to relegate to an explanatory footnote, and so I had to keep thinking. For much of the twentieth century, the established practice of textual scholarship derived from the principle that the last edition published during the author's lifetime should be taken as a copy text, provided that the author was involved in its preparation. Austen was demonstrably involved in preparing *Mansfield Park* for a second edition, so I was obliged to wonder whether she, in her wondrous refinement, moved the comma in the second edition in order to produce this nuance. Or, might an editor or typesetter of the second edition have moved the comma purposefully in order to "improve" the punctuation of the 1814 edition? Or, could the typesetter of the second edition have changed the position of the comma by accident, while he was distracted, perhaps by his lunch? Is there any justification for assuming that the first edition is "closer" to Austen's intention, as Kathryn Sutherland has claimed, and that the second represents the imposition of correctness and propriety? Could the comma in both cases be the work of the typesetter to begin with and so not Jane Austen's? Again and again, I read the two sentences aloud quietly to myself to settle this question until, finally, under these inauspiciously pedantic circumstances, a startling thing happened: I heard Jane Austen breathe.

As I read and reread those passages, I heard a clear intake of breath, and I reeled around in my chair to see if anyone had quietly slipped into my office. The respiration, I realized immediately on discovering myself quite alone, seemed very important at that particular moment, for in older practice, still in force when Austen wrote, a comma did not so much indicate a separation of ideas or of syntactical elements within a sentence as it indicated a pause during which a reader was to breathe. Was I living momentarily in a novel by Ann Radcliffe, and did the sound proceed from some occult air duct connecting my office to a subterranean passage where a prisoner sighed? Or, had I inadvertently invoked Austen's ghost by murmuring some abracadabra constructed out of the charm of her own words, and was breath telling me where to place the comma?

Even though scholars and biographers often feel connected to their subjects, often sense them tugging at the other end, so to speak, I am sure that this story sounds a bit loony and certainly inconsistent with the cool rationality we associate with academic scholars or, for that matter, with Jane Austen. But most of the writers I will be examining here are not academics, and the Austen they adore has more to do with the world of wonder than with the world of reason. A review of literary commentary suggests that Austen's devotees are particularly inclined to see her ghost. Sheila Kaye-Smith—coauthor (with G. B. Stern) of *Talking of Jane Austen* (1943) and *More Talk of Jane Austen* (1950)—wrote about a ghostly encounter in an essay titled "Personal Appearance," an essay not about Austen's looks but rather about a spectral visit from her. Here, the translucent shape of Austen appears unbidden on the settee in Kaye-Smith's parlor—"Did she know," Kaye-Smith asks, "I was writing a book about her and so had come to help me, or even stop me?" The conversation Kaye-Smith and Austen proceed to have is underwhelming, tedious in the extreme. To be sure, Austen expresses her bewilderment at electric lamps and radio broadcasts. But for the most part, their conversation rehearses a few critical truisms that we don't really require a ghost to tell us: Austen tells us that she is afraid that *Northanger Abbey* is too out-of-date for modern readers, that no one other than herself would like Emma Woodhouse, and that Anne Elliot is almost too good for her. Kaye-Smith and Austen converse unremarkably about literary opinions, until Kaye-Smith reads aloud from a poem by Kipling, narrating "Jane's" entry into heaven and her marriage to one of her own characters, Captain Wentworth. "Who is this Mr. Kipling," Austen asks indignantly, "and by whose leave does he call me *Jane*?" Austen's agitation is so intense that her ghostly "manifestation" begins to tremble and blur, and when she learns that Kipling no longer walks this earth, she departs in a huff, no doubt to box his ears in heaven for taking liberties with her Christian name.[4]

Encounters with Austen's ghost are not merely the zany chatter of lady novelists. Men of science do the same. As late as 1917, Sir Francis Darwin—Charles Darwin's third son, and a distinguished botanist and member of the Royal Society (in short, no flibbertigibbet)—recommends the game of asking children and adults alike what questions they "would put to the ghost of Jane Austen," averring that he himself wishes to secure from her genetic information about the offspring of Elizabeth and

Darcy.[5] Likewise the English journalist Henry Woodd Nevinson—famed for such manful pursuits as his reportage of the Second Boer War, his exposés of slavery in Portuguese Angola, and his war correspondence from the western front of World War I—published what he titles "A Letter from a Ghost," purported to be "spiritually conveyed to [him]" during one of his stays in Bath. This ghost is more impish than Kaye-Smith's— much like the Jane Austen of her letters—but like Kaye-Smith's she is altogether ordinary in her posthumous remarks, archly commenting on the short, mannish haircuts and boyish figures women sported in 1926. What is most notable in Austen's letter is her affectionate description of Nevinson himself, who amused her by reading passages from the liberal weekly magazine the *Nation* to her, which riles up the bishop and the general sitting at her table. When they later scorn Nevinson as "some inky fellow," Austen writes, "Was not Walter Scott the same? And Maria Edgeworth? And for the matter of that, what else was I?"[6] You will notice that for Kaye-Smith and Nevinson (as for myself), the appearance of Austen's ghost seems to guarantee or supplement their own authority as writers.

To be sure, all of this is tongue in cheek, but the playfulness also hints at the genuinely phantasmal quality that has always been a feature of *Janeism*, which we may define as a self-consciously idolatrous enthusiasm for "Jane" Austen and every primary, secondary, tertiary (and so forth) detail relative to her. In 2009 Seth Grahame-Smith's *Pride and Prejudice and Zombies* was a best seller on three continents. It has generated prequels, sequels, graphic novel versions, and video and iPhone games and at present is scheduled for release as a major motion picture in 2013. The gag at the heart of this mash-up of Regency and zombie fiction is that Jane Austen—whether we take her gentle or prefer her subversive—is probably the last figure we would associate with zombies. Yet the last laugh must surely be ours. It is conceivably possible that Grahame-Smith was aware that Austen's *Northanger Abbey* ironized the gothic a long time before he did and thus in a way wrote a novel that, rather than violating her proprieties, actually followed in her footsteps. But he was almost certainly not aware that Austen's admirers have always felt her presence in a way that is more than a little out of this world. William Dean Howells readily affirms that Austen "has never yet died." Consoled by the "sympathetic irony or ironical sympathy" and the "smiling intelligence" of Austen's "haunting presence" at her grave site in Winchester

Cathedral, he and other "pilgrims" ask, "Why was she so persistently, so increasingly, so, next after Shakespeare, Shakespeareanly alive?"[7]

For many readers, the principal answer has been that she never properly died. Even in literary commentary where Austen does not explicitly figure as a ghost, she is often somehow ghostly, still alive or at least undead, and the effect can be unnerving. Constance Hill's influential 1902 book, *Jane Austen: Her Homes and Her Friends*, is a sustained effort to channel Austen by visiting the places and recollecting the people associated with her, with well-thumbed copies of Austen's novels, letters, and biography in hand. More than once, Hill fancies that she sees the "girlish forms" of Jane Austen and her sister, Cassandra, walking among the trees and flowers at Steventon or entering the ballroom at Basingstoke, perhaps much as Catherine and Heathcliff might be glimpsed roaming the moors.[8] At the outset of the twentieth century, Hampshire still felt haunted by Jane Austen, as if she never really departed. For Oscar Fay Adams, Austen's *characters* are as palpably alive as Austen is. In Bath, he writes, "The people of 'Persuasion' and 'Northanger Abbey' meet us at every turn," and "the novelist herself is just as constantly before us."[9] In claiming—fancifully to be sure, but also with some seriousness—to see not only Austen but also her characters in the twilight zone of Bath and Hampshire, Adams is first of all paying tribute to Austen's uncanny gift for creating a sense of the living presence of otherwise utterly insubstantial beings, a gift for creating character (raising spirits, if you will) that Macaulay found to be equaled only by Shakespeare. As Reginald Farrer put it, she and Shakespeare alone enjoy "their solitary and special supremacy by dint of a common capacity for intense vitalisation," a phrase that conjures the gothic laboratory of Frankenstein to mind (RF, 2).

As the following pages will show, the reason Janeites tend to see ghosts has at least as much to do with the nature and practice of Janeism itself as it does with "Jane" herself. In a volume titled *A Name to Conjure With* (1953), G. B. Stern observes that "to be a Janeite is really a form of possession, with a profound contentment in being thus possessed."[10] The contentment Stern describes may call E. M Forster's "Austenites" to mind—readers with a "fatuous expression, and airs of personal immunity" who take up Austen's novels with "the mouth open and the mind closed." Forster's Austenites (among whom he freely if somewhat inaccurately includes himself) are what he describes as "regular churchgoers," however, and as such they do not really pay any attention to what is being said—mannerly high church folks, we infer, who accept the creed without making a fuss about it.[11] But Stern ups the ante. For her, Janeites are more maniacal: they are taken over by what they worship with a zealous intensity. They can spot an impostor Janeite with something more than rational deduction:

> *By the pricking of my toes,*
> I knows![12]

she writes, speculating that these lines derive from a Grimm's fairy tale. More likely, the source for these lines is the second witch in Shakespeare's *Macbeth*, who (hearing Macbeth approach) says:

> *By the pricking of my thumbs,*
> *Something wicked this way comes.* (*Macbeth* 4.1. 45–46)

Stern's buried allusion to *Macbeth* nicely conveys the demonic quality of Janeites. They are not ordinary readers, but readers possessed, as Stern puts it, readers uncannily sensitive to Austen and to her faithful, readers who know how to conjure with Austen's name, to harken back to the title of G. B. Stern's volume, *a name to conjure with*.

The particular name—Janeite—entered the English vocabulary via George Saintsbury in 1894. But an extraordinary zeal for Austen clearly predates this. Yes: even as early as the 1850s, pilgrims (many of whom were American) would solemnly visit Austen's grave at Winchester and, as Deirdre Le Faye puts it, puzzle the cathedral verger, who asked one visitor: "Pray, sir, can you tell me whether there was anything particular about that lady; so many people want to know where she was buried?"[13] But Janeism did not coalesce as an identifiable practice until after the publication of J. E. Austen-Leigh's *A Memoir of Jane Austen* in 1870, which spurred a more extensive interest in Austen, the republication of her works, and the development of a literary marketplace for her that has operated steadily ever since. By the end of the nineteenth century, Janeites were a discernible and decidedly (though not exclusively) masculine readership of publishers, professors, novelists, and literati such as Montague Summers, A. C. Bradley, Walter Raleigh, R. W. Chapman, and E. M. Forster, to name only a few. At the Royal Society of Literature in particular, Austen's novels were celebrated with an enthusiasm that would seem crazy if it were enacted in classrooms or conferences today. These Janeites flaunted their devotion: Austen was their *dear* Jane, their *matchless* Jane, and they are her *cult,* her *sect,* her *little company (fit though few),* her *tribe* of adorers who discuss and rediscuss the *miracle* of her work in extravagant, patently hyperbolic terms. As Montague Summers (incidentally, an expert on demonology and vampires) put it in a 1917 address to the Royal Society of Literature, "To-day the world is divided between the elect and the profane—those who admire Jane Austen, and those (one shudders to speak the phrase)—who do not."[14] Our modern term *fans* derives from the pejorative term *fanatic,* and Janeites dare the world to mock them for their adoration. The very term *Janeitism*—a rabid, quasi-religion of "Jane"—calls to mind seventeenth-century English Protestant sects, such as Adamites, Ranters, and Diggers, "enthusiasts" all, where the word *enthusiasm* means not, as it does today, a brisk interest, but rather a belief in private revelation, a belief that the faithful have a direct, privileged, personally felt rather than dispassionately reasoned or institutionally mediated relation to the Almighty, in this particular case (as Janeites freely call her), to "the *Divine* Jane."

By proud admission, then, Janeites are possessed of and inspired by a divine madness. To be sure, their excess is in part a subtle joke about the apparent incongruity between the extravagance of their devotion and the slenderness of its object, a form of play, perhaps even a performance of overvaluation that among other things is a disguised form of self-love: the world at large cannot see what's there in Austen, but *we* can! Even granting such self-parody, however, Janeite zeal is quite genuine. Before Austen was the darling of mass culture, being a Janeite was a badge proclaiming the privilege of election, a membership in the ultimate high-status minority culture. And even now, when Austen is touted everywhere, many Janeites still manage to assert their superiority to market-driven readers or (nowadays) viewers and—perhaps like *Clueless*'s Cher (Emma), who scorns Amber's (Mrs. Elton's) reeking, "designer-imposter perfume"—proclaim the distinction of their sensitivity to the supposedly Austenian gospel of less-is-more. In either case, Janeites know they look silly in the eyes of the world, and they feel frank superiority over the generality of folks who are blind to Austen's fabulousness, who cannot see what the fuss is about. To be a Janeite—more so than would be the case with devotees of any other literary figure—is precisely to be able (by virtue of a special, privileged relation to the divine Jane) to see what is invisible to others. Virginia Woolf phrased this best in 1923 when she remarked that of all great writers, Jane Austen was the "most difficult to catch in the act of greatness"[15]—so difficult as to be impossible for many, for that greatness has been as imperceptible to some as the difference in meaning produced by comma placement, between *to shew especially* or *to urge especially*, the impasse I was at when Austen literally in-spired me, with her breath. In some ways, then, being a Janeite is already in some sense to see a ghost, to commune with Austen's invisible but powerful legacy, whether that legacy takes the ghostly form of the author or the words in the novels she has bequeathed to us.

As an official organization, the Jane Austen Society was formed far later than groups devoted to the enjoyment of other major authors: in England, the Jane Austen Society (JAS) was founded in 1940, and the Jane Austen Society of North America (JASNA) was launched in 1979. But as we have seen, ever since Austen's death, adorers of Jane Austen have historically made up a prominent and very distinguished, if uncollected, body of readers, including scholars, scientists, and authors. Since World War II, the same time when she becomes a major part of curricula in English Departments, the public adoration of Jane Austen, along with her vigorous marketing in the form of print, television, and motion pictures, has been feminized, and Janeites are likelier to be seen as batty ladies than as supremely discerning connoisseurs. Writing on the cusp of this change, G. B. Stern writes that her niece, a girl of seventeen and a half, "really did imagine that Jane Austen was only read by maiden aunts in drawing rooms, or by cissy men," and she is thus perplexed to learn that even her manful beau, a distinguished soldier in his mid-30s, is "bats" on Austen and always "took a couple of Janes with him when he went away,—even to the Burmese jungle in the war."[16] But despite the magnitude of this gender shift for the general public, Janeites on both sides of the gender divide share a presumption of—or is it an aspiration to?—intimacy. Jane, she is called, as if she were the *familiar*, the friend, the intimate of those who adore her. In his "Biographical Notice" prefixed to *Northanger Abbey* and *Persuasion*, Henry Austen wrote of his sister, "No one could be often in her company without feeling a strong desire of obtaining her friendship, and cherishing a hope of having obtained it" (BN, 140).[17] This "strong desire" has produced in Janeites a tendency to collapse distance. Sometimes this distance is personal, as in the familiarity of first-naming her. At other times, the collapse of distance is historical. Calling up Austen's ghost is one instance of this. But just as frequently, Janeites themselves are the time travelers, taking themselves back into Austen's world by staging Regency costume balls, devising quizzes drawn from minutiae in Austen's novels, knitting Regency reticules, preparing banquets out of late-eighteenth- and early nineteenth-century cookbooks, discussing how a character from one novel might converse with a character from another, and setting tables according to the protocols of Austen's time, all with a distinctive combination of gaiety, fervor, and exactitude. Most of these activities can seem trivial, unprofessional, and even chastening to academic scholars—how mortifying to encounter one's own earth-shattering essay on Austen printed alongside a recipe for white soup, as somehow equivalent exercises—but they also produce real information and knowledge along with a sort pleasure that Clara Tuite has brilliantly described as "period euphoria."[18] To determine how Mrs. Bennet would set her table for the dinner she would host for her two new, very rich sons-in-law at the end of *Pride and Prejudice*, in what order guests would enter or leave a room, and where they would sit at the table is to understand the class structure of early nineteenth-century England and to recognize how it was supported by the rituals of daily life, even if it also carries with it the fantasy of being an invisible guest.

To recur to my ghostly frame of reference, we can say that Janeism in its past as well as its current forms allows us to foreclose the gap between Austen's time and our own, between the dead and the living, the fictional and the real, and to occupy Austen's novels as they are—not were—lived, in an eternal present, where they commune with her familiarly. Janeites commune with their divine Jane and her characters in a sort of suprahistorical time warp where past and present get blurred. And if JASNA's passion for costume balls seems trivial in the eyes of the nonelect, what could seem more so than my labors over comma placement that morning in my office, when Jane Austen seemed to me to inhale? As Stephen Greenblatt (inspired by Hamlet) has so memorably put it, "It is the role of the scholar to speak to the dead and to make the dead speak."[19] The textual scholar in particular does nothing if not attempt to channel an author's hand and voice, preparing a text she would regard as correct, and, as is the case with fans, that labor is also a matter of intense intimacy and devotion.

❦ As the foregoing makes abundantly clear, Jane Austen is not and has never been any old great author, whom we might discuss more or less rationally, but a fabulous figure and the paragon of popular and elite audiences alike. Certainly no other author—perhaps not even Shakespeare himself, who, despite his preeminence, is no longer popularly accessible—has inspired such widespread and intense devotion that is itself worthy of study. It was Lionel Trilling, in his 1957 essay, "*Emma* and the Legend of Jane Austen," who first remarked, "It is possible to say of Jane Austen, as perhaps we can say of no other writer, that the opinions which are held of her work are almost as interesting, and almost as important to think about, as the work itself." Trilling half retracts this already qualified claim ("*almost* as interesting . . . *almost* as important"), immediately adding that interest in such opinions is, strictly speaking, "illegitimate" for readers, who ought to approach texts without any "preconceptions" about the author. But Trilling also acknowledges that it is impossible to separate Austen from the "aura" of her compelling "legend":

> Her very name is a charged one. The homely quaintness of the Christian name, the cool elegance of the surname, seem inevitably to force upon us the awareness of her sex, her celibacy, and her social class. "Charlotte Brontë" rumbles like thunder and drowns out any such special considerations. But "Jane Austen" can by now scarcely fail to imply femininity, and, at that, femininity of a particular kind and in a particular social setting. It dismays many new readers that certain of her admirers call her Jane, others Miss Austen. Either appellation suggests an unusual, and questionable, relation with this writer, a relation that does not consort with the literary emotions we respect. The new reader perceives from the first that he is not to be permitted to proceed in simple literary innocence. Jane Austen is to be for him not only a writer but an issue. There are those who love her; there are those—no doubt they are fewer but they are no less passionate—who detest her; and the new reader understands that he is being solicited to a fierce partisanship, that he is required to make no mere literary judgment but a decision about his own character and personality, and about his relation to society and all of life.[20]

If Trilling partially disapproves of meditating on an author's legend, in the present case his prose positively revels in describing literary emotions "we" don't "respect"—consider, for example, the sonorous riff on Brontë's thunderous and Austen's cool elegance; the telling alliteration of sex, celibacy, and social class; the attic clarity of the final, long sentence, where a reader's literary judgment on this matter is said to take on the urgency and magnitude of all of life itself—and no doubt even more urgently so if that reader is a university professor whose name is "Lionel Trilling." In some ways, of course, Trilling is wrong. He confidently avers that Austen "by now can scarcely fail to imply femininity"—an odd and oddly evasive formulation, which nevertheless implies a consensus of which he approves—when no less insightful a reader as Reginald Farrer proudly professed misogyny and simply did not consider Austen really to be a woman in the first place, and certainly not a feminine one. Likewise, Austen's class placement, which Trilling suggests we all unproblematically intuit from her now legendary name alone, has actually always been a vexed question.

Still, Trilling is right to insist that the "literary emotions" aroused by the Austen legend are not purely personal and temperamental, but are rather responses to the texts themselves, and thus they repay examination, and his magnificent essay does just this. By calling the world of *Emma* an "idyll," gently but pervasively ordered, yet flexible enough to accommodate positive social change slowly and surely, he is describing the appeal Austen and her world had for actual and latter-day Victorians, who were spellbound by its prelapsarian simplicity and repose, by its wondrous sufficiency to its own forms and rituals. But of course Trilling is inevitably also describing the appeal of this Austenian idyll for himself, a twentieth-century Jewish American intellectual who, though typifying the same sort of "modern" restlessness and detachment that Emma does, could also imagine his own assimilation into this ideal of intelligence and authority.

In this book, I shall explore, with none of Trilling's (clearly half-hearted) apologies, how various "legends"—and the plural is important, for there is no single "Jane Austen"—came about, to ponder how Jane Austen became "Jane Austen," the deathlessly divine Austen, venerated with a peculiar intensity. In doing so, my book joins a number of studies historicizing the canonization of authors, particularly Shakespeare, most prominently among them Jonathan Bate's *Shakespearean Constitutions* (1989), Gary Taylor's *Reinventing Shakespeare: A Cultural History from the Restoration to the Present* (1989), and Michael Dobson's *The Making of the National Poet: Shakespeare, Adaptation and Authorship, 1660–1769* (1992), all of which consider Shakespeare's stature not as a given but as a historical process unfolding through many vicissitudes and carrying different cultural meanings over time. Perhaps oddly, given Trilling's vivid description of the conspicuousness and the importance of the Austen legend in 1957, Austenian scholars were not so quick to historicize her reception, despite the two monumental *Critical Heritage* volumes edited by B. C. Southam (1979, 1987) and David Gilson's massive *A Bibliography of Jane Austen* (1982), which paved the way. When I first published essays on Austen's readerships and reception in 1996 and 1997 (dry runs for this book), Victorian and early to mid-twentieth-century commentary held little interest, while the amateur Janeites of today were downright discomfiting: as with Trilling before us, we were nonplused by obviously well-read and sometimes even quite erudite readers gaga for Jane Austen, but whose protocols of reading and converse differed radically from our own, particularly with respect to authorial veneration.[21] That would not be for long, however, for Austen soon became an important case study of sorts for scholars increasingly interested in how literature and criticism alike have been institutionalized,[22] and in how Austen in particular has been re-created or transmitted in texts, biographies, and movies, or how her reputation has grown.[23]

Jane Austen's Cults and Cultures is everywhere in dialogue with all these studies, but it sets its distinctive course from them as well. I begin this project by exploring the most important monuments to and portraits of Jane Austen, in some ways as crucial as the novels in forming her legends. By their very nature, these artifacts stage the peculiar problem of an author who is apparently invisible and disembodied and yet whose image is inseparable from those of her characters and from the seemingly small fictional worlds she creates. The subsequent chronologically organized chapters focus on four critical phases in the history of Austen's reception—from the Victorian period, through World War I, World War II, to the establishment of Jane Austen's House Museum, formally opened to the public in 1949. My aim is not so much to trace Jane Austen's reputation as it is to ponder what loving her has meant to readers from the nineteenth century to the present, charting how the contingencies of their historical moments mingle productively with their literary appreciations, so that Austen in some sense both produces them—arousing specific enjoyments, consolations, and pleasures in her acolytes—while they in turn are also producing her for us, enabling us to read through their eyes and see in Austen's novels properties and possibilities we rarely if ever suspected were there.

By respecting the intelligence and the dignity of their commentary on Austen, even when—indeed precisely when—it seems vacuous, uselessly antique, and undisciplined to us, we are able to turn back to the novels themselves and to find them reenriched by their own literary history. How might the preoccupation of Victorian readers with Austen's "charm" and "magic," for example—words we pass over as drivel—say something about the enchantment produced by Austen's novels in particular, and the realistic novel in general, both of which seem to us so foundationally committed to the probable? How might the radically disenchanted Janeite readers of World War I, who considered Austen masculine and one of their own, invite us to see again the consolatory potential of designification in her novels, which they love precisely because they seem to be about nothing at all; or the bombarded readers of World War II identify with feminine vulnerability and heroic endurance; or the collection of Austenian relics for Jane Austen's House Museum read back to the novels' representation of the equivocal power of things? As we shall see, "Jane Austen" has mobilized powerful and contradictory ideas and feelings about taste, history, class, nationality, desire, manners, intimacy, language, and the everyday for very diverse readerships, and their complex histories of emotional, intellectual, and imaginative faith in Austen can inspire us to reread Austen in surprising and stunning ways.

By the way, I decided to print the comma after *especially*. This placement is just too odd, too distinctive, too ineffably good to be anyone's but Jane Austen's.[24]

Jane
Austen's
Body

I
n the late 1920s and early 1930s, when the aisles of Winchester
Cathedral were dug up to install pipes and cables, laborers had
to remove and rebury the human remains that had long rested
beneath—except, one workman remembered, for Jane Austen,
whom they managed to move gently to one side. This workman,
who related the story in 1999 when he was eighty-six, was, if
not the last person to have touched Jane Austen, then the last to bear
witness to what is (in the manner of all things Austenian perhaps) the
quiet miracle of her reposing singularly undisturbed since 1817, save for
what was probably modernization's tenderest nudge.[1] This story resonates with a sense of Jane Austen's enduring presence. Many English
readers consider their understanding of Austen sounder than that of, say,
North Americans, or Australians, or New Zealanders because—cultural
and national differences quite aside—they are closer to that presence,
to the ground Austen touched, the air she took in, the landscape that
met her eye. And within England itself, there is some jockeying for the
pride of place closest to her. Visiting Chawton Cottage one summer, I
overheard a Janeite from Bath bragging about acquisitions to the Jane
Austen Study Centre there, but her enthusiasm was crushed when a Janeite from Winchester rejoined, "But *we* have her bones." Clearly, the
cult of Jane Austen is not merely—or even primarily—a book club, but
rather retains an affiliation with habits of veneration rooted in the devotion to local saints and their relics. As we shall see, Austen's things—and
there are precious few of them—have the status of sacred remnants: the
lock of her hair, her writing table, her autograph. They serve as instruments of presence that, in closing the gap created by her loss, give lovers
of Jane Austen what they want, a closeness to her that is imagined to
confer insight and authority and, more profoundly, to heal and to cheer.
But Austen's bones trump all other relics. To possess them is to have the

best part of her. Better than any autograph letters, trinkets, or Regency fashion displays, better by far than the novels themselves—which give rise to ceaseless disputation—they evoke her real presence because they are that presence, and they are potent on this count.

Such anecdotes about Austen's bones, even as they testify to her etherialization via a process of secular canonization—one 1902 essay about her is aptly titled "Legends of St. Jane"—at the same time remind us of something that feels impertinent to remark even as it has always been in one way or another the foundation of Austenian appreciation: her body. Literary history is downright avid for the bodies of male authors; their oddities or even deformities present no necessary obstacle to their appreciation. Ever since Boswell, loving Samuel Johnson involves vividly reimagining scenes of his at once grotesque and sublime embodiment— Johnson's forehead perspiring and his veins swelling as he ate, Johnson's face and legs twitching, Johnson "rolling his majestick frame in his usual manner" on the beach at Harwich as Boswell's boat sails away, and even, as Helen Deutsch so brilliantly shows, Johnson's autopsy.[2] Understanding his prose style, dubbed elephantine, entails inhabiting that body for a moment and feeling how he huffs and puffs through a maze of subordinate clauses and parallel phrases before resting at an end stop that turns out to be all-too-provisional and preparing again for another effort of strenuous qualification. Johnsonians in this manner think and breathe through the body of their master, and in the process their very love keeps that body alive. In his own *Lives of the Poets*, Johnson leaves a space of discreet indeterminacy between the work and the life, yet his powerful evocations of Pope dressing or Pope eating clearly promote his sense of Pope as a poet of discipline and fastidiousness, much as appreciative as well as derogatory readings of Keats would emerge from and return to an apprehension of his body as robust, hale, and coarse on one hand or as delicate, sickly, and effeminate on the other. For the most striking test case, consider, for example, as Susan Wolfson has shown in her brilliant discussion of Byron's iconography, "images and imaginations of Bryon liberated (exhaustlessly, it seems) male as well as female swoons" throughout the nineteenth century and beyond. If the literary marketplace became more impersonal in the late eighteenth century, and if, furthermore, as Michael Warner and Lauren Berlant have argued, the public sphere during this period developed as a site open only to abstract, generic "men," the public itself compensated for the abstraction of print culture through a process of personalization, working on and through the bodies of beloved or despised celebrity authors.[3]

The bodies of women authors were never easily or unproblematically assimilated into the structure of literary appreciation, however. To put oneself forward as a specific body into the sheer publicity of print entails risks, embarrassments, and vulnerabilities that can threaten to discredit rather than describe or intensify female authority. Some female authors, most notably Charlotte Smith, consciously managed their portraits as an element of their literary personae and in the process attempted proactively to control their representation in the public eye. Still, a work such as Polwhele's *The Unsex'd Females* (even allowing for the customary satirical ploy of hyperembodiment during an intensely polemical period, as in his infamous description of Wollstonecraft as a "hyena in petticoats") puts even the bodies of women authors *not* under attack squarely on the line, making their writing redundant, just as, much later, allusions to George Eliot's "equine face" would imply that her prose was too lumbering to bother with, a poor substitute for the attractions her body supposedly lacked. Jane Austen eluded such embarrassments because she seemed to her readers to possess no body at all by virtue of a retirement that—whether by accident or by design—rendered her serenely invisible. For this reason, she is a particularly compelling case for testing Catherine Gallagher's contention in *Nobody's Story*. At the same time that the emerging novel, as distinct from previous narratives, represented vividly imagined but purely fictional characters, no-bodies, rather than actual characters along with their scandalous political or sexual intrigues, the increasingly disembodying and depersonalizing effects of the literary marketplace—as distinct from earlier systems of literary patronage—enabled women novelists themselves to perform "vanishing acts" in expansive and enabling ways.[4]

In this chapter I shall discuss how notions about Austen's body or nobody developed through the nineteenth and early twentieth centuries alongside ideas about Austen's novelistic art, and I will suggest that the belief in Austen's uncanny textual power has for the most part depended on the vanishment of her body, that one's presence has required the other's absence. George Henry Lewes, preeminently, makes his inability to imagine Austen's body at all the basis of his pathbreaking critical assessment of 1859. Playing off Samuel Johnson's witticism about the man who "managed to make himself public without making himself known,"

Lewes writes that "Miss Austen has made herself known without making herself public" (*CH1*, 150)—as if, of course, making oneself "public" could possibly imply the same things for male and female writers alike.[5] Picking up on Hazlitt's praise of Shakespeare and anticipating Stephen Daedalus's ideals of authorship, Lewes celebrates Austen as more than merely modestly retiring, but as essentially unseeable: she is "a great actor *off* the stage" stunning us with her "dramatic ventriloquism" (*CH1*, 157) but always remaining just outside our view. Austen's bodilessness has a corollary in Lewes's sense of the vivid but strikingly unvisual character of her fiction, which, even as it attests to a triumph of dramatic method, derives from a concomitant failure of descriptive art.

What accounts for Lewes's sense of Austen's invisibility? Not only the possibilities and the problems of vanishment attendant on the modern novelistic marketplace. To a degree hard for us to reimagine, early Victorian admirers of Jane Austen found her bodiless in part because they simply had no idea what she looked like: "There is no portrait of her in the shop windows," Lewes remarks in evidence of Austen's status as a connoisseur's rather than a popular writer, "indeed no portrait of her at all" (*CH1*, 150). In part, Lewes is simply referencing the fact that the 1833 Bentley edition of Austen's novels, like the editions of Austen's novels published during her lifetime for that matter, did not carry a frontispiece of the author. In saying so, however, Lewes is implicitly absorbing and reproducing Maria Jane Jewsbury's 1831 article on Austen published anonymously in the *Athenaeum*, the first publication about Jane Austen by a woman. There, Jewsbury maintained that even as Austen's ladylike seclusion shows that "literary reputation is attainable" without any "sacrifice to notoriety" incompatible "with female happiness and delicacy," in Austen's case the seclusion proves so rarified as to verge on disappearance, a point Jewsbury underscores by alluding to lines 5–6 of Wordsworth's "Song" ("She dwelt among th'untrodden ways"): "So retired, so unmarked by literary notoriety, was the life Miss Austen led, that if any likeness was ever taken of her, (and the contrary supposition would seem strange,) none has ever been engraved; and of no woman, whose writings are as numerous and distinguished, is there perhaps so little public beyond the circle of those who knew her when alive—A violet by a mossy stone / Half hidden from the eye."[6] As it turns out, virtually all we know or think we know about Austenian iconography—or, to be more precise, about the apparent nonexistence of "likenesses" of Austen drawn from her life—derives from this puzzling statement, and it deserves close attention. On what basis does Jewsbury aver that no "likeness" was ever taken of Jane Austen? There is no evidence that she corresponded with Austen's brother Henry on this matter—and the many inaccuracies throughout her article (Jewsbury often wrote quickly to meet weekly deadlines) confirm that she did not go out of her way to get facts straight, much less to vet them with Austen's family. Some of Jewsbury's discussion here surely is developed from Henry Austen's "Biographical Notice of the Author" prefixed to the 1818 edition of *Persuasion* and *Northanger Abbey*, but this text has nothing whatsoever to say on the subject of likenesses, averring only that Austen shrank from notoriety and "in public . . . turned away from any allusion to the character of an authoress" (BN, 330). To make matters more puzzling, when Henry Austen does say something about likenesses of his sister in his later "Memoir" in October 1832, he actually quotes Jewsbury's article (published more than a year earlier), rather than speaking in his own voice and out of his own knowledge: "So retired, so unmarked by literary notoriety, was the life Miss Austen led, that if any likeness was ever taken of her, none has ever been engraved."[7]

Because Jewsbury, then, and not the Austen family, is the source of the public's impression that Austen shyly retreated from any artist's gaze, we would do well to query what compels her to describe Austen in this matter to begin with. Her account seems to come to us as a disinterested, even quite tentative, statement about biographical fact ("if any likeness was ever taken of her . . . none has ever been engraved"). This is only her assumption, however, and a personally motivated one at that. An urban, professionalized, and ambitious writer who despite a posture of general anonymity wanted important people to know who she was and what she wrote (she sent her work to Wordsworth, for example), Jewsbury plays up the distinction between herself and Austen, who exemplifies a particular kind of woman writer Jewsbury emphatically is not. As a feminist woman of letters, inclined toward emancipation and craving fame in the literary marketplace, however ambivalent she was at times about her ambition, she challenges what seemed to her to be the *via Austeniana*, the idea that women writers negotiate their "careers" through withdrawal. Jewsbury's appreciation is thus implicitly oppositional; Jewsbury's likeness *was* taken (though not with the same play that Hemens and Smith managed), and so it follows as a matter of course that Austen's was not: "the contrary supposition would seem strange," as she puts it. The enlistment of Wordsworth's "Poem"—not an association that would likely spring to the minds of modern Austenians—underscores the stakes in establishing Austen's reclusiveness. Austen is deemed a mistress of "light literature," and Jewsbury renders her weightless indeed by absorbing her into Wordsworth's anonymous, phantasmatic "she," a placidly unselfconscious, airy figure without biographical specificity, not available for view, someone withdrawn from the public notice so remotely that she seems finally to disappear into sheer transparency, or perhaps even a "she" who never existed at all, a pretext for the poet's elegy that takes her place. Sequestration by this account is a secularized version of St. Jane's monastic isolation, as Austen is imagined as denying herself the worldly pleasures and stimulations of the city and submitting to the spare but redemptive rituals of country life before passing away without leaving any material trace, except the novels. In some ways, then, the logic of Jewsbury's presentation dictates that Austen *must* be "half hidden from the eye." There is no "likeness" of Jane Austen because there cannot be one, testifying as it would to a protrusion into bodily publicity that Jewsbury denies the better to demarcate her own.[8]

Whether Austen's uneasiness with notoriety was genuinely her own, or whether it was to one degree or another foisted on her by her family, Jane Austen—as distinct from "Jane Austen"—surely did not dwell among untrodden ways. Among literati, she was far from anonymous, and her letters show her to be extremely gratified by her developing reputation as a novelist. So it is with a mixture of irony, self-mockery, and sheer fantasy that this self-described admirer of portrait exhibitions in London describes her growing fame in terms of portraiture: "I do not despair of having my picture in the Exhibition at last—all white and red, with my Head on one Side" (*L*, 250, 3 November 1813).[9] Her early writing—exercises in excess that have never been popular, perhaps not coincidentally—is intensely physical and raucously oral: in the madness scene of *Love and Freindship*, repressed appetites return with hilarious vengeance when, after the death of her impecunious lover, the sentimental but famished heroine hallucinates first a leg of mutton and then a cucumber; in the gothic spoof "Henry and Eliza," as the heroine begins to feel what no hyperconventional heroine worth her salt ever feels—that is, "rather hungry"—she concludes "by their biting off two of her fingers, that her Children were in much the same situation" (*J*, 43); and in (my favorite) "The Beautifull Cassandra" the spirited young lady goes to a pastry shop, devours no less than six ices, knocks down the pastry chef, and runs away without paying, returning home to the maternal bosom with more ecstatically unalloyed satisfaction than Austen's later heroines would ever achieve: "Cassandra smiled & whispered to herself 'This is a day well spent'" (*J*, 56).

Austen's early work sides with the body and its vigors, particularly as these give the lie to restrictive, high-blown notions of female delicacy. Failing to meet her new sweetheart at a gathering, the young Catherine Morland, for example, violates all heroic decorum by returning home, appeasing her extraordinary hunger, and then enjoying nine deliciously refreshing hours of sleep. Elizabeth Bennet's "animal spirits" are more conducive to pleasure than those of her more boisterous but also more querulous sister Lydia, and after she runs through muddy lanes to Netherfield to visit Jane, we are pleased to observe that the flush imparted to her complexion by the exercise turns Darcy on, despite—or is it because of?—her dirty petticoats. In the later work it is the pain rather than the vigor of the body that seems to occupy Austen's attention. In *Persuasion*, the narrator's notorious attack on Mrs. Musgrove's "fat sighings"—on the degraded too-muchness of her sentiments and body alike—appear to enhance the prestige of daintiness, elegance, and restraint and so vindicate the superior claims of containment over excess. This by no means erases the body, however much it may demean Mrs. Musgrove's bulk. Indeed, the body is foregrounded as never before—its liability to broken bones, to debility, to knocks on the head, to foot blisters the size of a three-shilling piece (about one and a quarter inches in diameter), to crow's foot, to sunburn, to nervous fits of agitation that reason cannot manage. In this novel we are to understand Captain Wentworth's tribute to the impermeability of the sturdy hazelnut not only as playful but also as itself willfully obtuse: getting punctured, cracked, crushed, and trodden under foot is what hazelnuts have in store for them, at least if they are the elect, the worthy ones. Nothing productive or admirable is to be expected from hazelnuts or people who are too smooth, the ones who, in Anne Elliot's disapproving words, *endure too well* (like William Elliott or those whose complexions are unfurrowed (like Sir Walter). And while it is true that not everyone's liability to suffering is entitled to equal respect in a culture of complaint where all clamorously insist that deference be paid to their sensitivities, bodies that submit quietly to penetration by time and by pain are honored, and only unguardedness and involuntary losses of self-control are prized as reliable indicators of deep feeling. The body with all its excesses is still valued, but in an economy where the feeling body has so much prestige that one's own can only get the credit it deserves by distinguishing it through an (almost) perfect self-command.

It would be convenient to chalk up "Jane Austen's" disembodiment to Victorianism, but the case seems more complicated. True, Austen was less squeamish about the body than the Victorians who formed and maintained her reputation, though, as it happens, some of the garden-variety grossness that tinges her letters does not seem to bother Lord Brabourne, the great-nephew who edited the first edition of her letters. He lets stand the rather nasty comment, "Miss Langley is like any other short girl, with a broad nose and wide mouth, fashionable dress and exposed bosom. Adm. Stanhope is a gentleman-like man, but then his legs are too short and his tail too long" (*L*, 86, 12–13 May 1801). Yet Brabourne does delete the carnal matter-of-factness that runs through many of Austen's letters. References to "breeding" neighbors or suggestions that one prodigious couple, after the birth of their eighteenth child, might consider "the simple regimen of separate rooms" (*L*, 330, 20 February 1817) get the knife for sexual knowingness. Austen's wry description of a London girls' school—"it was full of all the modern Elegancies—& if it had not been for some naked Cupids over the Mantelpiece, which must be a fine study for Girls, one should never have Smelt Instruction" (*L*, 211, 20 May 1813)—is also deleted, as David Nokes has aptly put it, to "project an image of Jane Austen whose ignorance of the naked body extended even to gilt cherubic miniatures." What is important to recognize here is that posterity's insistence on Austen's ignorance of the body has its origins in *our* discomfort with her body, not in *her* discomfort with it.[10]

How and when, then, did Austen lose her body? The effort to detach Austen from the bodily begins early, as a counterresponse to the shocking hypercorporeality of illness and death—as an effort to detach the contemplation of Austen from the contemplation of her body in its last agonies. Whether we think Austen suffered from Addison's disease or lymphoma,[11] we know that starting in 1816 she was afflicted with nausea, vomiting, weakness, immobilizing back pain, and other muscle aches, along with fever and night sweats, and that the discolorations of her complexion distressed her (turning her looks "bad enough, black & white & every wrong colour" [*L*, 335, 23–25 March 1817]). We know further that in early April, her symptoms grew so alarming that, though ordinarily stoic, she pressed for the return of Cassandra, who had been away in Berkshire, to nurse her and that by the end of the month she privately drew up her will. Austen's recent biographers have attempted to demythologize the loving tranquility of the Austen family, and David Nokes took some aim at the Jane/Cassandra relationship, foregrounding tensions between the younger sister, who described herself, with only mocking self-criticism, as a "wild Beast" (*L*, 212, 24 May 1813), and the supposedly starchier elder determined to cast her as an angel of the house rather than memorialize her in all her particular—sometimes dark—complexity.¹² As much needed as revisionary efforts are, on the score of Austen's embodiment they may confuse effects for intentions. It is true that Austen's beatification begins immediately, as Cassandra describes her last (probably heavily sedated) moments: "There was nothing convulsed or which gave the idea of pain in her look, on the contrary, but for the continual motion of her head, she gave me the idea of a beautiful statue, & even now in her coffin, there is such a sweet serene air over her countenance as is quite pleasant to contemplate" (*L*, 345, 20 July 1817). Here, even in intense bodily agony, Austen has already become a statue, albeit a statue in motion. As Deirdre Le Faye's editorial notes help us to see, Austen's exaltation is inscribed onto the text of Cassandra's letter: Cassandra originally wrote "sweet serene air in her countenance" but scratched out "*in*" and replaced it with "*over*" in superscript, as if already to register the sanctification of her sister's "precious soul" as it lingers on its way up to its "far superior Mansion."

And yet at the same time, Cassandra's eloquent letter about her sister's death is so absorbed in the bodily intimacies nursing entails, intimacies that are still vividly felt, that more than anything else it conveys her attachment to Austen's body: to her languors, to the changing rhythms of her sleep and waking, to the ebbing of her strength, to the downwardly spiraling alterations of her looks, to her worsening seizures of faintness, to the head she supported in her lap for seven long hours, to the eyes she closed—"I was able to close her eyes myself & it was a great gratification to me to render her these last services"—and to the care of her dead body as it lay in the drawing room at College Street, Winchester, in a coffin open for, if not all, then at least a good part of seven days in mid-July, so already sanctified, we may presume, as not to stink or decompose (the sure sign of sainthood). In short, if Cassandra seems at times to abstract Jane from her body—describing her as a "treasure," as the "sun of my life, the gilder of every pleasure"—it is an impulse wishfully to imagine a beloved beyond the reach of pain, rather than a submission to propriety or an effort to whitewash the truth, because that specific, dying, and dead body is still so real and present before her.

However moving Cassandra's exaltation of her sister, it remained private until the publication of the letters in 1884, and so it did not directly contribute to the emerging tradition of disembodiment I am outlining here. Not so Henry Austen's "Biographical Notice." This first account is more immediate than the generalized account of Austen he prepared in his 1832 "Memoir," where the story of Austen's waxing literary reputation, as filtered through lengthy citations from Whatley's article of 1821 and Jewsbury's of 1831, takes precedence over fresh, particularized recollections of brother and sister. The 1817 "Biographical Notice" cannot forbear conjuring the physical vitality of a woman alive only five months before: "She was fond of dancing, and excelled in it" (BN, 139). This moment is atypical. Henry's account is more often given to strikingly bland, generalized terms of description—"middle" height, "graceful" carriage, "good" features, and "true" elegance, terms that tell us even less about how Jane Austen looked than Jane Austen herself tells us about her heroines. Its most striking figure, an allusion to Donne's funeral elegy "On the Death of Mistress Drury" (carried over to the 1832 "Memoir") seems to superembody Austen by casting her person rather than her pen as her expressive instrument: "her eloquent blood spoke through her modest cheek," Henry writes, (mis)quoting the line, no doubt via Fielding's description of Sophia Western in *Tom Jones*. The conjunction of Jane Austen with Sophia Western seems an odd one—*Tom Jones* is one of the novels beloved by John Thorpe, Austen's most fatuous boor—and it probably tells us more about Henry's literary tastes than it does about Jane Austen's appearance. In any event, Henry's allusion invites us to finish Donne's thought about "eloquent blood": "and so distinctly wrought / That one might almost say her body thought." In addition to rendering actual authorship unnecessary, this figure so evacuates Austen of authorial agency that it accomplishes via Fielding's allusion to Donne what Jewsbury accomplished via Wordsworth's "she." Henry's "Biographical Notice," doubtless heartfelt, has the effect of despecifying Jane Austen, as if the price for bringing her into public view in one way—that is, finally "outing" her officially as the author of *Northanger Abbey* and *Persuasion* and the four previous novels, published anonymously—were retracting or occulting her in another way. Henry insists that Austen was never satiric, barbed, unusual, funny, or simply particular in any way, but was rather generically sweet-tempered, mild, and gentle in word and deed — precisely the kind of "picture of perfection" that Austen once described as making her "sick and wicked" (*L*, 335, 23 March 1817).

Fittingly, then, Austen's first monument — her gravestone at Winchester Cathedral (fig. 1.1) — is as imposing as it is curiously vapid:

JANE AUSTEN,
youngest daughter of the late
Revd. GEORGE AUSTEN,
formerly Rector of Steventon in this County.
She departed this Life on the 18th July 1817,
aged 41, after a long illness supported with
the patience and the hopes of a Christian.

The benevolence of her heart,
the sweetness of her temper, and
the extraordinary endowments of her mind
obtained the regard of all who knew her, and
the warmest love of her intimate connections.

Their grief is in proportion to their affection
they know their loss to be irreparable,
but in the deepest affliction they are consoled
by a firm though humble hope that her charity,
devotion, faith and purity have rendered
her soul acceptable in the sight of her
REDEEMER.

We all know by now that beyond alluding to the "extraordinary endowments" of Austen's mind, the inscription omits any reference to Austen's authorship. Most of the obituary notices Henry placed in local as well as national venues did mention Austen's novels, so it would be ludicrous to accuse him of suppressing his sister's achievement. Pious decorum alone does not seem sufficient to explain why Henry would omit here what he mentioned everywhere else.[13] What is also unusual is that the stone, resting closely to Austen's body, covers her with such a crowd of words — as if the edges can scarcely contain them — rewriting her, as it were, to give the impression of both fullness and emptiness. No one expects profundi-

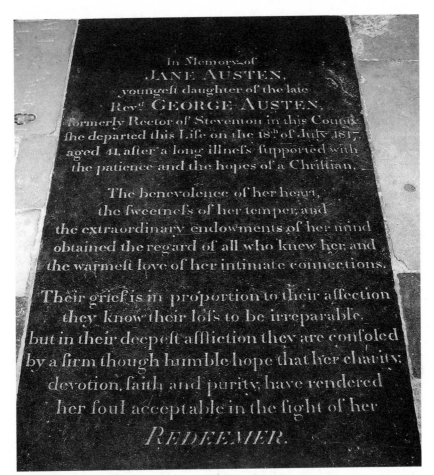

Figure 1.1. *Austen's gravestone at Winchester Cathedral (1817).*
Photograph courtesy of Allan Soedring.

ties on gravestones, of course; conventionality itself carries a positive, consolatory force on these occasions. The inscription, almost certainly of Henry's composition, is quite copious. Coming in at 122 words, it exceeds what so many other mourners in the cathedral saw fit to inscribe on the stones of their dearly departed. Henry has thus gone to much effort and expense—each chiseled character costs, after all—to say the usual, conventional things.

We might well ask, why is this Austenian monument here at all? The Austen family was not particularly attached to Winchester, even if nephews did attend school there. True, Cassandra avers that Jane admired the cathedral, but we have no indication that she ever worshipped there or wished to do so. Though Austen jokes in a letter of 27 May 1817 (*L*, 342) that if her doctor fails to cure her she will "draw up a Memorial [i.e., memorandum] & lay it before the Dean & Chapter [of Winchester Cathedral] & have no doubt of redress from that Pious, Learned & disinterested Body," the idea to bury Jane in the cathedral instead of taking her home to the churchyard at Chawton was probably, most agree, Henry's—having been recently examined by the bishop of Winchester in connection with his ordination, he could have used this connection and others with the dean and chapter of the cathedral.[14] No doubt he felt his own prestige was enhanced by bragging that "the whole catalogue of [the cathedral's] mighty dead" does not "contain the ashes of a brighter genius or a sincerer Christian" (*Memoir*, 138). Henry's monument to Jane prominently announces both Jane Austen's extraordinary worthiness and her family's extraordinary awareness of it.

This extraordinary tribute did not come for nothing. Austen's funeral expenses were, relatively speaking, unusually steep—£92, almost twice what Austen left to Henry himself. It is possible that the privilege of being buried within the walls of Winchester Cathedral was costly.[15] The precise breakdown of other fees—what the handsome and very large black marble stone cost, what expense the lengthy inscription entailed, and what fees if any were paid to the officiating priest—we do not know, but it is still hard to imagine them amounting to almost £100. We do know, however, that the sum came not from Henry's pocket—which was empty, in any case, due to his recent bankruptcy—but Cassandra's.[16] And yet it was almost certainly Henry, not Cassandra, who informed John Britton, then in the process of preparing his *History and Antiquities of the See Cathedral Church of Winchester* (1817) for publication, that his sister was buried there, in effect ensuring her status as a tourist site in the very year of her death. Britton writes: "Among the interments in this pile, is one of a lady whose virtues, talents, and accomplishments entitle her not only to distinguished notice, but to the admiration of every person who has a heart to feel and a mind to appreciate female worth and merit. The lady alluded to, Miss *Jane Austen*, who was buried here, July 1817, was author of four novels of considerable interest and value. In the last, a posthumous publication, entitled 'Northanger Abbey,' is a sketch of a memoir of the amiable author."[17] Pride no doubt inspired Henry to advertise Jane Austen in this way. Much to her vexation, he had violated her wish to remain anonymous years before, in a fit of what she described equivocally as "the warmth of Brotherly vanity & Love" (*L*, 231, 25 September 1813).[18] Novelizing women were not the thing in polite society: in skewing the so-proper Lady Middleton's censure of the Dashwood sisters as being "satirical" because "they were fond of reading," Austen seems to be satirizing the stupid censure to which she and Cassandra were subject, and possibly by wealthy relations. Seen in this way, Henry's pride is touching. But Austen was also aware that Henry's pride was inflected with selfishness distinctive to himself. In so speedily advertising Jane Austen's monument in Winchester Cathedral, he was seeing to it that her cultural capital accrued, and his along with it, not only as her brother but also as the author of the "Biographical Notice." Austen's first monument thus announces the substance behind Jane Austen, the loving family she left behind—and so what Jane Austen loses in specificity on her way to sanctification, her family gained in celebrity. The inscription, in other words, both situates Austen in her family circle and uses Austen to situate her family.

᠅ Austen's desubstantiation is perhaps the most important feature of her reception from 1817 until the present. Whether we encounter what Virginia Woolf memorably described as "twenty-five elderly gentlemen living in the neighborhood of London who resent any slight upon her genius as if it were an insult to the chastity of their Aunts," or whether we find D. A. Miller describing the disciplinary spareness of her style as "anorectic," bent on self-evacuation, we see a tradition—never single or uncontested, but certainly predominating—insisting rather aggressively on her immaculateness.[19] The investment in this tradition is so strong that one feels irrelevantly pedantic about observing that Jane Austen is not the same as "Jane Austen" or about opining further that when Austen remarks, "You know how interesting the purchase of a sponge-cake is to me" (*L*, 128, 15 June 1808), she appears to have every intention of eating it and keeping it down. Yet when we turn to the question of Jane Austen's iconography, it is impossible not to address this resistance squarely, for pictures of Jane Austen perforce oblige us to consider what she looked like, something that Jewsbury by 1831 had already found strange, incompatible with the very idea of "Jane Austen." At the same time, paradoxically, few faces have come to inspire so many people with so much devotion as Jane Austen's. Whether standing for the glory of the English novel or for the idyllic heritage of village life, Austen's face purveys something as grand as England itself, and as a result much depends on how we are invited or permitted to imagine it.

So what did Jane Austen look like? The question is worth considering in detail in part because answering shows, first, how different branches of Austen's family—sometimes together and sometimes separately—attempted to form and disseminate Austen's image in different ways, and, second, how what we might call institutional considerations subsequently influenced how we may be permitted to imagine how Jane Austen looked. So far as the National Portrait Gallery (NPG) has been concerned since 1948, there is only one authentic likeness of Jane Austen: the pencil and watercolor sketch of Austen by Cassandra that the museum purchased for £130 and exhibited that year (fig. 1.2). This unsmiling sketch bears out my claim about Austen's decorporealization, particularly when one encounters it as an actual object, rather than in reproduction, which considerably emboldens its outlines. This small (a little more than 4" × 3") sketch now hangs in a darkened display case that can be (faintly) illuminated only (briefly) when a visitor wishes to see it. Formerly, it reposed beneath a heavy velvet shroud protecting it from damage caused by light, and one would need to remove the shroud in order to peer at it. Though of course many pictures in the NPG are similarly protected from this kind of damage, one cannot help feeling that even the *likeness* of Jane Austen shrinks from being seen: deciding to see her seems a bit like intruding on her privacy, making one uneasily aware that the more one looks at her the less visible she will be. And yet the sketch represents no gently smiling household saint. The expression is, if not downright acerbic, then at least pursed. Moreover, the glimpse is informal, private. She is at home, but hardly looking like an angel of the house. She is not dressed for company and is not sitting as a lady ought, but rather is leaning against the back of her chair with her arms folded across her chest, in a posture implying less than infinite patience with her sister's drawing project. And finally, although the face rather than the figure receives the lion's share of Cassandra's attention, the body pictured here, however receded, is not diminutive: the shoulders slope slightly but are broad, and the body is substantial and comfortable. Altogether the image gives a characteristically paradoxical impression of being at once definite and faint, solid and imminently evaporable.

Figure 1.2. *Pencil and watercolor sketch of Austen by Cassandra (ca. 1810). The National Portrait Gallery purchased this sketch in 1948 and displayed it as the only authentic image of the author. Photograph:* © *National Portrait Gallery, London.*

Although R. W. Chapman dismissed it as "a disappointing scratch" (*JAFP*, 214), Cassandra's portrait of her sister in its own way is exceedingly impressive, and over the course of more than a half-century custom has surely endeared it to the public. But we must not let its familiarity obscure questions surrounding its likeness and its very existence. First of all, when Richard Bentley asked Cassandra and Henry Austen in 1832 for a portrait to use as a frontispiece, Henry and Cassandra never mentioned this sketch. They may well have denied its existence because they judged it inappropriate for the purpose at hand—though one imagines that it might have been improved on by another artist more successfully in 1832 than it would be later in 1869 (see below). These surmises beg questions regarding authenticity. This sketch is neither signed nor dated, and though the NPG assigns its probable date of composition to "c1810," this is no more than a (good) supposition. Stylistically, it is rather unlike the other watercolors Cassandra is known to have executed, and it is not clear whether Cassandra is trying to produce a caricature or whether she is being clumsy at producing an informal portrait. In any case, the Austen family never said a word about its existence until it becomes the basis of the frontispiece of J. E. Austen-Leigh's *Memoir* of 1869–70. It is not mentioned in Cassandra's will, nor is it named in the detailed letter she wrote to her brother Charles spelling out all the other Austenian relics and keepsakes she wanted to distribute among nieces and nephews at her death—for example, a lock of Jane's hair, her topaz cross, and her letters and manuscripts. Some forty years later, in W. and R. A. Austen-Leigh's *Family Record* (1913), we are told that Cassandra's great-niece came forward with the sketch in 1869 for use in the memoir, but none of Cassandra's papers corroborate this. J. E. Austen-Leigh attributes the sketch to Cassandra, but he does not say how he came by it. Provenance and custom attest to this portrait, in other words, not documentary evidence.

Cassandra's sketch was evidently not in that class of objects Harriet Smith in *Emma* called "most precious treasures." Only one descendent, Frank Austen's grandson, John H. Hubback, valued it enough to reproduce it, albeit in a coarsened version of intriguing austerity, in his *Jane Austen's Sailor Brothers* (1906), and because that image is now in the public domain and can be reproduced gratis, it is reprinted frequently (see fig. 1.3).[20] Later, the granddaughter of Austen's sailor brother Charles sold the sketch to a businessman in Cornwall named Frederick

"CASSANDRA'S SKETCH OF JANE"

Figure 1.3. *Reprint of Cassandra's sketch of Jane Austen appearing in John Hubback's* Jane Austen's Sailor Brothers *(1906). This sketch was the only published version of Cassandra's sketch until 1948.*

Lovering—certainly one of the first collectors of Austeniana—and everyone appeared to forget it until Lovering's collection was auctioned at his
death by Sotheby's in 1948, when the NPG purchased it. Evidence suggests considerable dissatisfaction with it as a likeness. Charlotte-Maria
Beckford (née Middleton), who knew Jane during some of the Chawton
years, objected that Austen's face was "by *no means so broad & plump* as
represented" in the Cassandra sketch, and she recollected Austen as "a tall,
thin, spare person, with very high cheek bones, great colour—sparkling
eyes, not large but joyous and intelligent."[21] When J. E. Austen-Leigh
wanted a frontispiece for the *Memoir*, he considered it so obviously defi-
cient that he commissioned Mr. John Andrews of Maidenhead to prettify
it in his watercolor miniature of 1869 (fig. 1.4). In this privately owned,
infrequently seen intermediate adaptation, Austen's face is rounded, the
lips fuller, and the eyes larger, softer, and less arched. The expression
as a result is mild, and the straight lips of the original are curved into
the trace of a smile. Austen has become more equable and more mannerly as well. The figure is seated upright, and the arms are no longer
crossed but rest in a ladylike fashion unseen on a lap no longer visible.
Andrews also changes the style of the chair, which in Cassandra's sketch
appears to be of the plain straight-backed kitchen variety, into something more formal, with curved side rails, bringing Austen into a drawing
room. Andrews also decreases Cassandra's emphasis on Austen's expressive yet enigmatic face by detailing her dress and bringing forward and
delineating the shoulders and neck, which were only faintly sketched in
the original.

As twee as Andrews's permutation of Cassandra's sketch is, it would
get worse in the steel engraving based on it by the Lizars firm in 1870
(fig. 1.5). The Lizars engraving embalms Austen in gruesome quaintness.
Her face has become narrower, her neck is grotesquely elongated, and
her shoulders are sloping acutely (shoulders that in Cassandra's version
were sketchy but rather square). The engraving further develops Austen's dress and its frills, crimps, and folds, especially emphasizing the
empire-style riband. This emphasis calls attention to Austen's bosom,
but though Austen's figure now stands out more, takes up more space
in the frame, it seems narrow and diminutive to the point of deformity,
a spinster's arrested body perhaps. And finally there is the chair, which
shows the grain of the wood. Perhaps like the chair, Austen herself is an
antiquated domestic furnishing, a cozy figure in an old-fashioned parlor.

Figure 1.4. *Watercolor miniature based on Cassandra's sketch of Jane Austen, by Mr. Andrews of Maidenhead (1869). This miniature "improved" Cassandra's sketch by sweetening Jane's facial expression and correcting her posture. Reproduced by permission of the owner. Courtesy of the Jane Austen Memorial Trust.*

JANE AUSTEN.

Figure 1.5. *Steel engraving of Andrews's watercolor (1870). In the public domain, this is the most widely reprinted portrait of Jane Austen.*

Her demeanor bears no trace of sarcasm (and cannot be imagined as capable of it) and also no trace of life.

This transformation did not occur without family discussion. J. E. Austen-Leigh asked his relations to judge how the engraving squared with their childhood memories of their aunt, memories dating back more than fifty years, and—to their credit perhaps—they were far from enthusiastic. His sister Anna was hardly impressed, regarding Cassandra's sketch itself as "hideously unlike" Austen but conceding that there was "a good deal of resemblance" in Andrews's version. J. E. Austen-Leigh's cousin Cassandra Esten Austen is also cool: "I think the portrait is very much superior to any thing that could have been expected from the sketch it was taken from.—It is a very pleasing, sweet face,—tho,' I confess, to not thinking it *much* like the original;—but *that*, the public will not be able to detect." What recommends Andrews's version here is the "pleasing, sweet" expression on the sitter's face, which is frankly acknowledged to be unlike the original. This is not an endorsement, exactly, because Cassandra Esten Austen thinks that the public will never know the discrepancy. Less harsh but equally equivocal are the remarks of Elizabeth Rice (daughter of Edward Austen Knight): "How well the portrait has been lithographed! I think it very like only the eyes are too large, not for beauty but for likeness, I suppose making them so was Aunt Cassandra's tribute of affection."[22] Elizabeth Rice seems to sign on with less dubiety than her cousins, but because she judges that the engraving is based on a sketch that, to her recollection, is already inaccurate, the value of Lizars's engraving is still limited.

If for different reasons, Austen's descendants seem as ambivalent about the Andrews/Lizars frontispiece as we are. R. W. Chapman judged these remarks to add up to "very guarded and qualified approval" (*JAFP*, 215) without inquiring too curiously into what these descendants were after, what exactly they were approving of. Even "very guarded and qualified" seems an overstatement. Lizars's engraving is never "approved" exactly, but it was accepted because it gives a face and body to an auntly sweetness acknowledged to be inaccurate or unreal. Chapman's inference that "it is probably not significant of misgiving that it was omitted from the second edition, since most of the other illustrations of 1870 were suppressed in 1871" (*JAFP*, 213) does not strike me as valid, for a frontispiece is not like other illustrations, and it is equally possible that J. E. Austen-Leigh decided to retract the frontispiece because he was aware of its insufficiency. In any case, he went on to memorialize his aunt in another, nonfigural way. With characteristic grandiosity, he cites Lord Macaulay's intention to "write a memoir of Miss Austen . . . and from the proceeds of the sale to erect a monument to her memory in Winchester Cathedral." Accordingly, he uses proceeds from his own *Memoir* of Austen in order to keep her celebration in the family—commissioning James Wyatt to design and install a brass plaque set into the wall above her grave (fig. 1.6). This tablet acknowledges that Austen is "known to many by her writings" but stresses her feminine virtue, "the varied charms of her Character" that "endeared" her to her family, the "Christian faith and piety" that "ennobled" her, the wisdom and loving-kindness of her tongue. In *Winchester Cathedral—Its Monuments and Memorials*, John Vaughan calls this a "chaste and excellent piece of metal work."[23] The chasteness and excellence Vaughan finds in the brass J. E. Austen-Leigh finds in Austen, and in the interests of such chasteness Austen's body vanishes from the memorial.

The elevation of "Jane Austen" that begins with her gravestone and continues with the brass tablet culminates in the installation of a three-paneled stained-glass window commemorating Austen in the north aisle of the nave above her grave, designed by Charles Eamer Kempe (fig. 1.7). Unlike the gravestone and brass tablet, this monument does not domesticate Austen; indeed, it gives her to the public. In the *Times* of 21 February 1898, the following letter was published:

> Sir,—Among the distinguished natives of Hampshire who are buried in Winchester Cathedral there are few names more worthy of record than that of Jane Austen; yet the only memorial of her (beyond the stone slab which marks the site of her grave) is a brass tablet let into the wall, which was placed there by her nephew and biographer, the late Rev. J. E. Austen Leigh, in 1870.
>
> We feel that we shall be appealing to a large circle of warm admirers, who have been charmed and cheered by her works, if we ask for subscriptions to enable us to fill one of the windows in the Cathedral with painted glass in her memory. The selection of the window will depend upon the amount of support that we may receive. The cost of a window in the Lady Chapel is estimated at £600, of one in the nave £300. We may add that our proposal has the cordial approval of the Dean of Winchester.

Figure 1.6. *Memorial tablet above Austen's grave, Winchester Cathedral (1872), extolling Austen's piety. This monument was commissioned by J. E. Austen-Leigh and paid for out of the proceeds of his* Memoir of Jane Austen *(1870). Photograph courtesy of Allan Soedring.*

Figure 1.7.
*Memorial stained
glass window
designed by
Charles Eamer
Kempe, Winchester
Cathedral (1900).
Courtesy of the
Dean and Chapter
of Winchester
Cathedral.
Photograph by
John Crook.*

Contributions not exceeding five guineas may be paid to Messrs. Hoare, 37, Fleet street, London, who have kindly consented to act as treasurers of the fund.

NORTHBROOK.

SELBORNE.

W. W. B. BEACH.

MONTAGU G. KNIGHT

By the end of the nineteenth century, it is clear, Austen's people are no longer exclusively that circle of family witnesses authorized and hallowed by association with her, nor are they confined to Hampshire (though her status as a local worthy is clear). Rather, she belongs to all of England (prominent conservatives in the national government are signatories of this letter) as well as the larger community of English speakers (this letter appeared in the United States as well). Although family members and local worthies are claiming their privilege of association, Austen belongs to the world. Financed by a widely advertised public subscription, the window thus testifies to Austen's status as a public figure. The subscription drew contributions ranging from a few shillings to the upper limit of five guineas at a time, from donors from the United States as well as England, from family members, literati, nobility, and ordinary lovers of Jane Austen, eventually reaching the targeted £300 rather than £600, and thus securing the window's place above her grave rather than at the enormous site in the Lady's Chapel.[24] The lower amount does not signal a lack of enthusiasm. During this period, when the cathedral was undergoing repair and renovation, the *Hampshire Chronicle* frequently ran melancholy notices attempting to squeeze more shillings from a citizenry weary of charitable subscriptions. After receiving the initial announcements, Austen's public was never dunned again. The account at Hoare's Bank opens on 11 February 1898 and closes 19 July 1900 with the £300, and on 13 October of the same year the window was filled.[25]

Kempe's stained-glass designs were well respected during the second part of the nineteenth century, and Kempe worked extensively on the windows at Winchester Cathedral during this period. Although no one would claim that the Austen window is inspired work, the very fact of its existence is astonishing and deserves more attention than it has received. Remarkably, the window has made virtually no impact on the imagination of Austenians, who ever since the mid-nineteenth century flocked to

Austen's grave as if it were a sainted spot, and who even today frequently leave flowers and scribbled notes of thanksgiving, praise, and supplication. Yet despite placards announcing its lofty presence, I have rarely seen tourists or pilgrims look up to take due notice of the window. With the exception of Sir Izaak Walton, who also has a stained-glass window in his honor in the cathedral, how many other authors have been honored so reverently? As if it had taken its sense of Jane Austen from the gravestone rather than the novels—the *Winchester Diocesan Chronicle* announces after it was installed that the "object of the figures and texts is to illustrate the high moral and religious teaching" of her works[26]—the window is designed out of conventional allusions and typology that do not connect with the particular kind of veneration Austenian pilgrims bring to this site. Its implications for Jane Austen seem at once inevitable and ludicrous: inevitable because Austen was indeed praised in mildly hagiographical terms from the get-go, and ludicrous because constructing her as a devotional writer rings false. Inasmuch as there is no record of this window ever being publicly dedicated—as one would expect given Austen's celebrity—it is hard not to infer some disappointment with it. It consists of two rows of three figures, the central top figure showing David playing his harp, the central figure beneath him showing St. John displaying the opening page of his Gospel, no doubt alluding lamely to Austen's work in words, and these central figures flanked by lights representing the sons of Korah, whose banners display verses drawn from the Psalms attesting to the religiosity of Austen's writing. The force of the window, of course, is commemorative—the Latin inscription between the two rows enjoins us "Remember in the Lord Jane Austen, who died 19 July, A.D. 1817"—but the effect is to celebrate her not merely as a sincere Christian (which few could doubt) but also as an inspired one, in the tradition of David and St. John (which few could not doubt). In some ways, the most impressive image is the one standing at the head, superintending the scene, and that is St. Augustine (fig. 1.8), whose name contracted in English is Austin.[27] Through the mediation of an English pun, then, Austen gets represented at the pinnacle, but in St. Augustine's body rather than her own. The window thus demonstrates that Austen's bodily effacement is the condition of her apotheosis. And, as we have seen to be the case throughout the century, that apotheosis is not Jane's exactly, but her family's: the lights on either side of St. Austin show the Austen family coat of arms (fig. 1.9) so that though Jane Austen's sanctification

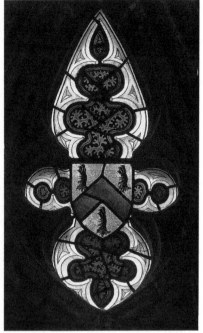

Figure 1.8.
Detail of *memorial window: St. Augustine, who often goes by "Austin" in English. Courtesy of the Dean and Chapter of Winchester Cathedral. Photograph by John Crook.*

Figure 1.9.
Detail of *memorial window: Austen family coat of arms. This window omits the crest and the decidedly secular motto,* Qui Invidit Minor Est *(Whoever envies me is less). Courtesy of the Dean and Chapter of Winchester Cathedral. Photograph by John Crook.*

is now a public rather than coterie concern, it also and rather literally accomplishes the family's project of upward social mobility.

Austen's gravestone, the brass plaque, and the stained-glass window monumentalize without embodying her and in a sense complete the trajectory Jewsbury started when she celebrated Austen's withdrawal from representation in favor of another, chaster and more feminine sort of blessedness that gladly recedes into the paternal. Seen in this way, the engraving J. E. Austen-Leigh prints as a frontispiece in 1870 is an interruption of invisibility, an interruption he attempts to correct in the second edition by leaving it out. But once Jane Austen's portrait was out, once she received a body, so to speak, however morbidly saccharine and attenuated, it could not be retracted. The engraving reappears in the third and all subsequent editions of the *Memoir* because the text refers the reader to the cap Austen wears in the frontispiece, thus making its restoration necessary. And because the engraving is in the public domain, it has circulated ubiquitously, sometimes in modified form, ever since the 1870s. One mutation demonstrates by its very peculiarity the argument I have been developing about Austen's body trouble (fig. 1.10). This portrait, engraved specially for Evert A. Duyckinck's *Portrait Gallery of Eminent Men and Women of Europe and America*, certainly gives Austen a body, and quite an ample, monumental-looking body at that, restoring the fuller view lightly sketched in Cassandra's original drawing but mostly cropped in the Andrews and Lizars versions.[28] The Andrews and Lizars versions attempt to represent a loving aunt, and this is in keeping with J. E. Austen-Leigh's vision of the woman who modestly disclaims authority, who does not repair the creaking door so that she can hide her manuscripts before her nieces and nephews sally in, and who writes for the amusement of a charmed private circle and not for something so large as a public. By contrast, even as this later engraving endows Austen with a serenely vacuous demeanor, it also supplies her with an inkpot, a writing tablet, and several volumes, and thus establishes her as a professional writer. In the process, it also gives Austen a wedding band, and this error is the most telling detail. The engraving can give Austen the fullness of her body and her profession only because the engraver manifestly has no idea who Jane Austen is, other than the fact that she is a woman and an author. Ignorant of Austen and her legend, he merely added a body and accessories to an image he was given to execute his task.

⁊ Having cast around for a portrait of Austen since the 1920s, the National Portrait Gallery acquired Cassandra's sketch in 1948 and has thereafter presented it as the only true likeness of Austen. The canonization of Cassandra's sketch is, in other words, a relatively recent event that enhances the sketch's value by surrounding it with an aura of singularity: there are no pictures of Jane Austen, except this one, and Jane Austen was so retiring that we are lucky to have it at all. A sense of legitimacy in this matter owes much more to custom than to anything else. For those who take the long view, the legitimacy of quite another

Figure 1.10. *Portrait engraved for Duyckinck's* Portrait Gallery of Eminent Men and Women of Europe and America *(1873). Sometimes referred to as the "Betrothal Portrait," this image prominently features a wedding ring.*

likeness, the controversial "Rice Portrait" (fig. 1.11)—once called the Zoffany Portrait, an attribution that has muddied much water—was established into the 1930s, though it is today considered controversial. Far from being an upstart, however, virtually all of the family authorities who tell us everything we believe about Jane Austen also tell us about its legitimacy and reprint it in their books: for example, her great-nephew Lord Brabourne, editor of *Letters of Jane Austen* (1884) and son of Austen's favorite niece; great- and great-great nephews William and Richard Arthur Austen-Leigh, who wrote *Jane Austen: Her Life and Letters* (1913); and great-niece Mary Augusta Austen-Leigh in her *Personal Aspects of Jane Austen* (1920). Many other figures in or close to the family also testify to it, such as great-nephews Cholmeley Austen-Leigh (eldest son of Austen's first biographer), John H. Hubback (grandson of Austen's brother Francis), who coauthored *Jane Austen's Sailor Brothers* (1906), and Fanny-Caroline Lefroy.

The Rice Portrait was first published in the 1884 edition of *Letters of Jane Austen*, edited by Lord Brabourne, the son of Fanny Knight Knatchbull (1793–1882), to whom Cassandra willed most of Austen's correspondence. The publication of the first biography of Jane Austen, J. E. Austen-Leigh's *A Memoir of Jane Austen*, was a major literary event, and Lord Brabourne's edition of his great-aunt's letters, which he undertook to edit immediately after inheriting them from his mother and which he dedicated to Queen Victoria, was to be comparable. He took seriously the responsibility of finding and authenticating a portrait for use as a frontispiece. This care is set forth in letters recently recovered at Chawton Cottage, having lain neglected there for years. In a letter of 7 May 1884, Brabourne explains to publisher George Bentley, "I have discovered that one of my cousins [J. Morland Rice] has a picture said to be of Jane Austen." Brabourne does not press for the portrait, but appealed to Bentley's judgment: "Tell me whether you think an engraving or photograph of it would be worth while, if [Morland Rice, the portrait's owner] would permit it." Nor does Brabourne take up the portrait on the unsupported say-so of Morland Rice, whose view might be partial. Instead, he goes to the other side of the family to seek corroboration from Cholmeley Austen-Leigh. This corroboration came because Austen-Leigh, initially assuming that a portrait of Austen as an *adult* was in question, averred that "the evidence seems *against the authenticity* of the picture, which must be *if* authentic, of Jane when a young girl of 14 or 15." Because the

Figure 1.11. *Ozias Humphry (1742–1810)*, Portrait of Jane Austen, *known as the "Rice Portrait" (ca. 1792–93). Oil on canvas. Private Collection. Courtesy of the Bridgeman Art Library. There is strong evidence in family testimony and provenance to believe that the "Rice Portrait" represents Jane Austen in her early teens, and it was commonly reprinted as such up until the 1930s.*

Rice Portrait indeed represented a girl of this age, Brabourne explains that his inclination is "to think it *is* a true Bill."

Brabourne still collected information from other family members and authorities. A letter dated 23 October 1883 from Fanny-Caroline Lefroy to Mary Augusta Austen-Leigh shows that the portrait was discussed among relations and that questions were aired and settled. "I never heard before of the portrait of Jane Austen. I feel sure it never was either at Steventon or Chawton," she writes. Of course, because no one ever claimed the Rice Portrait hung at Steventon or Chawton, Lefroy's inability to place it there means nothing. She opines that George Austen could not afford a painting and concludes with unaffected curiosity and candor: "If it is genuine would not Mr. M. R. [Morland Rice] generously allow it to be photographed? I should greatly like to see it." When Lefroy *did* see a photograph of the Rice Portrait, she recollected a family tradition about it and pronounced it genuine, affirming that it was executed in "1788 or 9 making [Austen] not 14." Lefroy was, then, satisfied, and so was Austen's great-niece Mary Augusta Austen-Leigh, who used it in her later *Personal Aspects of Jane Austen* (1920). We know further that at least on one other occasion, her brother, Cholmeley Austen-Leigh, affirmed the existence of a portrait of the young Jane Austen to Morland Austen, the nephew of Colonel Thomas Austen. As Morland Austen's sister reports it, "Mr. Austen-Leigh assured Morland there was no picture of the authoress but the one at the beginning of her life."[29]

These attestations are particularly important. While it is clear that a certain contention over the stewardship of Austen's memory developed between the Hampshire Austens and the Kentish Austens (descendants of Austen's wealthy brother Edward), here both sides testify that there was a portrait taken of Jane Austen *in the early part of her life*. On the basis of its one-time ownership by Thomas Austen (who knew Jane Austen when she was the age represented in the portrait), the knowledge and interest of the Harding-Newmans (who knew and/or admired Jane Austen the novelist), the later testimony of collateral descendants to the existence of a portrait of the young Jane Austen, especially the testimony coming from Cholmeley Austen-Leigh, who assisted J. E. Austen-Leigh with the *Memoir*, Brabourne concluded that the portrait was authentic and used it as a frontispiece. Thereafter, it appeared in widely circulated sets of Austen's works as well as in authoritative biographies, preeminently in William and Richard Arthur Austen-Leigh's *Jane Austen: Her*

Life and Letters: A Family Record (1913), which impartially rehearses arguments for and against its authenticity and decides in its favor. Indeed, so secure was its standing through the 1930s that the NPG evidently tried to acquire it. The Rice family had no intention of giving up a family treasure, but Sir Henry Hake of the NPG did not give up easily. According to a memorandum of 6 October 1932, he combined graciousness with a politely menacing reminder that the family might have to sell it before too long: "I said that I was entirely in sympathy with this attitude so long as it was realised that in the event of the picture having to come to this Institution we would like to have the opportunity of acquiring it."[30] Had the Rice family been (in Hake's impatient words) less "tenacious of their inheritance," the portrait would be in the NPG today, alongside the now famous watercolor by Cassandra.

This widely reprinted picture is without doubt the finest, for unlike Cassandra's watercolor, it is professionally executed. The artist, Ozias Humphry, had also painted Austen's very wealthy great-uncle Francis Austen and was a frequent visitor to Sevenoaks. This attribution is important, for early doubts about the portrait derived largely from its misattribution to Zoffany, who was in India when the portrait was executed. Whether it is because the painting itself is imposing (55.5" × 35.5"), whether it is because the face, hands, and gown are extremely well achieved (in contrast to the arms and parasol), whether it is because it clearly resembles Cassandra's drawing (the shape of the face, the slightly asymmetrical setting of the eyes), or whether it is because we feel for the girl depicted here all of the awe inspired by the extraordinary woman she grew up to be, the image is irresistibly arresting, quite unlike the demure, often generic-looking young ladies shown in more conventional portraits of the period. The young Austen looks spirited, arch, and disarmingly intelligent, altogether capable of sitting in her corner of the parlor and laughing at the world, as Virginia Woolf imagined on reading the raucous sketch *Love and Freindship*, which Austen wrote at fourteen or fifteen, about the age represented here. Of course, the figure is also radically incompatible with the mythology about Austen's reclusiveness developed decades after it was painted. The young woman here is vigorously forward. Unlike Wordsworth's Lucy, half hidden from the eye, this girl solicits the gaze of the beholder, and she returns it confidently.

Clearly, portraits convey all manner of cultural meanings, but at least one thing they are also supposed to do is show us what someone looks like. Pondering the Rice Portrait invites us to collect descriptions of Austen in her youth—before she became "Jane Austen," before she acquired an aura of bodiless generality. Mrs. Mitford, mother of Mary Russell Mitford, described the young Jane Austen as "the prettiest, silliest, most affected, husband-hunting butterfly she ever remembers," an allegation that prompted the ever-reverent J. E. Austen-Leigh to write a postscript in defense of "the modest simplicity of character which I have attributed to my aunt" (*Memoir*, 133).[31] J. E. Austen-Leigh's indignation notwithstanding, Mrs. Mitford's description of the young Jane Austen is not anomalous. The peevish Philadelphia Walter, who alone regarded Austen as unpretty, similarly described her cousin Jane Austen as "affected and whimsical," which assessments square with the pert girl in the picture.[32] So does the description of Austen's niece Caroline, who recollected that Austen's face "was rather *round* than long—she had a *bright*, but not a *pink* colour—a clear brown complexion and very good hazel eyes" and that "before [Austen] left Steventon she was established as a very pretty girl. . . . Her hair, a darkish brown, curled naturally—it was in short curls around her face (for *then* ringlets were *not*)."[33] Recollecting Austen as she appeared in the late 1780s, Egerton Brydges wrote that she was "fair and handsome, slight and delicate but with cheeks a little too full," an opinion validated by the facial plumpness in the Rice Portrait, though Austen's later biographer Elizabeth Jenkins, taking umbrage at Brydges's remark in 1939, before the Rice Portrait was verboten, thought the portrait absolved Austen from this disgraceful charge of bodily excess: "A portrait of [Austen] as a young woman suggests that she outgrew this defect." And in 1838, Fulwar-William Fowle recalled that Austen "was pretty—certainly pretty—bright & a good deal of colour in her face—like a doll—no that wd. not give at all the idea for she had so much expression—she was like a child—quite a child very lively & full of humor," a view once again resonant with the portrait.[34]

These descriptions of Austen's person and air—along with the Rice Portrait itself—run counter to the familiar myth about Austen because they endow her with such a vibrant physical exuberance. The publication of the portrait in 1884 gave the Victorian public an entirely new image of and outlook on Austen, and this enabled readers to articulate their dissatisfaction with the saintly and shy figure she cut in the *Memoir* and encouraged them instead to imagine her as energetic, mischievous, high-spirited, and satiric. Doubtless Margaret A. Doody and Douglas Murray are correct to observe that "the reluctance to accept the Rice portrait" in some quarters "comes from psychological rather than scholarly sources. There has been relatively little desire to see Jane Austen as a young and sexual woman, and a constant desire to associate her with a safe and slightly-wistful oldmaidishness."[35] What bears stressing here is that the tension Doody and Murray describe between a safe and sedate Austen and a vivacious and sexed one has its origins in one branch of the late-nineteenth-century reception of the Rice Portrait. Arthur Quiller-Couch, for example, praises Oscar Fay Adams's biography of Austen in telling ways: "Other biographers leave us with the impression that she was slightly prim, old-maidish, addicted to papa, potatoes, poultry, prunes, and prism; whereas in fact she was light-hearted, gay-humored, at times almost 'giddy,' and always fond of dancing and dress."[36] Quiller-Couch's vision of Austen derives in no small part from Brabourne's edition of her letters, which features the Rice Portrait, which from this time forward presided over a countertradition in Austenian reception stressing her vigor rather than her attenuation, a split persisting to this day.

The existence of the Rice Portrait returns us to the spurious authenticity of Maria Jane Jewsbury's assertion that no "likeness" of Austen was ever "taken," an overdetermined surmise that was retrofitted into family history. In 1832 Bentley contacted Henry Austen to ask for a portrait of Austen that might be used as a frontispiece for the 1833 edition of *Sense and Sensibility*. Henry and Cassandra made no mention of the Rice Portrait. As all readers of Jane Austen's novels know, silence is difficult to read, and what it might mean here is very hard to say. Does it mean that the Rice Portrait is not authentic? That is possible, though that argument might have to be extended to Cassandra's sketch as well, now proudly displayed by the NPG as the only genuine portrait of Austen, for that sketch could more easily have been improved and engraved under Henry and Cassandra's supervision than it would later be by their nephew James Edward Austen-Leigh. Could it mean that the age of the figure disqualified it from consideration as a frontispiece, for, as we have already seen, later family members, when asked about a portrait, always assume from the start that a portrait of an *adult* is meant and wanted? Could it mean that Cassandra and Henry lost track of a portrait that had been executed forty years earlier and that had since changed hands? In light of Austen's developing reputation for virtually beatific retirement, the fact that Cassandra and Henry do not provide Bentley with a likeness may also mean that they were unwilling to place *any* images of Austen into commercial circulation, least of all a portrait of a robust girl who, far from shrinking modestly from view, fronts the beholder dauntlessly, whose expression conveys all the sauciness and satire Henry already insisted she never had, and whose boldness belied the view of Austen articulated by Jewsbury in her 1831 article, a view Henry clearly treasured, a view that was already developing in the dominant "legend" of Jane Austen. [37]

᠅᠅ The publication of the *Memoir* and the *Letters* prompted a burgeoning and highly commercialized phase of Janeism, featuring reprints of her novels and a steadily increasing volume of reviews and commentary on her, all of which whetted an appetite for Austenian images on the part of a large public who had not shown much previous interest in her. Sometimes, readers were presented with images with no provenance and no claims to authenticity, as in Agnes Repplier's brief 1900 article accompanying a portrait of "Jane Austen" (fig. 1.12), which is actually of the translator Sarah Austin (1793–1867). The mistake is certainly not Repplier's, whose many remarks on Austen are quite astute, and who was familiar both with Lizars's engraving (a "pudding faced likeness [which could never have been a likeness"]) and with the Rice Portrait ("charming").[38] Whoever made the error, it says as much about an eagerness to see or represent Jane Austen as it does about a lingering unfamiliarity with her. At times, lovers of Jane Austen evidently felt free to invent her image altogether, as in Violet Helm's sketch (fig. 1.13), the frontispiece to William Henry Helm's *Jane Austen and Her Country-House Comedy* (1910). In its purely frontal attitude and stylish approach to Austen's dress and demeanor (no old-maid's cap here), it calls the figure of the Rice Portrait to mind as its prototype, maturing it (especially by ridding the face of the plumpness contemporaries observed), softening some of its impertinence, and insisting on writerly pastimes if not professional authorship.

This desire for more Jane Austen and this sense of entitlement to invent her body is nowhere more striking than in the astonishing—and obscure—bust of her (fig. 1.14) crafted by the ever-industrious Percy Fitzgerald, a photograph of which appears in the frontispiece of his *Jane Austen: A Criticism and Appreciation* (1912). Fitzgerald's bust of "Austin" was unveiled in the Pump Room at Bath on 26 April 1912 to the delight of local dignitaries, who claimed Bath as her "dearest home" (much as denizens of Chawton or Winchester had or would) and suggested that

Figure 1.12. *Portrait of "Jane Austen" (Sarah Austin) in the* Critic *(1900).*
This sketch actually represents editor and translator Sarah Austin (1793–1867),
which says as much about editorial carelessness as it does about the public's
unfamiliarity with Austen's likeness.

Figure 1.13. *Frontispiece portrait to William H. Helm's* Jane Austen and Her Country-House Comedy *(1910). The portrait is drawn by Violet Helm.*

Figure 1.14.
*Bust of
Jane Austen
by Percy
Fitzgerald
(1912).*

she was the city's spiritual patron who "reconstructed and ordained and decorated all the innermost life of the place," accomplishing for the city's soul what Woods had for its architecture.[39] Fitzgerald clearly feels none of the inhibitions about embodying Austen that predominate in Austen memorializing: "Jane Austen herself must have been a delightful personage, attractive in many ways. Judging from her picture we can note a sort of piquancy in her face and figure: delicate, finely formed features, closed lips, with an almost sly glance of reserve. One has almost a personal affection for her. She was a tall, slender, graceful creature—with a slim, rather languish neck on which was poised a delicately shaped head—a slight ribbon passing across the forehead to confine the clustering curls.

Add her slight, gentle humour—her sweetness of voice and manner, and we have her before us."[40] Fitzgerald used the Lizars engraving as the basis of the bust, though it also comports with Violet Helm's rendition, featuring a hair ribbon rather than a cap restraining Austen's curls.

Fitzgerald clearly believes that putting Austen "before us" in three dimensions—conjuring her, so to speak—poses no challenge and no particular sensitivity. I bet that most Janeites viscerally feel this statue to be wrong, not simply in its particularities but in its very conception as a statue. A writer such as Samuel Johnson, as Kevin Hart has shown, lent himself to the *monumental*—to being cast in busts and statuary, in hefty tomes, and to being conjured as an imposingly substantial figure every bit as solid as the rock he struck with his foot—even before he was *canonical*, before his actual works were commonly read. For Hart, authorial monumentality requires that one be "a focus of a large and usually diffuse cultural will, the centre of a network of imaginary relationships and real desires."[41] As we shall see, Austen certainly has been the focus of a large and diffuse cultural will as well, but she could never be monumental in the same way. By acknowledging that Austen has a place "among the Immortals," Lewes is also quick to add that her "pedestal is erected in a quiet niche of the great temple," so even her imaginary statue is almost hidden from view (*CH1*, 166). Throughout the nineteenth century, Austen was canonical precisely without having body enough for monumentality; or, to recollect Lewes's (or rather, indeed, Johnson's own) terms, she was *known* through her novels without being *public* as a specific person. And so casting her figure in public statuary, as Fitzgerald blithely does, endows her with a substantiality that feels more radically inapt than a painting. In much the same way, Austenian pilgrims prefer the purely textual memorial tablet to Austen made from Roman stone and dedicated in the Poet's Corner of Westminster Abbey in 1967[42] (fig. 1.15)—the idea for this memorial originated not from some communal will but evidently from a single member of the Jane Austen Society—to the bust of Jane Austen overlooking the Cobb at Lyme Regis (fig. 1.16).[43] This astonishingly infelicitous bust, shown here in 1971, is located within a garden dedicated to Austen by the Jane Austen Society during the bicentennial of 1975. But despite its semiofficial status as a point of interest, it is seldom visited, and I have not been able to find out anything about it. Its appearance now (fig. 1.17) is more tolerable only because it has been worn down by the elements. Like the gravesite at

Figure 1.15.
*Tablet in
Poet's Corner of
Westminster
Abbey (1967).*

Winchester Cathedral, where pilgrims throng without paying much attention to the stained-glass window or the brass tablet, Janeites flock to the Cobb, where Louisa Musgrove fell, without adding the bust to their itinerary.

Fitzgerald's bust of Jane Austen, not surprisingly, scandalized contemporary Austenian descendants. In a remark that reminds us that the status of Austenian representations always implies larger questions about authority, Mary Augusta Austen-Leigh expressed umbrage first of all that a statue could be made and publicly dedicated without consulting, much less deferring to, the family and their expertise: "No intimation

Figure 1.16.
Bust of Austen overlooking the Cobb at Lyme Regis (1971). Presumably this is how the bust of Jane Austen looked when it was first crafted. Alberta Hirshheimer Burke Collection. Special Collections and Archives, Goucher College.

of this intended proceeding [at the Pump Room] had been made to the Austen-Leigh family nor was any member of it invited to the ceremony of the unveiling of the bust." When she and her brother William Austen-Leigh saw the bust, they were shocked by its unlikeness and requested the mayor of Bath to remove it from the Pump Room on these grounds. He evidently complied.[44] Clearly, William and Mary Augusta Austen-Leigh were concerned that Fitzgerald's performance might detract from the éclat of *Jane Austen: Her Life and Letters* (1913), featuring the Rice Portrait as a duly authenticated frontispiece. It may seem strange that a frankly imaginative bust be removed on the grounds of inaccuracy, but it is indicative of Austen's emerging status as a national icon that public officials recognized that suspect images of Austen must not be displayed. Getting Jane right is now a public concern, and Fitzgerald's bust was immediately ushered into an obscurity from which it has never emerged, except for one later drubbing at the hands of another descendent, who wrote in 1978 that "the bust was undoubtedly a travesty, a most supercilious, arrogant and apparently Jewish Jane."[45] Unlike

Figure 1.17. *Bust overlooking the Cobb at Lyme Regis (2005). The sea air has rendered the bust virtually unrecognizable.*

those of us who today believe that the sublime *Clueless*—where Emma Woodhouse reappears as the Jewish American princess Cher Horowitz—intelligently refigured rather than profaned Austen and the heroine with which she is often identified, in the late 1970s family guardians of Austen's memory wished to preserve not merely her likeness but also her religio-national identity, felt to be travestied, perversely turned against its own nature, by association with Jewishness. A quick review of extant portraits of the Austen family confirms that the prominent nose in this bust, presumably what drives this writer's indignation, is perhaps the only accurate thing about it.

 As we have seen, the conviction that Jane Austen has no "likeness"— in the sense both of having no portrait or drawing taken from life and of

Figure 1.18. *Silhouette, "Done by herself in 1815." Despite its excellent provenance, and its frequent reproduction, evidence suggests that this silhouette was executed in the late nineteenth century. Courtesy of the Dean and Chapter of Winchester Cathedral.*

having no peer—has been in tension with the intense wish to behold that "likeness" anyway, the sense that she is what Kipling's Janeites called "a non-pareil" in tension with a market-driven determination to reproduce her works and her image everywhere. Efforts to preserve the singularity of her one true image have thus failed as her celebrity has brought to the surface more and more images possibly taken from life. Among the most familiar of these are the silhouettes—one of which has the words "Done by herself in 1815" written on the back and which was donated by Austen great-grand-niece Jessie Lefroy to the dean and chapter of Winchester Cathedral in 1936 (fig. 1.18), and the other of which, bearing the description "L'aimable Jane," was found in 1944 pasted into the second edition of *Mansfield Park* (1816) acquired by the NPG in 1944 (fig. 1.19). Frequently reproduced on mugs and websites, both images have some

Figure 1.19. *Silhouette, "L'aimable Jane," undated. R. W. Chapman was inclined to regard this widely circulating profile as authentic; it probably does not represent Austen. Photograph: © National Portrait Gallery, London.*

claims to legitimacy, but raise questions. The pedigree of the Winchester silhouette is excellent, and certainly the prominent nose is an Austenian trait, but it seems likelier that the silhouette is Victorian. "L'aimable Jane," professionally executed and somewhat idealized, seems on surer ground—as R. W. Chapman put it, "Who would insert, in a copy of *Man-*

sfield Park, a portrait of any other Jane than its author" (*JAFP*, 214)—but it has neither provenance nor documentary evidence in its favor.

To this pair of unauthenticated images ostensibly contemporaneous to Austen can be added three candidates that have appeared more recently. One of these is a 4" × 6" watercolor painted by the Prince Regent's librarian, James Stanier Clarke, whom Austen is known to have visited in November of 1815 (fig. 1.20), and included in his *Friendship Book* along with other signed and dated drawings of authors and artists of Clarke's acquaintance. The watercolor in question, however, is not signed or dated, and its identification as Jane Austen is a matter of surmise, based largely on the similarity between the clothing worn by the subject and the clothing and fashions described by Austen herself around the same time and on computer-generated comparisons among this drawing and Cassandra's sketch, the Rice Portrait, and L'aimable Jane, using the E-FIT process. The dress and bustling air of the figure here certainly contest in interesting ways the myth of Austen as sedately withdrawn, and given Clarke's interest in Austen, it would not be surprising if he did sketch her. And the mole beneath the lips? No letters mention this feature of Austen's physiognomy, but *if* this is 1815 and *if* Jane Austen was beginning to manifest the epidermal discolorations characteristic of Addison's disease, this may be a sign. The case is an intriguing one, but the documentary evidence linking the drawing to Austen is tenuous.[46]

Equally fascinating, though as yet without any established provenance or documentation, is a plumbago and chalk sketch acquired by Roy Davids in 1980 and now in private ownership (fig. 1.21). It measures 6" × 4.75" and inscribed on the back in a small contemporary hand is "Jane Austin," with mounted letters on the contemporary gilt frame identifying "Jane Austin B 1775–D 1817." The name "Austen" is not infrequently spelled "Austin," so that "i" is certainly no impediment to the portrait's authenticity, and the birth and death dates invite us to regard this as a genuine attempt to evoke Jane Austen. While the sitters for the Rice Portrait and Cassandra's sketch seem very alike to me, the resemblance of this sitter to either of the former is somewhat less so: although the asymmetrical setting of the eyes is similar, the gauntness of face is not. Nor does the cat ring any bells, beyond signifying spinsterhood, which would seem redundant to anyone acquainted with Jane Austen in the first place. But the drawing in every other respect appears to be making a determined effort to display what we all

Figure 1.20. *Watercolor by James Stanier Clarke (1816). Although there is no direct evidence identifying this woman as Jane Austen, indirect evidence makes it a tantalizing possibility. Courtesy of Simon and Victoria Wheeler.*

know today to be Janean signifiers—her locket, her cap, her gown, her writing table, her writing implements, her pens and paper, and her window overlooking what appears to be a cathedral (though this could hardly represent ad vivum Austen's College Street view of the cathedral at Winchester)—all of which suggest a familiarity with the author. The

Figure 1.21. *Plumbago and chalk sketch of "Jane Austin," undated. This is possibly a memorial sketch of Jane Austen, as the dates and writing implements identify her clearly as a writer. Photograph:* © *Paula Byrne.*

very thoroughness with which these signs are collected suggests that this may be a memorial drawing made shortly after death rather than a "likeness" taken from life. Surely this image deserves the sustained study that it is now beginning to receive.

And, finally, we have an intriguing photograph printed in volume 1 of *Christies Catalogue: Godmersham Park, Canterbury, Kent, The Property of the Late Mrs. Robert Tritton,* from an auction that took place 6–9 June 1983 (fig. 1.22). When Mrs. Elsie Tritton and her husband bought Godmersham in 1936, most of the valuable property was no doubt already removed, but this item, which Christie's merely identifies as English School, circa 1780, is minor enough in size and quality to have remained as a not particularly valuable household item throughout the nineteenth and most of the twentieth centuries. What the picture seems to be celebrating is the good fortune of the boy at the center, proudly holding

Figure 1.22. *Family portrait, English School (ca. 1780). This image was recently spotted in a Christie's 1983 catalog for the sale of the entire contents of Godmersham.*

up a bunch of grapes (typically representing good fortune in heraldry) and standing before a table featuring more fruit, particularly pineapple (symbol of luxury), while his parents and siblings appear to congratulate him. The design above the mantle appears to represent Ganymede who, favored by Zeus, was carried away by an eagle, perhaps Zeus himself, to Olympus. If this picture is a true Godmersham piece, then it very plausibly represents Edward Austen at the time the Knights decided to adopt him as their heir, thus elevating him if not to Olympus then at least to the ranks of the great gentry. This would surely be, for the entire family, an event worth memorializing. And furthermore, if the picture indeed celebrates Edward's good fortune, then we also have a picture of Cassandra and the very young Jane Austen and probably Francis Austen as well (James and Henry being away at Oxford and Charles being too young). All of these as yet uncanonical images deserve close study. Together they demonstrate that the belief that Cassandra's sketch is the only true image of Austen needs rethinking. Certainly it has made us stop looking and thinking, and that is always a bad thing.[47]

In light of efforts by such recent artists as Tom Clifford and Melissa Dring to supplement an archive of Austenian "likeness" wrongly imagined to be exceedingly scanty by inventing Jane Austen anew in portraits, sketches, and even motion pictures, all these images deserve more attention, regardless of their authenticity or accuracy, because they testify to how the story of Jane Austen's body gets imagined and reimagined. After all, almost everyone in Austen's immediate family has at least one likeness—a painting, a silhouette, a miniature, or a sketch—to their credit, and the fact that Austen stands apart in having none that we are absolutely sure of is one of the many mysteries of her "legend."

⅏ Even though we of the twenty-first century want to see Jane Austen everywhere, we are also ill at ease looking at her, and I have heard Janeites denounce various images discussed here as though they were outrages offered to the queen. The vehemence that images of Jane Austen can arouse shows that more is at stake than academic questions of authenticity. General readers are probably familiar with Cassandra's portrait, but the images of Austen we see most frequently are its horridly saccharine improvements, and if this has something to do with the costs of permissions rights and the business of reproduction, it also has something to do with the haunting quality of the original that, as I have argued, seems to come to us asking not to be seen. No wonder Austen inspires a certain amount of discomfiture in those who wish to behold her. How could any image be commensurate to what we think and feel about her? How could so momentous and yet so intimate a figure, one so divine and so domestic, one who has become the site of such different and such contradictory visions and fantasies—about civility, love, history, and England itself—survive figuration without arousing disappointment or anger? How fitting, then, in the only entirely authenticated, undisputed image we have—which Cassandra signed "C.E.A. 1804" and which depicts Jane (as Anna Lefroy later wrote), "sitting down out of doors on a hot day, with her bonnet strings untied" (*JAFP*, 213) (fig. 1.23)—Jane Austen finally reaches us, much as the celebrated irony of her writing does, only in the act of turning away.[48]

Figure 1.23. *Watercolor of Jane Austen sitting outdoors (1805), by Cassandra Austen. This is the only unequivocally authentic image of Jane Austen. Privately owned.*

Jane
2 Austen's
Magic

enry James called it "twaddle"—the sometimes quietly burbling and sometimes expansively gushing ef-
fusions of enthusiasm for Jane Austen abetted by a
"body of publishers, editors, [and] illustrators" who
find "their 'dear,' our dear, everybody's dear, Jane so
infinitely to their material purpose."[1] Repelled by (or
is it envious of?) the ubiquity of Austeniana in "pretty reproductions of
every variety of what is called tasteful . . . form," James saw Janeism as
the regrettable outcome of Austen's commodification during the Victorian period.[2] He had a point. Although Austen's six novels had been
available separately since 1832 in the Standard Novels series published
by Richard Bentley, she was admired, even adored, relatively quietly by
a few, such as George Lewes and Thomas Macaulay. "Janeism" itself did
not develop until the last few decades of the nineteenth century. James
Edward Austen-Leigh's *A Memoir of Jane Austen* not only provided ador-
ing biographical information about his spinster aunt but also included
Lady Susan, the Lizars engraving of Cassandra's sketch of Austen, and
woodcuts of Chawton Church and Steventon Parsonage, thus putting
much of Austen's "world"—which would soon constitute the Janeites'
universe—into a tidy, determinate bundle. Bentley's deluxe *Steventon
Edition of Jane Austen's Work* appeared in 1882, the first collected edition of Austen's novels, and soon Lord Brabourne's 1884 edition of Austen's *Letters* appeared, putting before the public all the necessary accou-
trements of devotion. Thereafter, Austen's novels appeared often singly
and in sets, ranging from (and this list is not comprehensive) Routledge's
cheap issues of 1883 and the Sixpenny Novel series starting in 1886; to
Macmillan's 1890 issues, lavishly illustrated by Hugh Thomson; to the
quasi-scholarly ten-volume set of R. Brimley Johnson for Dent in 1892
and reissued five times in as many years.[3] Janeism thrived in the literary

marketplace from the 1880s on, and in America too she was "a household word."[4]

Though James acknowledged that Austen would not be so "saleable if we had not more or less . . . lost our hearts to her" in the first place, he censured the "special bookselling spirit" that, with all its "eager, active interfering force" whips up a "stiff breeze" and drives the waters of reputation above their natural levels.[5] Produced by readers deemed incapable of assessing Austen's just value or discriminating her real merits, Janeism was a purely commercial affair and as such distinct from serious criticism. Until quite recently, few literary critics challenged James's contempt. Yet Victorian devotees of Jane Austen were hardly hoi polloi, as James makes its sound, but often distinguished literati. We have already seen that the word "Janeite" dates back to George Saintsbury's 1894 preface to *Pride and Prejudice*, where he declares himself a "Jane Austen-ite."[6] It was Janeites of Saintsbury's generation who with their twaddle transformed Jane Austen into "Jane Austen" the "legend" that Trilling and all of us recognize. In this chapter, I shall give the twaddle of the Victorian period its due. In it we shall not only trace the development of that wistful and elegaic mood that, as D. A. Miller has rightly described, epitomizes Janeism and that is still familiar to us today, but also see how "Jane Austen" provided and relieved anxieties about modernity and its attendant exhaustion that were distinctively Victorian.[7]

Foremost among the "pretty" volumes James probably had in mind when he acidly described them as "what is called tasteful" is Constance Hill's 1902 *Jane Austen: Her Homes and Her Friends*. This volume is by no means the first published effort to recover Jane Austen by visiting the places and recollecting the people associated with her; but it is the most sustained (the book is 268 pages long) and the most elaborate (Hill and her sister undertake their journeys with well-thumbed copies of Austen's novels, Brabourne's edition of the *Letters*, and J. E. Austen-Leigh's *Memoir* in hand). It was also the most influential. In his "authoritative" editions of Austen's novels, R. W. Chapman cribs this book when footnoting the actual places visited by Austen's characters. Hill's preface begins by citing the altogether banal observation that "works of genius" are marked by "something intangible" that is *felt* but that eludes words: "This 'intangible something'—this undefinable charm—is felt," she writes, "by all Jane Austen's admirers." Generally we encounter such platitudes about Austen's genius—which make up a large part of Victorian commentary on Austen—without attending closely. If we listen carefully, however, something remarkable emerges. Austen's "undefinable charm," she continues, "has exercised a sway of ever-increasing power over the writer and illustrator of these pages; constraining them to follow the author to all the places where she dwelt and inspiring them with a determination to find out all that could be known of her life and its surroundings."[8]

In Hill's hands the word *genius* starts to dance across semantic boundaries, sometimes denoting the modern sense of talent or intellectual endowment and other times reverting to the earlier sense of a tutelary spirit attached to a place; and the word *charm* is similarly charged, surpassing its bland sense as *attraction* and moving toward something stronger, like *spell*. Only this could account for the delightful but nevertheless palpable sense of supravoluntary compulsion: under the "increasing power" of Austen's "charm," the writer is "constrained" to follow Austen's footsteps. Veering momentarily into the language of Christianity borrowed by literary tourism throughout the nineteenth century (one recollects the prominent example of Byron), Hill tells us that her book will take us on a "pilgrimage," but only, as it turns out, to observe a crucial difference from other literary tourists. Following "in the footprints of a favourite writer would, alas! in many cases lead to a sad disenchantment." Hill's book promises, by contrast, an enchantment that will never disappoint or diminish: "We would now request our readers," she writes, in "imagination, to put back the finger of Time for more than a hundred years and to step with us into Miss Austen's presence," a presence that is special. Our journey is, to be sure, an act of friendship, for to know Jane Austen, as we have seen, is to desire to be her friend. As is so often the case throughout this little volume, we also cross boundaries into the noumenal: Jane Austen is no ordinary friend, and the purpose is not simply to get to become acquainted with her in any ordinary sense; rather, it is to "'hold communion sweet'" with her "mind and heart." What is this enchanted place located at the intersection of space and time, a place from a bygone era, yet accessible today and still somehow permeated by the traces of Austen's presence? The title of the first chapter provides the answer: "An Arrival in Austen-land."[9]

In an 1885 review of Brabourne's edition of Austen's *Letters*, Thomas Kebbel describes his own pilgrimage to Austenian sites in Hampshire, and he laments that "Miss Austen's country" is so little known.[10] "Miss Austen's country" has a different valence from "Austen-land." I take Hill's

Figure 2.1.
Ellen Hill's signpost
"To Austen-land,"
from Constance
Hill's Jane Austen:
Her Homes and
Her Friends *(1902).*

unblushingly fanciful chapter title—and its accompanying illustration (fig. 2.1), guiding us toward a magical place—as an allusion to *Alice's Adventures in Wonderland.* The wonders that Hill's volume goes on to narrate are—like everything about Austen—infinitely less egregious than Charles Dodgson's, to be sure, but paradoxically they may also be more powerful for being so because, however palpable, most of the important ones are not, strictly speaking, visibly there at all, and this invisibility is in marked contrast to so many author pilgrimages of the earlier nineteenth century.[11] Unlike heritage-constructing books of roughly the same period, such as W. Jerome Harrison's *Shakespeare-Land* (1907) and Ward and Ward's *Shakespeare's Town and Times* (1896) or James Leon Williams's *The Homes and Haunts of Shakespeare* (1892), which, as John Taylor has shown, use *photographs* both to show literary tourists what traces to look for and, just as important, to testify to the reality/authenticity of those sites, Hill's volume relies mostly on *drawings* of Austenian places executed by Hill's sister, even though photography was available.[12] When Hill and her sister arrive at the village of Steventon, they cannot find the rectory where Austen was born (it had been torn down in the 1820s by Austen's brother Edward who, oblivious of its hallowed status as Austen's birthplace, built a better house there for his son's use). With the marvelous appearance of an aged informant related to servants in

THE SITE OF THE OLD PARSONAGE, STEVENTON

Figure 2.2. *Ellen Hill's sketch of the Steventon pump, from Constance Hill's* Jane Austen: Her Homes and Her Friends *(1902).*

the Austen household, they locate "a pump in the middle o' the field" that "stood i' the washhouse at the back o' the parsonage." Though "barely noticed before," the pump (fig. 2.2) "become[s] interesting now as the only visible relic of the Austen's home." As the sketch indicates, the view of the pump clearly lacks the patent if somewhat shabby materiality that countless photographs imparted to, say, Ann Hathaway's cottage, and the site and sight of the pump would look even more absurd as a photograph.

Its primary purpose, after all, is to represent the absence of the Steventon rectory. As a result, the burden of wondrous vision is placed on the visitant—as when Ellen Hill is drawing the pump, and Constance, gazing on the blank space, muses, "I can now picture to myself the exact spot where the parsonage stood, and can fancy the carriage drive approaching it. . . . I can even fancy the house itself."[13] In cases where Austenian remnants *are* actually extant, they are not always bewitching and, in the nineteenth century, made no part of the pilgrimage. Chawton Cottage, to take the most conspicuous example, is an authentic and extant Austenian home, but it was so far from charming that J. E. Austen-Leigh not only declines to represent it in his *Memoir,* but also actively discourages "any admirer of Jane Austen to undertake a pilgrimage to the spot" because it has now been "divided into tenements for labourers" and "reverted to ordinary uses" (*Memoir,* 69). A comparison between Ellen Hill's partial, highly idealized sketch and a contemporary 1910 photograph of Chawton Cottage (figs. 2.3 and 2.4) demonstrates just how much imaginative work is required from the visitor bent on Austenian enchantment when confronted with such refractorily unlovely but actual material.

Although the mood of Hill's book is certainly genial—having arrived near Steventon on the first night of her journey, she writes, "We fell asleep that night with a happy consciousness that we were really in Austen-land"—its most powerful encounters are dislocating. More than once, Hill can "fancy" that she can glimpse "two girlish forms . . . those of Jane Austen and her sister Cassandra" walking among trees and flowers at Steventon; she can watch "Miss Jane Austen as she enters the ballroom" in Basingstoke; or can hear "the pleasant echoes" of Jane and the Lefroys at Ashe Rectory. At its best, Austen-land, in other words, is haunted: Austen's "echoes" have not died away even if she herself has vanished. Hill's purpose is to conjure Jane's ghosts and put us into contact with them. It seems fitting, then, that having reviewed Austen's life chronologically by revisiting the places she dwelled and traveled and coordinating these visits with the *Letters* and novels, Hill concludes her review of Austen's life not, as one might expect, with Austen's death and burial at Winchester, but with her afterlife—evoking the mournful Cassandra returning to a home at Chawton, surrounded by memories of her beloved sister, speaking of her always with the voice of *"living* love" and becoming in a sense the first Janeite, a mortal guardian of the genius of the place.[14]

CHAWTON COTTAGE

Figure 2.3. *Ellen Hill's idealized sketch of what we now call Chawton Cottage,* *from Constance Hill's* Jane Austen: Her Homes and Her Friends *(1902).*

Figure 2.4. *Chawton Cottage (1910). Small wonder Chawton was not on the itinerary of most Janeite pilgrimages. Courtesy of the Jane Austen Memorial Trust.*

Other Janeite pilgrimages of the period also take on this distinctively haunted quality. Oscar Fay Adams—whose works on Austen form a substantial part of a literary career that also included essays, poems, and literary handbooks—followed Austen's "sweet shade" a decade earlier than Hill, and his journey is marked by more violent temporal dislocations. Remote enough to be not present, yet (unlike Shakespeare) not so very remote as to constitute downright history, Austenian emanations occupy a liminal space between the past and present. For Adams, Austen-land is a charmed place fixed in a curious sort of time warp. He observes, "The view from the higher ground beneath which Steventon village shrinks out of sight . . . is practically the same which she saw as a child a century and more ago." Yet Adams's very words belie him: "'Time that shifts and veers,'" he continues (momentarily quoting Swinburne's "Ballad of Bath"), "has not worked many or great changes here. Now *as then* Steventon and its neighborhood is a peaceful corner of the world, a countryside whose quiet is broken only by the whistle of the train which rushes past without stopping."[15] Why has Adams forgotten the stunning historical fact that train whistles never blew as they rushed past

Steventon *then*, for the simple reason that there were no trains in Austen's time? To dismiss this as a meaningless blunder would be to underread the time warps that frequently irrupt in Adams's essay. It is not only that reading Austen carries him into her quieter, simpler time, as this passage makes clear, but also that thinking about Austen brings her forward toward our time as well, making it hard to tell the difference between the past and the present, the really living and the really dead.

On this score, Adams is more extravagantly beguiled than Constance Hill—she, after all, had merely marveled at a pump in a field, fancied the presence of once-living people, and endowed a rather unattractive cottage with all the charms of the picturesque. Adams encounters not only people who were once living but now dead but also people who never lived at all—that is to say, Austen's fictional characters—and these seem to mingle before him. For Adams, Austen's reality and that of her characters are equally palpable presences in the charmed, supratemporal spaces, somehow contiguous to our own yet above or outside history, associated with Jane Austen and her characters. In Bath, "if we go to the Pump Room and watch the people who drift through the spacious room . . . it is *her* men and women whose faces we look for. . . . The people of 'Persuasion' and 'Northanger Abbey' meet us at every turn," and "the novelist herself is just as constantly before us." Like so many Victorian Janeites, Adams proudly cites Tennyson's visit to Lyme Regis: "Don't talk to me of the Duke of Monmouth," exclaimed Tennyson indignantly when someone wanted to point out the spot where the Monmouth Rebellion officially began in 1685. This ill-fated attempt to wrest the throne from James II has no interest to Tennyson, who wishes instead to learn one thing alone: "Show me just where Louisa Musgrove fell." Tennyson's story about Monmouth is a compelling one, but it is no precedent for Adams's own musings. For Tennyson, Austen's fictional world displaces the nation's history of centuries ago, but for Adams, Austen's fiction eclipses the past and present equally: "It is we that are the shadows, not the people that Jane Austen sent upon this scene," he exclaims, and gazing on the famous Cobb he adds, "One may see [Anne Elliott, Captain Wentworth, and the Musgroves] here still, and with them, but by them of course unseen, the 'divine Jane' herself."[16] Of course? What kind of work does *of course* accomplish for Adams here? It establishes that knowingness— that secret handshake—that Janeites exchange as they indulge their flights of fancy with an equal consciousness of their absurdity and their seriousness, as if it were self-evident (of course) that characters could not possibly see their author, even though inspired Janeites might be able to channel characters and author alike.

What do we call this whimsy that can describe hallucinations of what never existed in the same breath as the driest and most scrupulous antiquarian research into former building sites or social practices? Sometimes this whimsy is mixed with an archness verging on high camp, as when Lord Iddesleigh enthuses, "Glorious amongst its fellows, that pump had stood in the washhouse at the back of the Parsonage, and from the well beneath it had come the water of which Miss Austen had made use. It is sincerely to be hoped that a stone may be erected by this well to record the fact."[17] Even when campy, self-parodic Janeite whimsy proclaims pride in its own excesses and savors the fact that its passions and expertises look frivolous or peculiar to the uninitiated. How ought we to characterize this preoccupation with a charmed world, a world "light & bright & sparkling" somehow adjacent to history but not seriously impinged by it, a world whose reality surpasses that of our own and at the same time feels like more of a true home to us than the one to which we actually belong, a world all but invisible except to true believers and accessible to us only at the price of our appearing scatty in the eyes of the world? I think we call it *fay*.

⚜ Non-Janeites smirk knowingly at most of the women and virtually all of the men who proclaim themselves one of the tribe, considering them dotty at best and queer, arrested at worst. Seldom has this imputation of queerness been genealogized, taken as a subject worth pondering rather than a put-down to be uttered without thinking. Associating Jane Austen or her works with fairies—the fay—goes against our twenty-first-century grain. I have elsewhere discussed the "queerness" of "Austen" for twentieth-century writers and readers, where queerness denoted homosexuality in particular.[18] That is not the sense of queerness I am exploring here, though it is certainly a partial prehistory of it. The queerness Victorians were thinking about was oddity, and the fairies they were referring to were . . . well . . . fairies. In a number of not-always consistent ways, thinking of Austen in the context of fairies was an effortless association for Victorian Janeites and a positively foundational one. In the relentlessly idealizing biography by James Edward Austen-Leigh, linking Jane Austen with fairies and fairy tales is part a defensive effort, chiefly designed "to show her love for children" (*Memoir*, 73), a position falling short of the self-evident. Then, as now, many readers maintained that Austen's novels imply a chilliness toward children, a contempt for parental fatuity in general and maternal partiality in particular. Austen's detractors did not hesitate to hold this against her. In 1894, for example, Alice Meynell could complain, "The lack of tenderness and of spirit is manifest in Miss Austen's indifference to children. . . . They are her subjects as spoilt children. . . . The novelist even spends some of her irony upon a little girl of three. She sharpens her pen over the work."[19] Foregrounding Austen's affection for children, Austen-Leigh domesticates and normalizes his illustrious aunt, suggesting a continuity between her artistic processes and her behavior with her nieces and nephews and in the process implicitly making the case for his own importance to her writing. For Austen-Leigh, Austen is not a novelist of stunning detachment or (as Margaret Oliphant phrased it) of shocking "feminine cynicism," but a modest spinner of "trifling anecdote[s]" and "fictitious histor[ies]" that "could deceive nobody" because they were delightful and innocuous "nonsense" (*Memoir*, 74).

The preeminent instances of such charming nonsense for Austen-Leigh were the fairy tales Austen transmitted principally, it would appear, to girl children. Although Austen-Leigh himself wrote and illustrated *The Delightful Tales of Fairyland*, dedicating the little volume to his sister, in the *Memoir* he either forgets or omits to mention his own boyhood interest in the fairy mode and instead produces the recollections of Austen's nieces on the subject. One recalled how Austen "would tell us [children] the most delightful stories, chiefly of Fairyland, and her fairies had all characters of their own. The tale was invented, I am sure, at the moment, and was continued for two or three days, if occasion served" (*Memoir*, 72). Another niece reports in the same vein that "her long circumstantial stories [were] so delightful. These were continued from time to time . . . woven, as she proceeded, out of nothing but her own happy talent for invention. Ah! if but one of them could be recovered!" (*Memoir*, 73). As late as the 1930s, descendants of the Austen family did in fact recollect specific fairy tales for very young children scrupulously handed down from generation to generation and transcribed in 1922 by Marcia Rice as having initially been told by Austen's brother Edward Knight (her great-great grandfather), and in 1931 substantially the same tales were said by John Hubback to have been told to him by his grandfather, Francis Austen, one of Jane's other brothers (see appendix).[20] Whether Jane Austen ever had a hand in the composition or in the transmission of these particular tales, which Austen's juvenilia in places resemble, can only be a matter of speculation. What is not speculation is that Austen's nieces and nephews (and, later, their progeny) treasured fairy tales and that they link Austen with them. Austen-Leigh understands Austen's narrative mode to be compatible with that of the fairy tale, implying that her novels too were inventive tales, essentially full of fun and nonsense, and likewise continuable at the request of children: "She would, if asked, tell us many little particulars about the subsequent career of some of her people" (*Memoir*, 119).

The world of fairies by this account is used not so much to account for the potent magic of Austen's art but rather to render her a figure of marvelous dexterity when it comes to domestic handicrafts, weaving tales and writing novels, both taking on a domestic character. Her fastidious handwriting, her talent for tidily folding and sealing letters, and her accomplishments as a seamstress each receive Austen-Leigh's particular attention: "The same hand which painted so exquisitely with the pen," he writes with fervent praise, "could work as delicately with the needle" (*Memoir*, 79). The unwary reader might assume that Austen-Leigh is praising the quality of his aunt's temper that made it possible for her to turn from the stunning perfection of the word painting in her novels to the homely task of needlework, when he is referring to her penmanship rather than her authorship, thus initiating a tradition of criticism that would celebrate Austen for respecting her limits, for never using her pen to usurp the needle of female propriety. If we were tempted to mistake Austen-Leigh here, the error would not matter, where a diminished sense of scale and purpose are paramount. Accordingly, Austen-Leigh is deaf to his aunt's irony: he accepts at face value as a "description of her own style of composition" her self-deprecating contrast of her "little bit (two inches wide) of ivory on which I work with so fine a Brush" to his own evidently bombastic and manifestly failed attempts at novel writing, which she characterized as "strong, manly vigorous sketches, full of variety and glow" (*Memoir*, 122, 123). Austen-Leigh cannot conceive of the possibility that his aunt may be commending his artistic efforts with her tongue in cheek. The fairy aunt is a modest little person whose homely and unpretending miniatures are for the amusement of little people. Thus he tells us about Austen's little silken sewing bag, along with thread, needles, and a tiny scrap of paper containing two stanzas of verse, as an artifact. This "curious specimen of her needlework," he writes, is "the kind of article that some benevolent fairy might be supposed to give as a reward to a diligent little girl" (*Memoir*, 79). Throughout the *Memoir*, Austen-Leigh presents himself as a dutiful nephew who admires the largeness of Scott's historical romances and who considers Scott's superiority as a genius self-evident. For Austen-Leigh, Austen's fairy dimensions are precious exactly because they are diminutive. Austen-Leigh uses the fairy world, somewhat paradoxically then, to normalize Jane Austen, to represent her as wondrous only in that she accomplished the ordinary duties of feminine domesticity with such extraordinary benevolence, affection, and selflessness. An angel of the house of sorts, a benign and reassuring sprite, this is the Jane Austen adduced later, and with less fairy magic, by Alice King in 1882 as "a picture of what a female author and artist should be: true to home duties" and by Saintsbury in 1894, who offers her as a wholesome contrast to the "offensive . . . *viraginous* . . . 'New Woman.'"[21]

Austen-Leigh was not the only one to introduce Austen to a wide public via fairyland, however; Lord Brabourne also did so, and in a more fascinating, if less direct, manner. As B. C. Southam observed, Jane Austen is "dear Aunt Jane" for Austen-Leigh, but she is "the inimitable Jane" for Brabourne, and the celebratory valences of these epithets are different (*CH2*, 40). Austen-Leigh is, when all is said and done, extolling his own familial piety—honoring the now-illustrious kinswoman "dear" to him—whereas Brabourne is indulging in a hyperbolical but nonetheless professional admiration. By the 1880s, Brabourne was known to the reading public as a prolific author of fairy tales. Noting more than once that his "fairy tales have delighted a whole generation of readers," Oscar Fay Adams designates Brabourne as the inheritor of Austen's inventive genius: "It seems to me by no means improbable that her grandnephew, Lord Brabourne, whose talent as a weaver of fairy tales is so generally recognized by children of to-day, may have discovered his own peculiar gifts in the same direction from a knowledge of his aunt's abilities in that quarter."[22] Brabourne never makes this claim, but unlike Austen-Leigh, who reports on Austen's fairy tales for children but never represents himself as recollecting them, Brabourne clearly does take up the fairy mantle. The fairy that emerges from his work is not a figure of mawkish propriety—indeed, the view of Austen that flourished in his branch of the family was decidedly less idealized in the first place. Brabourne's mother—

none other than Fanny Knight, Austen's favorite niece—remarked in 1869, "Aunt Jane from various circumstances was not so *refined* as she ought to have been for her *talent*."[23]

No doubt this view of Austen as countrified or déclassé (perhaps as Elinor and Marianne perceive Lucy Steele, or as John and Fanny Dashwood perceived Elinor and Marianne themselves) circulated in the household of her parents. So for Brabourne, the charm instead is first the age to which Austen belongs, and second her voice as an artist. Austen-Leigh too regards Austen as old-fashioned enough to require him to swell his pages with general descriptions of what meals, dances, cookery, and manners existed sixty-odd years earlier, and at times he appears embarrassed by the rusticity of his aunts and uncles. But for Brabourne, the temporal change is made to feel vaster and is invested with real glamour: "The customs and manners which Jane Austen describes have changed and varied so much as to belong in a great measure to another age" (*Letters 1*, 206). While Oscar Fay Adams presents us with an Austen who is perpetually (yet impossibly) present, Brabourne's Austen belongs to a lost world. Editing Austen's *Letters* is accordingly an exercise in English local history, and the dedication of these hefty volumes to Queen Victoria is thus more than a matter of authorial self-promotion and puffery. To help us to understand Austen and her world better, Brabourne appends genealogy tables and material on the Kentish associations of the Austen family. Though some of the chattiest and most amusing of Brabourne's explanations involve firsthand anecdotes about the later life of persons mentioned in Austen's letters, the work of tracking down allusions, Brabourne forewarns us, often "awaken[s] old memories and recall[s] old stories" (*Letters 1*, 208), stories about the "old nurse" at Godmersham, whose own "stories" in turn Brabourne remembers "to this day" (*Letters 2*, 126–27), or a ghost story of sorts about the lawsuit against the property of his grandfather (Austen's brother Edward), fomented when "an old, long deceased Mr. Knight appeared twice or thrice in a dream to the claimant, and informed him that he [rather than Austen's brother] was the rightful owner of Chawton [Manor]" (*Letters 2*, 220). Part raconteur and part antiquarian, Brabourne prepares his edition of Austen's *Letters* as though Austen herself were situated just outside the boundary of history and just inside a discourse of lore.

Brabourne's own fairy tales circulate the same kinds of language about "old" times that he uses as an editor of Austen's *Letters*. I am thinking in

particular of Brabourne's—then Edward H. Knatchbull-Hugessen's—
1874 collection of seven stories bearing the provocative title *Queer Folk*.
"Well, and so they *are* 'Queer Folk,'" he affirms defiantly in the first sentence of his preface, an asseveration reminiscent of Austen's gloriously
intrusive "Yes novels!" harangue in the fifth chapter of *Northanger Abbey* (*QF*, v). The opening story, "The Warlock of Coombe," takes place in
Kent and is in a sense about Kentish land itself, "the legends of which
are so deeply impressed upon my memory" (*QF*, 2), the land that produced Austen along with the rest of his family and that is, he says, "fairyland to me" (*QF*, 2). Like the people and places of Austen's *Letters*, this
story floods him with memories of what he calls "the old, old days" when
"the habits of the people, too, were different—there was less cultivation
and more politeness; labouring men touched their hats to squire and
parson." This hardly sounds like the remote past when fairies roamed
the English hillside; in fact, it sounds a lot like Victorian evocations of
Jane Austen's novels, when class (and gender) relations seemed bliss-
fully nonconflictual and when "many things which are deemed necessary to existence in the days we live in were not even known" (*QF*, 2).
Indeed, Brabourne's description of the main character—"a firm believer
in all that his father, grandfather, and great-grandfather had believed
before him, and [who] shrank from new ideas and new theories with
a thorough old fashioned John Bull prejudice" (*QF*, 4)—owes more to
conservative, Burkean idealizations of the British yeomanry prominent
during Austen's time than it does to earlier periods of English history.
Accordingly, despite the supernatural powers represented in the story,
we are nonplussed at the very end to learn that it transpired well before
the Elizabethan era. My point is simply that Brabourne places in Austen
and his stories alike what we—taking a cue from his title—may call a
queer temporality, old and yet not that old, familiar and strange at the
same time.

Brabourne justifies the title of his volume by referring to the curious
and archaic personages who occupy it: "a Warlock—a Witch—a society of Pig-faced Ladies—a quantity of Elves, and several other things
and persons which any unprejudiced individual will at once allow to be
queer enough to justify the name I have chosen" (*QF*, v). In some respects, at once the queerest and the most Austenian of Brabourne's stories is the final one, "The Old Bachelor Married," which moves us from
the quasi-primevality of the Kentish countryside to a quasi-domestic

comedy of discernibly modern England. This story is about a rich old bachelor surrounded by servile relations — near and distant — who flatter, indulge, and fawn all over him in the hope that he will leave his money to them when he dies. They endure his cantankerousness with fulsome patience, displaying "a laudable readiness to visit and cherish him, to improve their acquaintance with him in every possible way, and even to assist him in the distribution of his superfluous wealth" (*QF*, 299). The archness of the narrator — particularly when the relations, anxious lest the rich old gentleman produce an eleventh-hour heir, unite in decrying the evils of marriage — places the tale so squarely within the realm of social satire that its few elements of the fairy-tale mode do not fundamentally disrupt its realism. Accordingly, the abruptness with which he decides to vex them by announcing his intention to marry within the year any woman whose finger fits his napkin ring merely intensifies the sharpness of the social comedy, demonstrating both the senile petulance of the old bachelor and the obsequiousness of his relations, who are momentarily flummoxed as they try to figure out how to discourage him and at the same time toady to him.

Like Austen's silliest bachelor, Mr. Elton, the old gentleman meets his match at a public place. Instantaneously captivated by a mysteriously veiled young woman, the old gentleman is thrilled to discover that she meets his absurd condition, as her middle three fingers have been fused together in a childhood accident, and proposes marriage on the spot. The old gentleman is brought up short, however, when no sooner does his shy young bride enter his house than she becomes ungovernable, refusing to observe the routines of ordinary civility, much less the niceties of wifely subservience — with the raucous violence reminiscent of Austen's juvenile writings, she throws a hot pudding in his face when she wants to be alone, for example; and far from playing the gracious wife, she not only refuses to greet his guests but even poisons them and behaves like a madwoman to drive them away. Galled to find himself imprisoned and intimidated within his own house by an almost preternaturally unpleasant woman of his own choosing, the once coddled and high-handed old gentleman is chastened — until one day quite by accident he discovers through the gypsies on his estate that she was in fact previously married to a tinker before turning actress and running away. Legally a husband no longer, the old gentleman remands the woman to his bailiff, delighted at last to have his house and his sycophantic relations back to himself, nettling them to the very last by leaving his vast wealth to be applied against the national debt.

Although "The Old Bachelor Married" is a modernized rendition of the fairy-bride-tale type, its treatment is particularly ironic, eschewing the marvelous by resolving it into banality, much as Austen had comically done via Ann Radcliffe in *Northanger Abbey*.[24] Except for the ludicrously fortuitous deformity to her hand, the fairy-bride here is nothing more or less uncommon than a maneuvering adventuress in the mold of *Lady Susan* (which had been published in J. E. Austen-Leigh's 1871 edition of the *Memoir*) or Lucy Steele and just as weirdly attractive as they are in her histrionic verve and in the effortlessness of her mastery over pompous and witless men. In other words, the queer personage that haunts the concluding story of *Queer Folk* is no witch or elf, but Jane Austen herself, not as an aunt, but as a novelist, or at least a belated novelistic permutation of her narrator. Austen-Leigh, too, has specifically associated Austen with a sort of queerness. After discussing Austen's juvenile writing, he explicitly likens Austen's earliest literary exercises to Scott's "early rambles on the borders" when he was practicing for his adult endeavors without knowing it, both figures similar in having spent their early years thinking of little "but the queerness and the fun" (*Memoir*, 43). Austen-Leigh, it must be remembered, upheld his family interest in decorum by withholding virtually all of Austen's brilliant, bumptious, youthful writings from publication, and so the message is clear: his aunt outgrew her queerness. For Brabourne, the opposite appears true: that queerness itself is a treasured legacy. His "inimitable" Austen is strange and wonderful, and she achieves her startling narratorial liveliness through a detachment from the dreariness of "modern" domesticity and its sentiments of sobriety. Her narrator, like fairies, lives in our world differently, queerly we might say, living in the same space but askance, and in the process imparting a wonder to it that, as we shall see, becomes nothing less than a cultural resource.

The foregoing suggests that the placement of Jane Austen and her novels within the charmed world of fairyland was not some aberrant development in Victorian Janeism. On the contrary, fairydom is one of the fundamental ways Austen was introduced from 1870 forward to a wider public that had hitherto not paid much attention to her, and such notions were immediately taken up. The very title of Anne Thackeray Ritchie's *Book of Sibyls* (1883) locates the power of the female tradition she is mapping out in the preternatural, thus countering the masculine tradition her father established. Her widely influential essay on Austen, originally published in *Cornhill* in 1871, presents Austen as the sibylline counterpart to Scott, whom her father called the "Wizard of the North."[25] After this essay, the discourse of magic is used almost reflexively as a way of alluding to or accounting for Austen's distinctive fascinations. The *Gentleman's Magazine* of 1885, for instance, meditates on Austen's "literary alchemy," and the *Spectator* of 1890 ponders the "secret of her charm" that "wields no spell at all" on a "very considerable number of remarkably able men," yet "wields a spell of quite curious force" on others.[26] Even as late as 1917, naturalist Sir Francis Darwin acknowledges the magical "quality of treasure-trove to the secrets" about the heroes and heroines Austen imparted to her little nieces and nephews, and he recommends, as we have seen, the game of asking children and adults alike what questions they "would put to the ghost of Jane Austen." Although Darwin's principal interest is in the genetic information Austen's ghost might share about the offspring of her heroes and heroines—in short, what kinds of traits did Darcy and Elizabeth pass on to their children—Darwin never brackets the world of wonder; indeed, the whole enterprise is rooted in fancy. Visiting the famous Cobb where Louisa Musgrove fell, he writes, "I quite suddenly and inexplicably fell down." Quite mysteriously, he continues, "The same thing happened to a friend on the same spot." These two men of science put their sage heads together and "concluded that in the surprisingly slippery character of the surface lies the explanation of the accident." To my ear, at least, if this reassuringly simple—and madly tautological—explanation were quite right, Darwin would not have described his and his friend's sudden falls as *inexplicable* in the first place. What really happened, we are to infer, is that he and his friend strayed momentarily into the fay world fellow Janeites such as Constance Hill and Oscar Fay Adams described more candidly.[27]

In order to consider how the placement of Austen within fairyland as well as other magical registers made sense to her Victorian readers and what that placement accomplished for them, it is necessary to pause for a moment and observe how deeply counterintuitive it is. Today, few writers seem more removed from, if not downright inimical to, fancy and fairyland than Austen, whose reception we have always thought was simply and clearly rooted in the discourse of probability. True, in highly attenuated forms, fairydom has appeared in the commentary of influential twentieth-century Austenians as diverse as C. S. Lewis and D. W. Harding, with respect to their assertions about the Cinderella structure of Austenian plots. What was far more emphatic in Lewis's essay was his effort to affiliate Austen with Dr. Johnson as vigorously empirical and unblushingly Christian in her moralism; and what has proved most memorable in Harding's essay were his claims about Austen's "regulated hatred" and her witheringly dis-illusioning irony. Diverse as their two apprehensions of Austen are, however, they both presume her to be categorically, even somewhat aggressively, grounded in common sense.[28]

Victorian Janeites also insisted, as Anne Thackeray Ritchie put it, that Austen's "literary hour" was "midday . . . bright, unsuggestive, with objects standing clear," and this is precisely what makes their habit of simultaneously enlisting her into the world of wonderment so peculiarly arresting.[29] After all, detractors had always complained not only about the absence of turbulent passion in Austen's fiction but also about the absence of fancy there as well. Transforming Scott's famous comparison of Austen's scrupulous attention to the commonplace to Flemish painting into a form of disparagement, Charlotte Brontë established a tendency to understand Austen's fictional method as photographic transcription and to equate such transcription with a failure of or hostility to imagination: Austen did no more than present "an accurate daguerreotyped portrait of a common face." Associating the photographic not (as we might) with the elegiac but with the mechanical and the literal, Victorian commentators recur to the transcriptive and the antipoetic when discussing Austen's work. The writer for the *Westminster Review*, probably George Eliot, appears to commend Austen's "accurate portraits of very tiresome and uninteresting people" by contrasting "a photographic picture" favorably to a "glaring piece of mythology." Such praise is so qualified, however, as to appear underhanded, for the review insists that Austen has no "imagination, depth of thought, or wide experience" and that she is absorbed in "the littlenesses and trivialities of life" (*CH2*, 198). Again and again, even professed admirers describe Austen's characters as "just and faithful transcripts of human nature" and her novels as "amusing but faithful picture[s]," "pictures of contemporary society," "faithful mirrors of a generation that has passed away," representing "things intensely real . . . intensely prosaic . . . without exaggeration, or deficiency, or adulteration."[30] Seemingly unaware that he is contradicting Austen's own quoted declaration that her aim was to "create, not to reproduce," J. E. Austen-Leigh himself describes his fairy-aunt's writings as "like photographs, in which no feature is softened; no ideal expression is introduced, all is the unadorned reflection of the natural object" (*Memoir*, 157, 153); and Lord Brabourne writes that "she describes men and women exactly as men and women really are, and tells her tale of ordinary, everyday life with such truthful delineation, such bewitching simplicity" (*Letters 1*, xiii).

These apparent contradictions call out for explanation. On the face of it, at least, it makes some sense that detractors could sniff at Austen's daguerreotypical art, but how does it make sense for professed Janeites to consider Austen as at once photographic and fay, truthfully delineative as well as bewitching, commonplace as well as enchanting? Such categories of description seem to belong to incompatible discourses, the one locating Austen's art in a world of mundane facts reflected or transcribed (however cleverly arranged), and the other locating it in a sublime and wondrous world created by and accessible only to the imagination. As such they pose a riddle we must solve if we are to understand what Victorians loved in Austen and what makes their Janeism distinct from ours. To some extent, the kind of boundary crossing we are encountering here is the general legacy of the realistic novel during the nineteenth century, the sort of novel Austen herself is so often said to have founded. As Catherine Gallagher and Stephen Greenblatt have shown, novels invite us to indulge in complex and increasingly self-conscious acts of credit and resistance. Unlike romance, for example, which is egregiously marvelous and imaginative, or unlike the miraculous narrative supposedly constituted by the Eucharist (the instance discussed at length by Gallagher and Greenblatt), the novel does not patently tax our credulity, does not come to us in any form remotely requiring what Coleridge memorably termed a "willing suspension of disbelief." Coleridge, after all, was trying to account for a process by which fantastic literature is enjoyed by enlightened readers. Because the Austenian novel "does not ask its readers to believe its characters actually existed or the events really took place, but instead invites us to appreciate the *believable* as such," it posits and privileges the reader who acquiesces to fictional representations without believing in them, who extends *credit* without becoming *credulous*. Novel readers, like the fetishists who interested Freud, never forget that the object of their regard does not really have the power they act as though it has, never forget that it is not really the thing itself. That knowledge does not make the object less powerful for them; if anything, there is a certain campy fun to be had precisely in sensing their originary power in making the transaction work: "We help fabricate a 'world' (which we know is not The World) for the purposes of achieving specific narrative pleasures."[31]

With these reflections on the nineteenth-century novel in mind, Austen's novels—unlike, say, Dickens's—will seem distinctive precisely because the "world" they represent is so ordinary, so little intensified as not to appear invented at all. If, as Gallagher and Greenblatt suggest, novels "limber us up to cross ontological levels with ease, to poise ourselves on provisional ground, to assent for the moment while keeping our readiness to depart from the fictional world," then it must be said Austen exercises us more rather than less vigorously than other novelists precisely to the degree that the boundaries are harder to detect in her fiction.[32] The Janeite's self-congratulatory pleasure in being able to discern them, and to cross over them and back again, is all the more delicious because they are invisible to the uninitiated. Austen's novels represent the ordinary so successfully as to be mistakable for it by the nonelect. The writer for *Chamber's Journal* observes of Austen's commitment to unsensational and even unremarkable events that "the more truly they are described, even, the duller they may appear." Recollecting the man whose opinion of *Emma* was so low that it could not be reported to Austen, the writer concludes, "He was doubtless a good deal bored,"[33] much like a scoffer Iddesleigh describes who damns himself by calling *Emma* "awfully stupid."[34]

Worse than the mere boredom that betrays vulgar readers who don't "get it" is the foolish fearlessness of those who think they do—for Janeites, all pretensions to civility notwithstanding, are censorious of other readers, aiming their most pointed barbs not at nonbelievers, so to speak, but at other Janeites who fail to love Austen in the right way. In perhaps the best essay on Austen to appear during the Victorian period, Margaret Oliphant detects a disturbing similarity between the fools in Austen's novels and the soi-disant admirers of Austen's novels. For Oliphant, Austen represents fools with a skill that is quite marvelous: "It is all so common—never rising above the level of ordinary life, leaving nothing (so think the uninstructed) to imagination or invention at all." Blind to the "marvelous," the uninstructed never think to quail before it. When Oliphant turns to the ridiculously pompous suggestions for a novel given to Austen by Mr. Clarke, librarian to His Royal Highness the Prince Regent, she writes, "Mr. Collins himself could not have done better." Oliphant goes even further, observing aptly that even Austen-Leigh himself is Collins-like in his blindness to the exultant irony with which Austen demurs from Clarke's suggestions, but instead treats Clarke like a wise man. Again and again, Oliphant perceives, Austen's admirers are confounded by her mistakability for the ordinary, for people such as themselves, and accordingly they are oblivious to the fact that they are in the presence of an intelligence somehow categorically different from and superior to their own: "It appears, however, that this was by no means a singular occurrence. Her friends, who could see plainly that Jane Austen was very much the same as other people, and not a person to be any way afraid of, were so kind as to give her many hints" about how to write novels.[35] More than most Victorian admirers of Austen, Oliphant insists that Austen is indeed to be feared and that the success with which she conceals the boundary between the ordinariness of what she represents and the marvelousness of her own art has made her dangerously misrecognizable as the ordinary, thus putting unwary, unfazed, and unafraid readers into the position of lumbering into fairyland without knowing it.

Yet Austen's simultaneous location in the mundane and in the marvelous, in the factual and the fanciful, also says something very specific about how Victorian readers use Austen to mediate their own sense of degraded modernity, where modernity itself is understood as disenchantment. We have already amply seen that Victorian Janeites place Austen on the other side of a historical gulf, and inasmuch as Austen might easily have lived to become, chronologically at least, a Victorian novelist herself, this insistence on her remoteness seems out of proportion to the actual number of years separating her from her Victorian readers. After all, it is not as though Austen were medieval or even faintly medievalizable. On the contrary, as Thomas Kebbel aptly observes, "Miss Austen belongs essentially to the eighteenth-century school of literature,"[36] and the eighteenth century seemed preeminently, in Matthew Arnold's famous words, to be the age of prose and, as such, party to the deplorably uncharmed and uncharming spirit of Enlightenment that has taken all the magic out of the world to begin with. At the same time, despite this unequivocal modernity, she is still considered to predate the most conspicuous phases of the Industrial Revolution, machine age, and railway boom that seemed so drastically to alter the economy, the landscape, and the mores of the nation.

Accordingly, Austen's location is somewhat indeterminate or, as Lord

Brabourne might have put it, more queer: she is not quite other than ourselves, nor quite like ourselves either. She is a mirror who passively reflects, but at the same time a magical mirror disclosing our modernity at a particularly utopian moment when even dullness and triviality and prose were still charmed. Contrasting "our modern times, when steam and electricity have linked together the ends of the earth, and the very air seems teeming with news, agitations, discussions" with the "tranquil, drowsy, decorous English day" of "a century since," Sarah Chauncey Woolsey attributes Austenian tedium to the sensibility of a better, less sensationally harried time: "People did not expect happenings every day or even every year. No doubt they lived the longer for this exemption from excitement, and kept their nerves in a state of wholesome repair."[37] Many readers joined Woolsey (an American) in celebrating this kind of boredom in Austen as precisely what makes her English and good. Janet Harper's 1900 account for Jane Austen's "renascence" emerges from her sense of what it means to be an Anglo-Saxon writer. Of course, she writes, Austen has "no music, no magic, no caressing phrases." What Austen has instead is a "thoroughly English, realistic and moral solidity" that, once again, seems to be akin to eighteenth-century commonsense ideals such as "knowledge, observation, toleration, and expression" that combine to create a "solid foundation" for "easy, graceful dialogue." If Austen is of the eighteenth century, however, hers is not the eighteenth century of, say, the *Rape of Lock*, miniature and fairylike, light and bright and sparkling though she may be. Hers is, rather, the eighteenth century of rational modernity, showing us "ordinary, unimaginative—indeed, commonplace—people," people presumably like us before we grew bored with ourselves, before our Anglo-Saxon sensibilities were denatured, debilitated, and denationalized by "the short, feverish, genius-filled lives of such people as Marie Bashkirtseff or Aubrey Beardsley."[38]

While Harper—somewhat like Edmund Burke and his infamous tribute to the bovine sluggishness of English cud chewers—finds herself in the difficult rhetorical position of trying to glamorize qualities definitionally exclusive of magic and imagination, other reviewers are more successful at drawing an aura around Austen's English dullness. Sometimes Austen loses any sort of personhood, as her English dullness becomes disembodied, dissolving into the landscape: her life "passed calmly and smoothly, resembling some translucent stream which meanders through our English meadows, and is never lashed into anger by treacherous rocks or violent currents."[39] Others see that dullness as a quality not of the landscape per se but of a world now lost. Thus a review of the *Memoir* appearing in the *Nation* calls the village life Austen lived and wrote about "the picture which resides in the mind of every Englishman when he thinks of his country," where "the gentry" dwelled "more numerous and, if coarser and duller, more home-loving and less like pachas than they are now."[40] Accordingly, as Thomas Kebbel makes clear, Austen's coarse and dull "picture" memorializes a vanished race who embodied England's quiet, domestic glory:

> There was in those days a particular grade of society, now all but extinct, which haunted these large villages and small country towns. . . . Mr. Woodhouse is just a man; Mr. Bennett was another. They were not country gentlemen; they were not professional men; they were not necessarily sportsmen; if they farmed, it was only for amusement. They would have shuddered at the thought of speculating; they vegetated quietly on a fixed income. . . . The residents in the neighbourhood of Chawton have noticed the gradual disappearance of families of this type, and I have noticed it myself in many other parts of England. Civilisation has been too much for them, and they are gradually retiring before its advances like the otter and the badger.[41]

In Kebbel's wistful, intensely Tory tribute, Austenian families—real and fictional—are beings of equivocal ontological status—they at once live like vegetation, without any visible means of support (a point to which I shall return in a moment), and like shy wildlife (the badgers and otters). who retreat before the "advances" of civilization.[42] Once all of England was the habitat of these amiable denizens who have long since, like the fairies, fled the countryside altogether. Clearly, the ordinariness Austen was thought to represent and to typify was already so idealized, so inflected with the marvelous, and so saturated with loss and longing that to characterize her novels as ordinary as well as wonderful, *photographic* as well as *fay*, is not, in some sense, to be contradictory at all.

The Victorian tendency to invest Austen's very mundanity with magical quaintness emerges as a reaction to its own disenchantment with modernity. If the "advances" of "civilization" seemed to be the lamentably demystifying culprit, so too are the violence of labor and the enmity of class. Overlooking the fact that Sir Thomas Bertram in *Mansfield Park*, for example, does indeed "speculate," Victorian Janeites such as Thomas

Kebbel place Austen in the old days before capital alienated people's social relations; as the review appearing in the *Nation* puts it, "Jane Austen
lived in . . . a society affluent, comfortable, domestic, rather monotonous,
without the interest which attaches to the struggles of labour, without
tragic events or figures."[43] Hence Austen's magic. Lord Brabourne's *Queer
Folk* features a mildly twilight zone sort of story titled "The Strange City,"
mysteriously accessible by train, where servants and workers not only are
extraordinarily pleasant, civil, and solicitous for one's comfort but also
refuse tips of any sort, taking umbrage at the slightest suggestion that
their wages are insufficient in and of themselves or that their pleasant-
ness and attention could be purchased so crudely. Similarly, the reassuringly patriarchal titular figure in Brabourne's "The Warlock of Coombe"
is moved to act in protective, intercessory ways against the violence of
robber barons solely on account of the heartfelt gratitude of the mortal who honors him, and not on account of any paltry offerings or re-
payments. In a world where farm laborers tip their hats to squires and
parsons, and squires take care of their tenants, the warlock's affective
economy is readily understood. Like these "queer folk," Austen appears
to live in a magical economy where bonds of gratitude and solicitude
suffice, where class relations are everywhere to be found but remain in
an unalienated and unexposed state, and where service and protection
cannot be bought.

When, as we have seen, James Edward Austen-Leigh observes that
Chawton Cottage is no longer a suitable destination for pilgrimage because it is now "divided into tenements for labourers" and "reverted
to ordinary uses," he betrays a comparable aversion to the exposure of
work in a capitalist economy (*Memoir*, 69). Where paid labor is visible,
magic cannot subsist, and so it is not surprising that Austen-Leigh's most
vivid recollection of his fairy-aunt is precisely the concealment of her
own work, which, as Austen-Leigh presents it, is not merely modest but
itself fabulously screened: she was "careful" that "servants, or visitors,
or any persons beyond her own family party" should not "suspect" her
writing, and so she employs "small sheets of paper" specifically because
they could "easily be put away, or covered with a piece of blotting paper;" and finally Austen forbears to repair the creaking door because "it
gave her notice when anyone was coming." It goes without saying that
Austen-Leigh stresses, contra everything we have since learned, that
Austen was disinterested in the profits and losses she incurred as a pro-

fessional writer. More than retiring, Austen is presented as downright secretive, as if she too believed that novels were written not by hard work but by what Austen-Leigh terms a "mystic process," as if this process had to be shielded from view in order to have efficacy (*Memoir*, 81–82). The marvel of Jane Austen, then, is that one never sees her work, and that marvel carries over to her novels as well, where her principal characters sustain their ordinary lives in perfect comfort (so it is thought) without material struggle or social conflict. Even as Austen's popularity in the Victorian period (and well into our own), as James lamented, is precisely a result of commodity culture, then, Austen herself is a magical, ghostly (dis)embodiment of the commodity as fetish, restoring the aura of richness and authenticity even to mechanically reproduced novels—much as the very binding of Constance's Hill's book reproduces the satin-stitch design Austen embroidered (i.e., "worked" in that earlier sense) on a muslin scarf, aiming to put us literally in touch with Austen directly as we hold her book, as if to escape the mediation of mass production (fig. 2.5).

⁀ Austen reenchants her Victorian devotees by representing the ordinary relations of life as effortless and nonconflictual, but finally and just as important, she does so as well by representing the supercommensurateness of desire and satisfaction: unlike her Victorian readers, Austen is never bored, never boring. This is a prodigious feat of magic considering that by all rights Austen *ought* to be both. As we have amply seen, she and her fiction alike were described not merely by detractors but by enthusiasts precisely as *un*interesting: "She would have no dealings with any circumstances which were not of an ordinary nature," giving us only "just such figures as would bore [us] if they were in the flesh."[44] At times, tributes to Austen's self-sufficiency sound more like detraction than praise: "She is just a simple-minded, well-bred English young lady, thoroughly satisfied with her lot in life."[45] *Just* a simple-minded English young lady? Yes, in the same sense that *Belinda* or *Camilla* or *The Mysteries of Udolpho* is *only* a novel, as Austen herself wrote in *Northanger Abbey*, transforming litotes into hyperbole, a put-down into the highest possible praise. It is true that some reviews of Austen's *Letters* especially betray some irritation with their incessant preoccupation "with small things, domestic arrangements, the merits of cooks and housemaids, country parties and balls, chaise journeys to Bath or London, new dresses, the little comings and goings, disappointments and hopes of genteel life."[46]

Figure 2.5. *Book cover of Constance Hill's* Jane Austen: Her Homes and Her Friends *(1902), depicting Austen's stitchwork; even the book cover of this commodity was to put us into contact with Austen.*

Austen's perceived readiness to represent the satisfactions of the prosaic appeared attractive when contrasted to contemporary sensational fiction, which was often judged of a sensibility so degraded that only the lurid and extreme could rouse it. B. C. Southam has persuasively argued that Victorian views of Austen, including J. E. Austen-Leigh's *Memoir*, are refracted through Ruskin's influential *Sesame and Lilies* (1865), with its affirmation of the quiet sanctity of home and woman's place in it, as well as through his vigorous criticism of sensational fiction and its pernicious tendency to render "the ordinary course of life uninteresting" (*CH2*, 8).[47] Thus we find that Austenian commentary of this period frequently takes the form of a list detailing the sensations and the incitements to interest missing from her novels—*St. Paul's Magazine* notes that the "wild pulsation, the stormy embracing, the hand-pressure which bruises, the kiss which consumes" are all "absent from Jane Austen's pages"; Andrew Lang playfully scolds her for being unperplexed by Esoteric Buddhism, Higher Pantheism, High Paganism, Analysis, Passion, Realism, Naturalism, Irreverence, and Religious Open-Mindedness; and the *Temple Bar*, drawing up a considerably shorter list, is grateful simply that "she has nothing to say about evolution and the Jews."[48]

Yet even though readers anxious to preserve Victorian pieties praise what is absent in Austen as a means of censuring what is present in novels by Braddon, Hardy, and Eliot, it would be a mistake to conclude that she was merely valued as a decorous or wholesome alternative to the excesses of sensationalism or that the ordinary in her fiction held no positive, productive charm in and of itself. On the contrary, it is cherished most importantly as a potent amulet. Anne Thackeray Ritchie's apostrophe—"Dear books! bright, sparkling with wit and animation, in which the homely heroines charm, the dull hours fly, and the very bores are enchanting"—was, as B. C. Southam has shown, widely quoted and reworked in essays, appreciations, and biographies from the 1880s through 1930. For him, Ritchie's "lyrical hagiolatry" typifies cloying, anticritical Victorian "twaddle" at its worst (*CH2*, 22–26). But Ritchie's tribute is worth pondering, precisely because it celebrates the wondrous immunity of Austen's novels and their readers to the Victorian malady of ennui. If boredom is that condition in which it is impossible to frame a desire the merest anticipation of which does not already pall, then for those readers susceptible to Austen's charm, at least, her novels are a cure, because they are fully and ceaselessly engaging. As Ritchie's testimony implies, boredom is always assumed to be our condition prior to reading: when we are not taking up Austen's novels, time presses ponderously on our shoulders rather than skimming by; the dullness of our companions is irksome; and the sheer dailiness of our homely lives stretches out before us, unrelieved and unanimated. Yet, as Ritchie maintains, our "friends of pen-and-ink" in Austen's novels are not merely always accessible to our desiring—"They are always 'at home;' they never turn their backs nor walk away as people do in real life, nor let their houses and leave the neighbourhood"—but are also always desirable despite their familiarity: "Perhaps the most fashionable marriage on the *tapis* no longer excites us very much, but the sentiment of an Emma or an Anne Elliot comes home to some of us as vividly as ever."[49] Austen's novels thus offer pleasures that are uniquely reiterable—for it is plain that we often call on our pen-and-ink friends and are never anything less than gratified to find them at home and ready for us—ever reawakening desires whose satisfactions deepen, so that even characters constituted by dullness—the bores in the novels, and the bored people like ourselves reading them—become bottomless sources of fascination. Ritchie's tribute describes Austen's effects on the genteelly jaded, on readers who have everything and therefore are excited by nothing. It holds as true of desires exhausted by indulgence as it does of those thwarted by monotony: Oscar Wilde wrote from Reading Gaol on 6 April 1897 that "there being hardly any novels in the prison library for the poor imprisoned fellows I live with, I think of presenting the library with about a dozen good novels: Stevenson's . . . some of Thackeray's . . . Jane Austen (none here)."[50]

The prevailing context of boredom, whether resulting from a fin-de-siècle oversaturation of desire or from the bleakness of desire's imprisonment, suggests that Austen's supposed "limitations" and the conviction that "Miss Austen's charm consists" precisely in her being "circumscribed and narrow" refers primarily to the affective economy she represents personally and artistically.[51] Stupefied by "the morning paper with its statements of disaster and its hints of still greater evils to be . . . when, lo! in comes the evening issue, contradicting the news of the morning," Victorian readers regard the prospect of ordinariness having intense interest with amazement.[52] The triviality of Austen's life, letters, and fiction—and their concomitant indifference to war and revolution erupting around them—testifies not so much to their isolation as it does to the enviable fullness of the objects of Austenian desire: limited though they seem, they are infinitely, ceaselessly rich in their satisfactions. And the fact that Austen was understood as unassuming and unaspiring, while it certainly speaks to the placidity of womenfolk in the good old days, hints at her very particular and marvelous self-sufficiency, a sufficiency that her sexlessness and auntliness together keep from being threatening: "It is something that Miss Austen's genius was sufficient for herself, that she was ready to delight others without caring for a reward, and that she shed abroad the gifts of her bright sunny nature and never paused to ask whether they were appreciated."[53] Victorian "twaddle," in short, carries a yearning for the amplitude of moderation, for a utopian world some-where or sometime when our sensibilities were so fresh that limitations left us not simply with enough to enjoy but with plenty.

Clearly, all the excess one never finds inside Austen's novels one finds outside of them in the enthusiasm of her readers, readers who, though surfeited or frustrated everywhere else, are never disappointed in Austen despite the boundlessness of their craving for her novels. This is how we might best understand the emergence of vaunted rereadings as a touch-stone of Janeism. Reporting that Disraeli read *Pride and Prejudice* sev-enteen times, Rowland Grey agrees that Austen's novels are best read "again and again" especially for the full savoring of their "bores"; and Sir Francis Darwin brags that Macaulay himself could not "have endured to read her as often as I have."[54] Even secondary Janeite discourses satisfy the measureless desires of confirmed fanatics, as Lord Iddesleigh con-firms: "It would be a very delightful thing if a magazine could be started that should be devoted entirely to Miss Austen. . . . We are never tired of talking about her; should we ever," he asks, "grow weary of reading or writing about her?"[55] No, for foreknowledge and anticipation never out-strip her; there is always more to wonder and to enjoy. Reginald Farrer's centenary essay on Austen's death was written in the shadow of World War I, and it stands in a highly critical relationship to the elegiac mode of Victorian Janeism. For him (and, as we shall see in the next chapter, many of his contemporaries), Austen is loved as a bracingly unsentimen-tal contemporary, far closer in spirit to the iconoclasm of the lost genera-tion than to the respectability of the Victorians. Yet even though he con-ceives of Austen as an artist of *dis*enchantment, he still carries over the hyperbole of Victorian Janeism—"the thousandth reading of 'Emma' or 'Persuasion,'" he declares, "will be certain to reveal . . . jewels unnoticed before." And he also cannot resist the established tendency for crediting her fiction with a marvelousness at once zany, awesome, and downright weird. Farrer ends his essay with an anecdote about an experiment he performed on a friend stranded for weeks in a tiny Chinese village. Being no reader and suffering in "sheer desperation of dulness," this friend at last consented to read Jane Austen and was taken "by storm," and for days and weeks made himself somewhat of a bore by talking of nothing else but her characters, summing up her work at last: "Why, all those people, they're—they're *real!*" (RF, 30).

Victorian enthusiasts enlist Jane Austen in a project of reinvesting the world with wonder, and as we have seen, fairy magic is a predominant means of imagining this. Austen at once instantiates the problem—the unlovely ordinariness of modern life—as well as the uncanny solution—the sufficiency of that life, as beheld through the charm of her artistry, which brings wonder and strangeness back into the world. Thus the mundanity and the marvelousness Victorian Janeites see in Austen, far from subsisting in spite of each other, actually keep miraculously producing each other, making Fairy-Jane look at one and the same time like St. Jane in her mystic capacity to transfigure the sublunary into the sublime: "Ordinary life," as the Earl of Iddesleigh put it, "was seen by [Austen] not dimly and partially as we see it but in all its actual vastness, and it was in this huge field that she worked with such supreme success. If the 'little bit of ivory' were only 'two inches wide,' those inches were not of mortal measure."[56]

3 Jane Austen's World War I

J ane Austen has always been loved or hated in part because of what she did not write about. During the nineteenth century, passion (of every sort) was the subject Austen was thought not to include. In the twentieth century, the great unsaid was just as likely to be war. Frederic Harrison's 1913 letter to Thomas Hardy is the locus classicus of this view: "A heartless little cynic was Jane, penning satires about her neighbors whilst the Dynasts were tearing the world to pieces, & consigning millions to their graves. A relation of hers was even guillotined in 1793, her brother was in the fleet that fought at Trafalgar—& not a breath from the whirlwind around her ever touched her Chippendale *chiffonier* or *escritoire.*"[1] Although Harrison had earlier written with measured respect about Austen's artistic achievement, here he decries not Austen's obliviousness to the turbulence of war—indeed, his whole point is that the Reign of Terror in France and the Napoleonic Wars reached into her very family—but rather her indifference to it, a failure of moral imagination and seriousness worthy of that mixture of scorn and faintly misogynist contempt that he can convey only by recourse to French words for furniture.[2]

Harrison's censure of Austen's silence about the dynasts tearing her world to pieces is so stinging because it was written on the eve of World War I, when the dynasts of our own century were clamoring to do the same thing; later, his son would be one of the millions consigned to their graves. What Harrison could not foresee, however, is that Jane Austen was often the cherished companion of the World War I generation in general and of English soldiers in particular during the war. Indeed, Reginald Farrer's appreciation of Austen, an extraordinary and influential effort of literary reflection written on the centenary of Austen's death in 1917, begins by drawing a similar analogy between her time and his: she died just as the "great conflict" of her time was concluding, and we celebrate her immortality a century later "amid the closing cataclysms of a conflict yet more gigantic." Far from deprecating Austen for ignoring the "tyrannies and empires" that "erupt and collapse" here below, he celebrates her for not writing about "all the vast anguish of her time." It is precisely on this account that Farrer finds that in "water-logged trench, in cold cave of the mountains, in sickness and in health, in dulness, tribulation and fatigue," her worshippers on the front fly "for comfort and company perennially refreshing, to Hartfield and Randalls, Longbourn, Northanger, Sotherton and Uppercross" (RF, 1–2).

To understand what it might have meant to seek the refreshing company of Jane Austen while in a "water-logged trench," I will turn to Rudyard Kipling's story "The Janeites," an extremely difficult text that is evidently more often referred to under the assumption that Janeism is a gentle thing than carefully read with an attention to what Janeism is and does in the story. A story within a frame story and further enframed by poems, "The Janeites" is set at a London Masonic Lodge in 1920, where a shell-shocked veteran named Humberstall talks about a "Secret Society" into which he was inducted in 1917 while serving under the supervision of Sergeant Macklin as an officers' mess waiter with his artillery battery in France. At the time, Humberstall has no idea who "this Jane" is or why his major and captain regard her as "a none-such." What most intrigues Humberstall at first is how Jane is the currency of fellowship, turning strangers into friends. A new lieutenant—a "young squirt"—is initially ignored by the officers, who are as usual absorbed in Jane-talk, but he is immediately befriended (and offered to share their port) when he shows that he too adores Jane. "It *was* a password, all right! Then they went at it about Jane—all three, regardless of rank. That made me listen" (*DC*, 129). As the three officers discuss whether "Jane" died without leaving "direct an' lawful prog'ny," Sergeant Macklin (who is "bosko absoluto" drunk at the time) loudly cuts in on what appears to be a private literary conversation,

> leanin' over a packin'-case with a face on 'im like a dead mackerel in the dark. "Pahardon me, gents," Macklin says, "but this *is* a matter on which I *do* 'appen to be moderately well-informed. She *did* leave lawful issue in the shape o' one son; an' 'is name was 'Enery James."

"By what sire? Prove it," says Gander [the new lieutenant], before 'is senior officers could get in a word.

"I will," says Macklin, surgin' on 'is two thumbs. *An'*, mark you, none of 'em spoke! I forget whom he said was the sire of this 'Enery James-man; but 'e delivered 'em a lecture on this Jane-woman for more than a quarter of an hour (*DC*, 129–30).

After delivering his lecture, Macklin falls on his face in a drunken stupor, and the officers then order Humberstall to take him off to bed. Once again, then, Humberstall is struck that club solicitude trumps rank and even class: "'e'd lectured 'is superior officers up an' down; 'e'd as good as called 'em fools most o' the time in 'is toff's voice. . . . An' all he got was— me told off to put 'im to bed! An' all on account o' Jane!"

Well might Humberstall marvel: what Janeite would not want to hear more about exactly how Austen begat Henry James! Whether Macklin is "sufferin' from shell-shock" or whether he is only bosko absoluto, he is sagacious in the ways of Jane, because this is not a silly or lightweight position. Intelligent converse about her and her novels seems to be crack-brained only because the setting is even more so. Talking Jane keeps the Janeites steady until their time runs out, and in the meantime it earns them other perks as well. Humberstall thus resolves to find out more from Macklin about the secret club whose membership brings such privileges. For one pound, Macklin sells him the password of the First Degree (*"Tilniz an' trap-doors"*), whose utterance before the Janeite officers gains Humberstall six Turkish cigarettes, and for another pound he gives him the six novels to read and puts him through a rigorous course of instruction. Janeite instruction makes the front companionable: "It *was* a 'appy little Group" (*DC*, 139), he later murmurs nostalgically.

Unlike most academic readings of Austen's fiction, this story relegates to irrelevant background the courtship plot, in which Janeites take no interest. Having more or less sworn themselves faithfully to Austen's novels (reading them, as Farrer put it, "in sickness and in health"), they are chilly about women in their civilian lives: Jane "was the only woman I ever 'eard 'em say a good word for" (*DC*, 128), Humberstall remembers. And they are chary of domesticity: the senior Janeites in their civilian lives are a divorce court lawyer and a private detective specializing in adultery cases, and Humberstall himself returns to the front after having earlier been discharged for injuries because he cannot tolerate the company of his mother, aunt, and sister. Of course, Humberstall recognizes that Austen's novels are "all about girls o' seventeen . . . not certain 'oom they'd like to marry" (*DC*, 132). For them, however, unlike non-Janeites in the story, this detail is leveled with other ones that are also part of what the novels are "all about"—including "their dances an' card-parties an' picnics, and their young blokes goin' off to London on 'orseback for 'aircuts an' shaves" (*DC*, 132), a fact that particularly intrigues Humberstall, who is a hairdresser in civilian life. As for Austenian plots, "there was nothin' *to* 'em nor *in* 'em. Nothin' at all" (*DC*, 134). The absence of striking incident in Austen's novels, which Victorian Janeites found charming and salubrious, is seen by Humberstall and his brethren as soothing in a more deadly serious way. Defended by "laddies," equipped with superannuated guns, the Janeites' battery is pitifully doomed. For them, Austen's novels are saving not merely because they are not sensationalistic but more particularly because "there was nothin' *to* 'em." Trench-bound Janeites ignore plot with its forward-moving momentums, its inevitabilities, its "maturity," and its closure—all of which spell death—and dwell instead on atemporal aspects of narration, minor descriptive details, catchy phrases, and, especially, characterization. In this story, talking Jane and identifying people and things in their own experience and renaming them according to her characters, the soon-to-be-slaughtered Janeites keep a shattering world in place.

Kipling's Janeites thus call attention to the pleasures of de- or nonsignification in Austen's novels. Goldwin Smith, writing earlier, put it aptly when he remarked, with fullest possible approval, that "there is no hidden meaning in her" (*CH2*, 190). This view is likely to irritate Austenian scholars, anticipating as it does antiacademic readers of today who bitterly complain that we "read into" Jane Austen's novels, designed for pure entertainment, all manner of weighty moral, social, or political significance. And yet this view, particularly as articulated in Kipling's story, also reminds us that a very compelling case has historically been made for a free play of nonmeaning in Austen. For one thing, it gives the lie to Leo Bersani's claim long ago that the realistic novel from "Jane Austen to the later Henry James" combines "a superficially loose, even sprawling narrative form with an extraordinary tightness of meaning," making everything "submit to the discipline of being revealing."[3] Kipling's Janeites find "nothing at all" in Austen's novels, and they enjoy a both absorbing and expansive triviality that releases them—temporarily, alas—from the grip of the inevitable. In celebrating Austen as the creator of novels of nothing, the Janeites further point us to swaths of merry blather in Austen's fiction, written with obvious gusto—say, the talk of Mrs. Allen and Miss Bates and a good deal of the youthful writings—that run wholly counter to the pointed, tight, epigrammatic style often (overly) associated with Austen. Such passages remind us that there is a good deal that may be gained by seeing Austen not as the first Victorian novelist, the inauguratrix of the Great Tradition, but as the last of the eighteenth-century novelists, committed to the protodeconstructive potential of formal parody rather than to realism, even, indeed especially, in a conspicuously "serious" novel such as *Mansfield Park*.

The narrator of the story, not a Janeite, closes by observing that Austen was "a match-maker" and that her novels were "full of match-making" (*DC*, 147) and by hinting at a secondary character's marriage to Humberstall's sister. Kipling also attaches a sequel poem, titled "Jane's Marriage," in which Austen enters the gates of heaven and is rewarded in matrimony to Captain Wentworth. These multiple efforts to reinstate the marriage plot are risible in themselves (Wentworth is not only fictional but already married) and at odds with the Janeitism elsewhere in the story: the frame story is thus a sop thrown to "a pious post-war world" (*DC*, 136), which requires what the narrator calls "revision" of the truth. One of these truths is that Janeites are committed to club rather than domestic society. They are as barren of "direct an' lawful prog'ny" as Austen herself, leaving no issue, the sole-surviving Humberstall being a stranger to women.

"The Janeites" presents several homosocial societies: the Masons, the soldiers, and the secret Janeites, a subset of the soldiers. Several details suggest that Austen's fiction promoted a secret brotherhood of homoerotic, if not homosexual, fellowship on the front. When Humberstall chalks the names of Austenian characters—General Tilney, Lady Catherine De Bourgh, and the Reverend Collins—onto the guns, he infuriates the battery sergeant major (B.S.M), who reads his Cockney spelling "De Bugg" (for De Bourgh) as a reference to sodomy. Convinced that Macklin is behind this, and determined to punish him for "writin' obese words on His Majesty's property" (*DC*, 137), the B.S.M. takes the case to the officers on the grounds that "'e couldn't hope to preserve discipline unless examples was made" (*DC*, 137). The B.S.M. is not a club member, of course. He does not realize that the Janeites even exist, that they share codes and

practices, and that they would not discipline one of their own for doing
precisely what Janeites are supposed to do: spreading Austen's word. The
officers dismiss the charges after sharing a glass of port with the B.S.M.
and proceed to entertain themselves by quizzing Humberstall at length
about why he named particular guns after particular characters. Clearly,
the reproduction the Janeites are interested in pertains to the dissemina-
tion of Janeite culture itself. Just as Austen brought forth Henry James,
Janeites bring forth other Janeites—by recruitment—hence Macklin's
pleasure when Humberstall rechristens the guns after Austenian characters: "He reached up an' patted me on the shoulder. 'You done nobly,'
he says. 'You're bringin' forth abundant fruit, like a good Janeite'" (*DC*,
137). Even after half the battery is blown up in a German artillery attack
and Humberstall is the only Janeite to survive, Humberstall finds that re-
making the world through Jane offers him club benefits in an otherwise
hostile world. As he struggles to board a hospital train, only to be pushed
back by a talkative nun insisting the train is too crowded, Humberstall
implores a nurse to "make Miss Bates, there, stop talkin' or I'll die" (*DC*,
145), and she—an initiate herself—praises the aptness of his allusion,
and she secures him a place and pinches a blanket for his comfort.

Some readers, as we shall see, did turn to Austen elegiacally during
World War I and the post–World War I period, marking a schism within
Janeism that will be explored more fully in the next chapter. Austen
enters the modernist imagination not despite the trenches but by way
of them. The power of Kipling's story does not, as commonly assumed,
derive from a conceit, memorable only because it takes two heteroge-
neous ideas—Jane Austen and World War I—and yokes them together
by violence. Unlike Victorian Janeites, Kipling's Janeites do not link Austen nostalgically to a gentle England whose beauty and vulnerability are
what menfolk must go to war to protect. By this reading, Austen would
offer a way out of the horror of war and into some more comfortable past
or imaginary place. For Kipling's Janeites, Austen is violent already (why
else would it be judged apt to rename the guns after General Tilney, Lady
Catherine, and Mr. Collins?). Austen is with them there on the front, offering a way to be in an absurd and doomed world beyond their control.
And after the war, Humberstall reads Austen's novels not because they
help him recover a prior world unshaken by war but precisely because
they return him to the world of trenches that are more real to him: "It
brings it all back-down to the smell of the glue-paint on the screens. You

take it from me, Brethren, there's no one to touch Jane when you're in a tight place" (*DC*, 146).

❧ Having been declared unfit for combat in 1917 and 1918, Reginald Farrer worked for the Foreign Office, writing letters to John Buchan that described combat from three fronts of the war. These war letters, collected in *The Void of War: Letters from Three Fronts,* were published in 1918 but written contemporaneously with his centenary tribute of the previous year, and the two texts speak to each other in telling ways. Generally speaking, the centenary tribute stands as the theory of Jane's brilliance, and the war letters document the practice of it. Farrer sometimes sounds Victorian in referring to the *miracle* of Austen's genius, but the frame of reference has changed radically. Victorian Janeites turned to Austen for reenchantment; Farrer and other writers of his generation celebrate their "radiant and remorseless Jane" (RF, 4) as the supreme figure of disenchantment, a strong-minded artist whose allegiance is solely to the truth of her art. And whereas earlier Janeites longed for the magical wholeness of Austen's lost world of England, Farrer professed to despise that world, along with Christianity and all of Europe, converting to Buddhism in part to distance himself from it. Not surprisingly, then, Farrer finds no fairyland in Austen's novels, but a different sort of magic, perhaps, a "new kingdom" of art that is "hermetically sealed" from our toils and frets, so that while worldly "tyrannies and empires erupt and collapse" here below, her art remains immortal, and immortally vibrant for us (RF, 5). In some ways, then, Farrer is adumbrating a theory of Jane Austen for the modernists—a lamentably understudied affiliation—whose lean and unsparing oeuvre is like a planet on the table, not a delightful miniature, but a semiautonomous fictive world. In any case, Farrer's 1917 essay has been canonical throughout the twentieth century, important for its foundational insistence that Austen's novels are not remote, not utopic, not particularly narrow, and certainly not in step with dominant values: "She is, in fact, the most merciless, though calmest, of iconoclasts," Farrer insists, in words that anticipate D. W. Harding's famous assertions in 1939 about Austen's "regulated hatred," which in turn would go on to become seminal.[4] Consumed with a "passion for the real," and intolerant of "the slack thought and ready-made pretenses that pass current in the world," Farrer's Austen does not seem like any ordinary warm and fuzzy source of refuge or comfort. So what could it mean for Farrer to have sought comfort in the "remorseless" Austen in a "water-logged trench"?

In Farrer's letters from the front, snippets from "the Divine Jane" (*VW*, 189) surface, much as they do in "The Janeites," in a strikingly fragmented, piecemeal form, detached from any narrative arc. Though surely not as discontinuous as "The Janeites," *The Void of War* likewise opts not to attempt the impossible, that is, to comprehend the incomprehensible with some grand, overarching unity of design. Instead, the letters come in short pieces, often no more than a paragraph long. In this tact and terseness, Farrer is actually following his sense of the *via Austeniana*, whose decision not to represent "supreme moments" he defends in this way: "In the supreme moments . . . humanity becomes inarticulate, and thus no longer gives material for art. Jane Austen, knowing this, is too honest to forge us false coin of phrases, and too much an artist to pad out her lines with asterisks and dashes and ejaculations. . . . It is notorious how she avoids detail in her proposal scenes; certainly not from 'ladylike' cowardice, nor from any incapacity, but merely in her artist's certainty that the epical instants of life are not to be adequately expressed in words" (RF, 9). Farrer's journeys to the front are nothing if not a series of "epical instants," and in *The Void of War* Farrer frequently uses the recollection of Austenian snippets—as distinct from the intensely graphic description employed by, say, Wilfred Owen—to suggest rather than to say such epical instants.

Although all these snippets are striking—passwords of sorts that establish a secret fellowship with a subset of readers—not all of them resonate with equal force. The devastated woodlands at Thièpval, for example, now "grey and leprous," must "have been a view like Donwell once" (*VW*, 93). As Farrer wanders through the wreckage of mud and woods and brick, he thinks of "the house-parties that once happened here," as if Mr. Knightley's estate in *Emma* were the benchmark for the loveliness and civility blasted away at the Chateau de Thièpval. The allusion saturates the scene in pathos, of course, but its import stops so far as Austen's novels are concerned. In another passage, however, Farrer's allusion resonates with Austen's novels more suggestively. Having arrived at the "front-line trenches," for example, Farrer feels sheepish and humble, as a noncombatant visiting and chatting with soldiers undergoing such hardship, "round-shouldered with apology, feeling that one must be a graceless nuisance and offence to the real people. However, we are told—and I am going to make a point of believing it—that they rather like these visitations, as bringing change and 'a little quiet cheerfulness' into their monotony" (*VW*, 120). This is a stunning feat. Farrer's transformation of Austen's ironic passage in *Persuasion* invites us to behold the soldiers at the front line as so many Mrs. Musgroves and Lady Russells, the trenches themselves either as a country house full of the "quietly cheering" clamor of screaming children or as the city of Bath astir with "quietly cheering" commotion, the "dash of other carriages, the heavy rumble of carts and drays, the bawling of newspapermen, muffin-men and milkmen, and the ceaseless clink of pattens" (*P*, 146). Clearly, this deeply embedded allusion is a tribute to the jauntiness of Tommies who love to chat and especially to laugh amid deafening noise, by Farrer's account (though certainly not by Kipling's) as unruffled by the whirring and booming of shells as Mrs. Musgrove and Lady Russell are by their respective cacophonies, which are (conversely) now made to sound earsplitting. It is a tender allusion also, but it does not rebound on *Persuasion* in any way that makes us understand that novel anew.

Other allusions are not only moving recollections but transformative ones as well. Wandering on Vimy Ridge, above a "castle of corpses, blown away into heaps and piles and masses in every direction," Farrer notes that though wandering on the "down-top of Vimy Ridge is difficult and grisly . . . with trenches meandering through the ranges and the odds and ends of battle lying about," still the scene "does not seem dead like the Somme." The presence of flocks of little birds makes this so: "They were not in the least concerned about the shelling: thousands of them were busily mobbing a hawk, and the sky was aflutter with tiny wings: and then, when they had successfully driven away their Boche, they went and sat in rows on the new telegraph-wires, and chittered about it passionately, 'all talking together, but Rebecca loudest'" (*VW*, 156–57). This quotation from *Mansfield Park*—uncited, uncontextualized, and far from self-evidently apt—might fly past even an accomplished Janeite: it is a phrase neither memorable nor dramatically prominent in the novel itself, and it seems to come from nowhere under the circumstances at hand. And that is the very point, as it is for Kipling's Janeites: springing from the fabric of Farrer's mind, the detail alone is saving, at least temporarily, to surmount trauma by describing it in terms of what is already known, thus offering psychic consolation to a mind boggled by unthinkable carnage. Folded quietly amid shocking spectacles narrated with Austenian detachment, the allusion helps Farrer to manage experiences otherwise too enormous to take in, much less to describe. And at the same time, once Fanny's doleful homecoming and the birds on Vimy Ridge have been brought into conjunction, the connection works in both directions, underscoring the quiet agony in Austen's novels that made this passage leap to Farrer's mind in the first place. Reading back to *Mansfield Park*, then, we see that the phrase "all talking together, but Rebecca loudest" (*MP*, 441) underscores and intensifies our apprehension of Fanny's (shell)shock to find herself amid a chaos at Portsmouth that now seems even more essentially battering and desolating than we realized before.

In a similar way, though (only ever so) slightly more apropos, a passage from *Northanger Abbey* comes to mind when Farrer stops in Saint-Omer to muse on the crisp and clean hospital barges he beholds, full of injured bodies being cared for,

> those long, cool rooms sliding by, filled with quiet and coolness and flowers, and the relaxed comfortableness of those men at rest among the cleanness and calm after the hells they have traversed. It is a paradox, but however ill they might have been in England, they would never have had anything like this, hardly even in the best of hospitals. While as for their own homes!—I suppose it is because these reflections are so obvious that they make one feel so sentimental. Do you remember how General Tilney was convinced that Catherine's fine mind must be gratified by "a view of the accommodations and comforts by which the labours of her inferiors were softened"? (*VW*, 165).

General Tilney does not fare well at the hands of Janeites on the western front. Humberstall calls him "a swine of a Major-General" whose behavior to Catherine is so horrid that "it made you ashamed," and Macklin judges that he is "shapin' to be a good Janeite" for thinking so (*DC*, 134–35). The same judgment surfaces here in Farrer's allusion, though less dramatically, and it has the effect of undercutting the sentimentality he momentarily feels on viewing the barge and being moved by its apparent humanity. Putting himself in the ingenuous Catherine's position as she is imagined to admire the arts by which the subjection of "inferiors" to the general's bullying domestic regime is dressed up and softened, Farrer undercuts any easy belief that the present-day authorities' care for their servicemen makes up for the calamities that injured them in the first place. In his centenary tribute, Farrer had written, "Everything false and feeble . . . withers in the demure greyness of her gaze" (RF, 11), and trust in the kindness of superiors is among those false, feeble things. At the same time, the direness of the present-day context projects backward ominously to underscore Catherine's vulnerability and to foreshadow the outcome of *Northanger Abbey*, suggesting that once Catherine herself is discovered to be an "inferior," the general's pretense of solicitude will drop, and he will order her out of the protection of his house.

How does all of this strike a twenty-first-century reader of Jane Austen? In conspicuous distinction to Victorian readings, Janeite allusion here produces an intensely tragic reading of her novels, where the world is not magically safe and uncomplicated, where the stakes are higher and the dangers keener than we imagined before. Austen's novels are about nothing if not the perils of living in a confined, narrow, profoundly bruising place where experience unfolds under the aegis of ordeal, where vulnerable, deferent young protagonists with next to no autonomy are exposed to adversities so brutal that they cannot be essayed, much less assailed directly. In Austen's world, that narrow place is called a neighborhood; during World War I it is called a trench, but in both, a premium is placed on behaving well during "epical instants" of duress. *Northanger Abbey*, a novel pooh-poohed as a fledgling effort in most academic readings after World War II, sides with the vulnerability of Austen's youngest heroine. It is plangent to imagine how Kipling's Janeites in their trenches, designed by their generals for cannon fodder, might have discussed Catherine Morland's misplaced confidence in General Tilney's intentions: certainly, she reassures herself, "he could not propose any thing improper for her" (*NA*, 160). Janeite allusion thus breaks down the false opposition between the arena of war and the arena of domesticity. From here it is a small step to Mrs. Dalloway's stunning imaginative intimacy with Septimus, her double, whose suicide is reported at her party: "She felt somehow very like him—the young man who had killed himself. She felt glad that he had done it; thrown it away."[5]

Furthermore, wartime Janeism derives from a gender dispensation almost impossible to imagine either during the Victorian period, when Austen's stature was virtually inseparable from her sex, or in our own, when sex and gender are crucial hermeneutic categories that sometimes open up new possibilities for meaning and sometimes shut them down as well. Here we find men devoted to Jane Austen readily identifying or identified with Fanny Price or Catherine Morland or Lady Russell. This is one of the underappreciated benefits of the discourse of "human nature" and atopical universality that academics shrink from nowadays, the apparent (and tentative) reawakening of interest in the human notwithstanding. As Farrer puts it, "Jane Austen can never be out of date, because she never was in any particular date . . . but is coextensive with human nature. . . . Jane Austen's heroes and heroines and subject-matter are, in fact, universal human nature, and conterminous with it, though manifested only in one class, with that class's superficial limitations, in habits and manner of life" (RF, 6). Note that Farrer does not mention sex along with class: the category is not definitive for him, or at least not consistently so. To be sure, he assumes that women readers do not like Austen (because she has their number), and he rehearses the too-familiar line that women are "vehicles of creation, not creators themselves" (*VW*, 189), but for him the sex of a character does not condition a reader's empathic or identifactory position, as it does for detractors who are evidently indifferent to the tribulations of young women: "A breaking heart is a breaking heart, no more no less, whether it find vent in the ululations of Tamburlaine, or in the 'almost screamed with agony' of Marianne Dashwood" (*SS*, 208) Throughout the nineteenth and much of the twentieth century, male critics discussed which Jane Austen heroine they would like to marry—many claimants for Elizabeth Bennet, of course, and virtually none for Fanny Price—not which heroine they could imagine being.

Other factors contribute to Austen's exemption from dismissively gendered readings during the Great War. Her reticence and understatement made her available in distinctive ways to notions about national character during this period. Quiller-Couch's jingoistic lecture "Patriotism in English Literature 1," written as young men were being urged on to war by elders full of claptrap about duty and patriotism, celebrates "the cheerful irony of the English private soldier, now fighting for us on the Belgian border." For Quiller-Couch, soldierly irony in the face of grandiose rhetoric about the duties of patriotism derives not from indifference or from a lack of feeling, but rather from a "shyness" about matters as close to the heart as love of country. Quiller-Couch proceeds by opposing the implicitness of the English soldier's patriotism to the "loud-mouthed" bombast of the German soldier, whose noisy *Deutschland über alles!* he dismisses as the shrill demagoguery of false patriotism. To

Quiller-Couch, understatement is the manful value of the English soldier, whose patriotic feelings are holy and true not because they emerge from the business of politics or of conquest but because the "true source that feeds them, the spirit that clarifies" is "home," the "green nook of his youth in Yorkshire or Derbyshire, Shropshire or Kent or Devon; where the folk are slow, but there is seed-time and harvest and 'pure religion breathing household laws.'"[6]

Although Quiller-Couch elsewhere celebrated "our incomparable Jane" and gladly professed himself among the tribe of her adorers, his rhapsody here on the reticence of English character and English patriotism cites the Old Testament and Wordsworth specifically, and elsewhere Shakespeare and Dryden, among others, and never Jane Austen. Still, the qualities he admires on nationalist grounds helps us to focus on what made Austen so companionable during this period. He articulates the reasons why that silence that we think of as so preeminently Austenian— silence about the nation during times of national crisis, about war during times of war—must be read as eloquence, that is, not as an absence, but as a presence of sentiment too deep and sincere to tout. For him, English silence is an implicitness, and implicitness as such is a positivity. "We do not, in our true hours—as all our glorious poetry attests—brag of England as a world-power, actual or potential. Blame it who will upon our insularity, we do habitually narrow and intensify our national passion upon the home and hearths now to be defended."[7] During the period of the Great War, I am suggesting, Austen was the beneficiary of efforts to see precisely such "narrowness" as national grandeur, and to define particular sites of rural life as England tout court, and with this to celebrate specific qualities of temper as befitting English character in general and English manhood in particular.[8]

Ever since Austen described herself as a miniaturist working on a "little bit (two Inches wide) of Ivory," narrowness has been one of the key words of her reception—the basis on which she would be either marveled at or sneered at—and one inseparable from her sex. Austen, by this reading, is the woman artist who knows her place—at home and in the larger world of literature—and accepts those "limitations" without longing after grander things inappropriate to her sex. Here, the circumscription of purview, the modesty of reference, the confinement to the neighborhood that Victorians denominated (and sometimes dismissed) as feminine now constitute for Quiller-Couch something as grand and as glorious as the nation itself during wartime. But Victorian readers have not been the only readers to have been blinkered in this respect. Indeed, the categories of late twentieth-century interpretation, particularly in light of feminism, have been skewed in comparable ways as well, for we too have been inclined to code "homes and hearths" as domestic and therefore as feminine and to place under the banner of *female modesty* affects that Quiller-Couch places under the banner of the English virtue of homey reticence that he recommends to men. This, of course, is the same kind of conduct—in another context called (perhaps slightingly) "manners"—that Austen's narrator in *Emma* describes as the "true English style." When the Knightley brothers greet each other, "'How d'ye do, George?' and 'John, how are you?' succeeded in the true English style, burying under a calmness that seemed all but indifference, the real attachment which would have led either of them, if requisite, to do every thing for the good of the other" (*E*, 107).

Implicitly here, as we later learn, "the true English style" is contrasted with the frenchified effeminacy of Frank Churchill, who can be *aimable* but not amiable, gallant but not sincere, and who irks Knightley with his hyperbolic style of writing: "He is a very liberal thanker, with his thousands and tens of thousands." One hundred years later, the French were allies, of course, and Teutonic thunder will be scorned instead, but the principle of preferring English containment over foreign excess, English reserve to alien grandiosity, remains the same. At the same time it is worth pointing out that Englishmen were not the only heirs to Austen's quietly manful love of the local, which is then equatable with the national. As Richard English has shown in his recent biography of Ernie O'Malley, the classics of English literature, among whom Austen figured prominently, were dear to the hearts of many IRA rebels during precisely this decade. Thomas MacDonagh, a poet and university professor of English in Ireland, devoted his last literature class before the 1916 Easter uprising to Austen's art: "'Ah, there's nobody like Jane, lads,' he sighed, closing his *Pride and Prejudice* for the last time."[9] Shortly afterward, MacDonagh was arrested and executed before a firing squad for his leadership in the rebellion. Clearly, this "lad's" passion for "Jane" was consistent with armed nationalist insurgency against Jane's England, and the attachment to the local, to the dust of one's neighborhood that Austen's novels both exemplify and produce, was transposable to other national contexts.

Discussing how the Great War left his generation with a "bitter cynicism" that transformed reading tastes, Hugh Walpole observed that while the "catastrophes and disappointments of the War left us with a deep contempt for what seemed to us a naive and desperately complacent idealism" of Victorian writers, "it was very natural and significant that the one novelist of the nineteenth century who expressed in her work no philosophy at all, whose observation was ironic, whose genius was mainly in the humours of little things, was our own Jane Austen, who might, in spirit at least have belonged to our post-War time."[10] "Our" Jane organizes a community around herself once again. She is the contemporary of a generation whose ideals have blown up, a generation that respects the humor of little things, home things, not because they are darling, diminutive, or manageable, but more tragically because big bombastic things have been shown to be shams. Frederic Harrison, as we have seen, meant to disparage Austen by calling her a "heartless cynic." But for the generation whom the Great War left with "bitter cynicism," Harrison's insult is high praise. Farrer sees Austen's serene pitilessness as the bedrock of her genius and the basis of her contemporaneity: she is impatient with "the slack thought and ready-made pretences that pass current in the world" and rejects everything that "fails to prove pure diamond to the solvent of her acid" (RF, 11–12). Similarly, Virginia Woolf, who also regards Austen's unsparing severity as the principle of her artistry, states, "At fifteen she had few illusions about other people and none about herself. . . . She is impersonal; she is inscrutable. . . . Never, even at the emotional age of fifteen, did she round upon herself in shame, obliterate a sarcasm in a spasm of compassion, or blur an outline in a mist of rhapsody."[11]

To take the full measure of the chasm between Harrison's late Victorian views before the war and the modernist views of Woolf, Walpole, Farrer, and others during and after it, consider for a moment the reception of Mary Augusta Austen-Leigh's *Personal Aspects of Jane Austen*, published in 1920. Mary Augusta Austen-Leigh (1838–1922) was Jane Austen's great-niece, and the daughter of J. E. Austen-Leigh, the author of the 1870 *Memoir*. Her career was spent honoring her last name, in 1911 with a privately published biography of her father, and in 1920 with the volume *Personal Aspects of Jane Austen*. In between, she compiled *Patriotic War Songs* (1914), which, in addition to cheering laddies on to war, also celebrated her family, as two of the thirty-four poems were by her brother Cholmeley Austen-Leigh (whose verse does not stand up to the other writers, such as Scott, Tennyson, Garrick, and Browning). Her book on Jane Austen was also a call to arms, designed to vindicate her illustrious relative from accusations she considers defamatory and plain wrong—accusations that Jane did not like children, that she could care less about the greater world, that she was cool or passionless, that she shunned sadness, that she did not care for the poor—all charges comprehended by Harrison's disdain. The review in the *Bookman* dismisses *Personal Aspects of Jane Austen* as "slight" to the point of superfluity, saying that it tells us nothing about Austen the novelist, damning it in effect by saying that only those "who like Jane and the Hepplewhite period" will value it. For Harrison, Jane Austen was inseparable from her escritoire and chiffonier, and Janeites were all alike, but for the *Bookman* reviewer Janeites fall into two camps, the Hepplewhite Janeites, who love period domesticity (hence Austen's persistent association with furniture), and modern Janeites, who are completely indifferent to whether or not Jane was "genteel."[12] Reviewing the book for the *Athenaeum*, Katherine Mansfield brushes aside Austen-Leigh's belatedly Victorian effort with an ever-swifter and more devastating quip: "Begging Miss Austen-Leigh's pardon—who cares?" Mansfield knows and endorses what she imagines Austen herself would say back to her detractors: "Ah, but what about my novels?"[13]

The presence of Austen on the fronts of World War I does not mean, of course, that she was always or only read as a contemporary writer. If Reginald Farrer celebrated a disenchanted modernist Jane Austen whose works could serve as a clean, well-lighted place, R. W. Chapman— the dean of Austen studies during much of the twentieth century and editor of authoritative modern editions of her novels and her letters— inaugurates a phase of Austenian study that is every bit as elegiac as Victorian Janeism but that is animated by a decidedly dry, philologically oriented conservatism. Chapman did not write a memoir of his experiences of World War I, but in 1920 he did publish *The Portrait of a Scholar and Other Essays Written in Macedonia, 1916–1918*, consisting, as the full title makes clear, of essays written under the influence of his wartime service, and his name on the title page underscores this by adding R.G.A—the Royal Garrison Artillery. In a brief prefatory note, Chapman explains that the composition of these essays "in camps and dug-outs and troop trains" gives the volume a "unity" (*PS*, 5), and I would suggest that a scholarly homesickness is the mainspring of that unity. The portrait in the volume's title refers to Ingram Bywater, an eminent scholar of Greek and a bibliophile who died in 1914, but in some ways the volume is Chapman's self-portrait as a scholar as well, drawn under deprivation and loss: "The graces of civilization and the delights of learning are far from me now. But my nomadic and semi-barbarous existence is still solaced by a few good books" (*PS*, 22). In Macedonia, where books in English are rare, Chapman imbues every essay with an almost sensuous yearning for English words—their spelling, their different pronunciations in different areas of Great Britain, their appearance in the typefaces of old books, their musicality when read aloud, their lamentable scarcity—and that sensuousness sometimes borders on the erotic: "To the lover [of books] whose fingers thrill to the touch of old vellum, whose eye lights to the appeal of faded print, an old book will yield something of the treasure of its experience, something of the bloom of its youth" (*PS*, 65).

In this context of deprivation, thinking about language and literature—place names in poetry, syntax, proposals for spelling reform, textual criticism, rhyme—is in part an exercise of therapeutic salvation, whereby Chapman can "beguile my tedium with pleasant speculations" (*PS*, 24). And because, excepting active combat itself (which Chapman never mentions), tedium is one of the great hardships of war, such beguilement is crucial.[14] Reciting "an ode of Horace," Chapman writes, "lightens the labour of dressing; and on long marches, or quiet nights at an observation post, I have soothed the aching hours with this harmless anodyne" (*PS*, 45). Beguiling the tedium, after all, is what Janeite conversation amid the trenches accomplished as well. And several of Chapman's beguiling musings relate specifically to Jane Austen, as when he complains that modern reprints of *Mansfield Park* fail to observe the break between volumes 1 and 2 and thus eliminate the intensity of Austen's dramatic emphasis on the dreaded Sir Thomas's return home. Chapman's scholarly speculations are also an assertion of stewardship over precious things that require care and conservation, at all times, of course, but more urgently so in a world that does not treasure them. *The Portrait of a Scholar* ends with a light-seeming essay on the gentle passion of spoon collecting: "I love my spoons," he declares candidly, not only for their beauty but for their higher service to what Norbert Elias calls the civilizing process. As Chapman puts it, "Not the least of the triumphs of civilization is to have fashioned for our daily use those utensils whose propriety and elegance refine the gross act of eating and lend a grace to social intercourse" (*PS*, 142). Remote from such grace and such civilization, Chapman recollects the pleasure of using lovely old spoons, displaying the dryness of his wit with a playful allusion to Milton's squib against cloistered virtue in *Areopagitica*: "I have little pleasure in a cloistered spoon" (*PS*, 142). So Chapman muses on spoon handles and spoon bowls, on the ornamentation of spoons, and on the golden age of spoons, all (he says) to "beguile my loneliness with fond memories, and sometimes with rash anticipations. Spoons of my dreams lie in the windows of little old shops in quiet streets of English towns" (*PS*, 147). Dreaming about spoons seems at least as zany and as touching (if not as sociable) as talking about Jane on the western front, and as marked by sharp pathos, for the last line reads: "There are no spoons in Macedonia" (*PS*, 147).

Jane Austen is a sort of silver spoon for Chapman (flatware now, rather than Hepplewhite furniture, but the same idea), to be treasured not only because she exemplifies the same soothing propriety, elegance, and grace that spoons do in the menacing, semibarbarous wilderness where he finds himself—"I recall a series of summer evenings in Perthshire, when a lady read *Persuasion* to admiration" (*PS*, 46)—but also because she is vulnerable to cultural trends at home that similarly threaten the refinements Chapman so values. *The Portrait of a Scholar* is as shot through with censure as it is with yearning: people do not read aloud anymore; his countrymen do not care that Americans are buying all the venerable old books once held in the libraries of great noblemen; the art of quotation has fallen into desuetude, and gentlemen cannot quote Horace in Latin anymore without arousing resentment; and, perhaps worst, no one knows how to write anymore, so degraded is modern English by jargon and verbosity. Chapman is beset from both sides, as it were, by a pernicious modernity at home and sheer desolation abroad, and his solemn determination—"To restore, and maintain in its integrity, the text of our great writers is a pious duty" (*PS*, 79)—takes on a special resonance; on his return to England he would undertake landmark scholarly editions of Samuel Johnson and, of course, Jane Austen.

Chapman's 1923 edition of *The Novels of Jane Austen* is the first scholarly edition of any novels written in English, and its authoritativeness is only now being seriously displaced in the twenty-first century by *The Cambridge Edition of the Works of Jane Austen*. As his title page announces, the text throughout is based "on Collation of the Early Editions," prepared scientifically, in short, according to principles of textual scholarship. According texts as "light" as novels—let alone novels by women—the dignity of textual scholarship was a major event not merely in Austen studies but in the history of the novel more generally, which was only beginning to enter into the ranks of high art. Preparing a scientific edition of Jane Austen's novels required a certain audacity we have not fully appreciated, for not all reviewers were pleased. It was one thing for scholars to unwind by reading Jane Austen—Edward Fitzgerald wrote that Edward Byles Cowell "constantly reads Miss Austen at night after his Sanskrit Philology is done: it composes him: like Gruel." It was another thing to edit Austen as though she were truly a classic. Reviewing the edition for *Bookman*, George Sampson (an anti-Janeite) remarks acerbically, "Shakespeare never has been, and never can be, edited so fully and finally as Mr. Chapman has edited Jane Austen." Chapman's textual loving care is misplaced because Austen is patently inferior to Shakespeare, a sexless "Peter Pan of letters," lacking a first-rate imagination working on first-rate experience. This could only have occurred by the happy convergence of two factors: Austen's extraordinary popularity among educated elites at the time and the importance of the notion of classics in English that World War I intensified. In any case, this edition was hardly for a wide public. Only 1,000 copies were printed, and of these only 950 were for sale, and by March 1925, 858 of those were sold, though later reissues in cheaper formats would become available.[15]

Although Chapman's practice and editorial principals are open to question, and the extent of his debt to the scholars he mentions in his preface is difficult to determine, there is no denying his command of Austen's novels at the level of words, or the judiciousness of many of his editorial decisions. Yet, as Kathryn Sutherland has so skillfully shown, R. W. Chapman's edition appears to owe a good deal to the scholarship of Katharine Metcalfe, whom he married in 1913. Chapman lifts the entire setting of the text to her 1912 edition of *Pride and Prejudice* into volume 2 of his 1923 set without acknowledging it or her, much less accounting for this wholesale duplication. The publication by Clarendon Press the same year of Metcalfe's edition of *Northanger Abbey* deepens the mystery, because *The Novels* also reproduces the setting of this text. Chapman's preface to *The Novels* mentions that he planned this edition "many years ago," and it is possible that he worked with Metcalfe on *Pride and Prejudice* as a trial run.[16] In "The Textual Criticism of the English Classics," included in *Portrait of a Scholar*, Chapman appears to take credit for at least some of the textual scholarship in this 1912 edition when he boasts, "The present writer claims to have restored dramatic propriety to a place in *Pride and Prejudice*" (*PS*, 73), moving the first word of a particular sentence slightly to the right and thereby the sentence to Mr. Bennet rather than Kitty. Chapman's later *Jane Austen: A Critical Bibliography* states that Metcalfe's "unassuming" edition of *Pride and Prejudice* "is equipped with a perceptive introduction and notes, and anticipates the textual rigours" of his edition of the collected novels in 1923—which certainly does not come clean about his indebtedness—while Metcalfe's 1923 edition of *Northanger Abbey* is not mentioned at all.[17]

Although Chapman had obviously been pondering editorial issues in Austen's texts before as well as during his war service, he was not the only one to do so. In some ways, indeed, the entire project of the 1923 *Novels of Jane Austen* was scooped from a Janeite of a different stripe, Reginald Farrer. In 1916, the year before the centenary of Austen's death—or of her "immortality" as he puts it—Farrer wrote a letter to the *Times Literary Supplement* from Tibet urging the public to undertake such a project. Among other things, he calls for a "Dream Edition" to include the six novels as "sumptuous, stately, final and perfect" as editors and publishers can produce; minor works such as *Lady Susan*, *The Watsons*, and *Sanditon*; etchings or drawings of sites where the novels take place instead of illustrations of scenes in the manner of Brock or Thomson; and appendices including background material important in the novels—for example, *Lover's Vows* for *Mansfield Park* and *Mysteries of Udolpho* for *Northanger Abbey*.[18] Farrer died in 1920, before seeing much of his dream come true. Chapman's 1923 edition, published in a large format with color plates, did not include any of Austen's minor works, as many reviewers complained, but the volumes are produced with the care and sumptuousness that Farrer called for; they banish Victorian illustrations in favor of Regency-period drawings of places, as Farrer specified; and they include *Lover's Vows* and excerpts from *Mysteries of Udolpho* and *Romance of the Forest*, exactly as Farrer directed. Whether Chapman was indebted to Metcalfe or Metcalfe to Chapman, we do not know, but clearly Chapman's conception of his authoritative edition of Austen's novels owes more to Farrer than he ever admits.

And yet finally the differences between Farrer's "Dream Edition" and Chapman's edition are what seem most striking. For Farrer, Austen is, as we have already seen, a contemporary in spirit and a living presence. For his "Dream Edition," Farrer calls on modern novelists "faithful to the school of Jane Austen"—such as Henry James, Edith Wharton, E. M. Forster, and Elizabeth von Arnim—to write prefaces to each of the six novels with the "discreet and solemn rapture of the hierophant."[19] Chapman is a textual scholar: his raptures in *The Portrait of a Scholar* are confined to old books. Accordingly, his edition of Jane Austen's novels has nothing to do with appreciation per se. His introductions are about dates of composition and editions printed during Austen's lifetime. Seeking to restore her texts from the corruptions introduced by repeated and often careless reprintings during the Victorian period and well into his own, Chapman aims to preserve her from decay, which takes her death for granted, rather than to celebrate her deathlessness, as Farrer does. It should be clear, then, that however immersed Chapman is in Austen's world in general and in the minutiae of her texts in particular, he is not any ordinary Janeite. Not for him the unrestrained, enthusiastic hallelujahs of Farrer and his ilk. Next to Farrer's heady and unequivocal claim that she is "our greatest artist in English fiction," Chapman's assessment sounds so measured, so qualified as to feel downright cold. His appendix on "Miss Austen's English" puts it thus: "Miss Austen's language deserves closer attention than it has received. She is not indeed one of the great writers of English prose in the early nineteenth century; but she is one of the greatest, because one of the most accurate, writers of dialogue of her own or any age; and of the writers of her period who furnish good and abundant specimens of polite conversation, she is to-day by far the most popular."[20]

Always the scholar, Chapman will not give himself over to enthusiasm. Assuredly, he regards Austen as great enough to deserve the preservation he accords. Yet his carefully qualified judgment—which sounds a bit like a concession to popular demand—justifies us in thinking more about the basis of her worthiness for him. Outside of dialogue, Chapman would later write, Austen's style "is not highly individual; it is just the ordinary correct English that, as Johnson had said, 'everyone now writes'" (*JAFP*, 209). Her greatness would appear, then, to be of a silver-spoonish sort. Like those beloved spoons, Austen's novels are ordinary exemplars and instruments of civilization before the Great Decline, when every literate person wrote well, when the elegancies and decorums he so missed in Macedonia were the regular currency of social life. And even today,

as Chapman has it, she furnishes "abundant specimens of polite conversation."[21] Farrer scornfully regards the practice of referring to Jane
Austen as "Miss Austen"—which he considers as absurd as it would be
"to speak currently of Mr. Milton, and Monsieur de Molière"—as one of
those "fantasies of propriety" that perpetuate false ideas about her ladylike limitations (RF, 8). Such ideas are precisely what Chapman wants to
perpetuate, and so he routinely refers to Jane Austen as "Miss Austen."

What stands out, then, is not the simple fact that Chapman's edition
"preserves" Jane Austen but that it is careful about precisely which elements to preserve. Fantasies of propriety—to recall Farrer's phrase—play
a large role here. The frontispiece to volume 1 (*Sense and Sensibility*) says
it all: "Evening Dresses" from Heideloff's Gallery of Fashion, November
1797, shows two women (sisters perhaps, like Elinor and Marianne Dashwood) decked out in full late eighteenth-century fashion, and in the 1923
editions this plate was elegantly tinted. The frontispieces to *Emma*, *Pride
and Prejudice*, and *Persuasion* likewise feature Regency fashion plates
of young women whom we might imagine to be the heroines of the novels or whom the heroines or their creator might have seen in books or
magazines. These illustrations emphatically (re)feminize Austen within
a world of fashion and elegance. To be sure, the illustrations Chapman
includes are not exclusively feminine. He also includes, in addition to the
facsimiles of the title pages of the first editions of each novel, pictures of
carriages; prints of London, Portsmouth, and Bath; and reproductions
of Gilpin, Rowlandson, Repton, Edridge, and so forth. Such illustrations,
having fallen out of favor during the heyday of New Criticism and later
of the "Theory Boom," seem to have reacquired their pertinence under
the aegis of Material Culture. But whether illustrating the distinctively
feminine world of fashion, bonnets, dancing, and domesticity or the cultural milieu of games, dances, and taste, Chapman stresses that quality of
politeness (which always includes the feminine) that he himself intensely
values, so the illustrations as a whole have the effect of fixing Austen
firmly and comfortably in her happy time, evoking a placid Regency sans
Napoleonic Wars, in order better to produce an Austen who is redemp-
tively light, and bright, and sparkling.

Fantasies of propriety also bear on Chapman's textual annotations.
Take, for example, Chapman's explanation of the following passage from
the first edition of *Sense and Sensibility*, which appeared in 1811:

"And who is Miss Williams?" asked Marianne.

"What! Do not you know who Miss Williams is? I am sure you must have heard of her before. She is a relation of the Colonel's, my dear; a very near relation. We will not say how near, for fear of shocking the young ladies." Then lowering her voice a little, she said to Elinor, "She is his natural daughter."

"Indeed!"

"Oh! Yes; and as like him as she can stare. I dare say the Colonel will leave her all his fortune."

Lady Middleton's delicacy was shocked; and in order to banish so improper a subject as the mention of a natural daughter, she actually took the trouble of saying something herself about the weather (*SS*, 77–78).

In his introductory note to *Sense and Sensibility*, Chapman observes that it is "worth recording" the fact that Austen deleted the whole of the last sentence of this excerpt—about Lady's Middleton's shocked delicacy— "in the interests of propriety" in the second edition of her novel, which appeared in 1813.[22]

Generations of students, reared on reprints of Chapman's edition, have read this note and reproduced its import. I am not taking issue here with Chapman's decision to follow the second edition, but rather with his account of this, her most conspicuous major revision in it. Austen did surely delete the sentence, but emphatically not in the interests of propriety. If Austen came to regard "the mention of a natural daughter" as a serious risk to propriety, then she obviously took the risk, because the text as emended actually retains that supposedly shocking phrase, "natural daughter." What Austen tones down in the 1813 edition is not impropriety but her full-on satire on the propriety-conscious Lady Middleton, who is so shocked that she turns the subject to the weather. These are very different things. In gliding over the distinction—with a carelessness not otherwise characteristic of him—Chapman creates the Austen he assumes exists, an Austen in step with the proprieties of her day, or at the very least anxious not to offend them. Much of Austen's saving virtues for Chapman, then, are to be found precisely in the fact that she predates Victorianism, which "by virtue of its instinct for ugliness" made not only spoons ugly but the rest of the world too, and his edition is thus a way of restoring a lost beauty. But on the score of propriety, Chapman owes far more to Victorianism than he does to modernism.

Chapman's edition widens the gap between Austen's time and our own, and as Kathryn Sutherland has noted, even the "faux Regency" typeface of his edition serves to take us back for a time to that better world.[23] The title page announces that these editions will have "Notes, Indexes and Illustrations from Contemporary Sources." But "Contemporary Sources" would have allowed for a broader sense of Austen's world than Chapman employs, particularly in his annotations. Most of Chapman's notes are textual, and he doubtless considered extensive explanatory notes of the sort we now expect to be intrusive and unnecessary. Just the same, when he does judge it fit to annotate a passage, his notion of what requires explanation is interestingly skewed, further ensuring, given the longevity of his editions, that his view of Austen would appear undisturbed for several generations as well. In *Northanger Abbey*, for example, Chapman writes a very long note on the whereabouts of the Northampton Light Dragoons, in which Frederick Tilney (a relatively minor character) serves, but deems it unnecessary to write a note explaining why Eleanor's fear of *riots* in London, riots menacing (as Henry Tilney says) the Bank of London and the Tower, is a reasonable fear, nor does he attempt any dating on the basis of this reference. On the same page that he notes that the phrase "sister author" refers to Frances Burney, he opts not to annotate contemporary landscape issues that lead Tilney to the subject of "oaks in general, to forests, the inclosure of them, waste lands, crown lands, and government" (*NA*, 113). In *Sense and Sensibility* he will annotate a reference to Mrs. Dashwood's age to inform us of what we already know—that she is forty (which would make me one of the old dowagers in Austen's oeuvre)—and then to observe that life spans were shorter in Austen's day, which has the effect of entirely negating the comedy of the passage in question, in which Fanny and John Dashwood are bitterly resenting how "people always live for ever when there is an annuity to be paid them; and she is very stout and healthy" (*SS*, 12). Chapman does not note what Willoughby means by imagining Colonel Brandon talk about "nabobs, gold mohrs, and palanquins" (*SS*, 61), for Austen's sense of the English empire holds no interest for him. In *Mansfield Park*, he annotates "the same interest" that Sir Thomas and Mr. Rushworth share, but he does not specify what that interest might be. It is perhaps needless to say that Chapman does not annotate the slave trade to which Fanny

Price (and later Mrs. Elton) alludes, but why he does not annotate Antigua seems willful given that Austen's father was a trustee of an estate there? In *Emma*, Chapman is aware that he is "exceeding [his] editorial function" on numerous occasions.[24] He calls our attention to a passage where Harriet hints to Emma that she has turned her affections from Mr. Elton to Mr. Knightley presumably so that we better savor the brilliance of Austen's subtlety, but he does not mention anything about the bawdiness of Garrick's "Riddle" ("Kitty, a fair, but frozen maid") that Mr. Woodhouse cannot quite remember, though doing so would certainly intensify the comedy, at the expense of the propriety, of the scene. In sum, though Chapman does not often annotate, when he does, his choices clearly suppress as much as they reveal. Chapman is doing more than preserving Jane Austen's texts; he is preserving a sense of the stability and loveliness of Jane Austen's time so that it may remain there, accessible for him and his like-minded contemporaries when modernity becomes too harsh, as it already has. As Kathryn Sutherland has elegantly put it, in place of history we have chronologies, which he appends to each novel: "If Chapman dismissed the disruptive forces of history, he remained fascinated by the quiet details of chronology. Was it on Thursday 12 January 1809 that Edmund dined at the Parsonage?"[25] These "quiet details" and all the other *detailia* of Chapman's editions have provided latter-day Janeites with a wealth of information for quizzes that have always tended to strike modern-day academics as beside the point (not that we can pass them).[26]

Many of Chapman's reviewers recognize Chapman's distinctive integration of scholarly apparatuses and enchantment. Writing for the *Edinburgh Review*, A. B. Walkley (an avid Janeite) mentions many aspects of Austen's novels that Chapman passes over entirely—the context of the French Revolution, the England of the Eldonine period, with its harsh penal laws, its unawakened Church, and its unreformed parliament. Walkley's Austen is not sealed off from politics, but her novels permit us to believe that ordinary life can be lived despite it. Accordingly. he praises Chapman's Georgian and Regency illustrations, his chronologies of the novels, and his notes on Austen's vocabulary because they "enable us to put ourselves in her place and, in reading, to recreate her work within ourselves." Walkley acknowledges that "we cannot . . . put the clock back," but we can enjoy the contrast. Putting an allusion to Wordsworth to rather un-Wordsworthian ends, Walkley continues, "It is something to have escaped, if only for a moment, from this 'world' that is 'too much with us' to that other world, the leisured, 'country-featured' and homely world of Jane Austen."[27] Desmond MacCarthy ("Affable Hawk") concludes that the edition is "covetable" and that Janeites will value it because "her books, besides being works of art and of unrivalled reality, are also to her readers a *refuge* from present realities." Yet in a remark that clearly shows that schism within Janeites produced by World War I that I have been tracing here, he also writes that minute textual scholarship into the commas and chronologies of Austen's novels "appeals only to an elderly childishness."[28] In her own review of Chapman's edition, Virginia Woolf hardly comments at all on the set itself and instead observes that present-day Janeism is the fruit of "masculine sensibility." Farrer's scorn for the Janeites given over to "fantasies of propriety" is transformed into Woolf's scorn for the fact that Austen is admired because—is Woolf thinking of the Rice Portrait?—"her dress was becoming, her eyes bright, and her age the antithesis in all matters of female charm to our own."[29]

When Shakespearean scholar and Janeite extraordinaire Caroline Spurgeon called Austen "a classic," she was not (merely) indulging in the ecstatic hyperbole typical of the Janeites among the Royal Society of Literature. By "classic," Spurgeon meant specifically that "every scrap of information we can gather, every ray of light that can be thrown upon her character, her outlook, her surroundings or her methods of work, are of intense and indeed of national importance." Presumably, those "scraps" would surely have included the information included in Chapman's textual notes, along with his annotations of all sorts. Unlike Chapman, Spurgeon does not look backward to Georgian England as a golden age: the "longer leisured vacuity of country life a century and a quarter ago" she dismisses as a "matter of antiquarian interest." Her Jane Austen, like Farrer's and Walpole's, is both ageless and contemporary. What most compels her is something, she writes, that remains permanent: the "English character" itself. Although this has been implicit both in the enchanted and the disenchanted Austens we have examined here, writing in 1927, Spurgeon finds that Austen's Englishness "is one aspect of her which has hardly been touched upon." And without going so far as to say, as Farrer did, that Austen is a man gone astray in a woman's body, for Sturgeon Austen's representative Englishness trumps gender altogether. No one, in Sturgeon's view, "had a clearer insight" into what is "characteristically English" than Austen, a character defined by delicate perceptions and moderation in expression, by reserve covering very deep feeling, by self-control, self-depreciation, and by a hatred of extremes, shams, and insincerity. And because Austen particularly excels in "the indirect revelation of character either through conversation or action, or sometimes letters," her books are full of what "Mrs. Wharton calls 'the magic casements of fiction, its vistas on infinity.'"[30] Vistas are large, expansive views, of course, not those confined, limited, diminutive views often associated with Austen's miniaturist's art. While Wharton's Keatsian "magic casements" opened out onto infinity, Sturgeon's open wonderfully and unexpectedly out onto Englishness itself, which for her amounts to the same thing. Austen's "classic novels" constitute a sort of national education.

In Austenian appreciation after World War I, *characters* in English novels, where English character is on display, create what Benedict Anderson so memorably called the "imagined political community" of the "nation," promoting a perception of fellowship across temporal as well as class borders, an esprit de corps over and against other nations, a sense of sovereign destiny.[31] At times, the contemplation of English national character is displayed as a tribute to the war that was: J. B. Priestley's *English Humour* was first published as part of the English Heritage Series, and its introduction was penned by Stanley Baldwin, then prime minister of England and president of the English Association. Baldwin's Janeism, as we will see in the next chapter, would some ten years later become the object of satire. For Baldwin, the English Heritage books—about English parish churches, the English county spirit, the English road, villages, and English humor—make him think immediately of the men lying in "our graveyards in Flanders and on the Somme."[32] Clearly, Austen is not the only English novelist to be implicated in these early stages of the "heritage" movement that burgeons in the 1980s. But she is certainly a key player. By the 1920s, Austen, in the minds of her admirers, served as a site of consolation and reprieve as well as a site of conflict, a site at once infinitely capacious and infinitely parochial. To be sure, during this period she *was* largely a creature of the elite, but she traveled with them to the trenches, and that experience makes early twentieth-century Janeism distinctive. The Austen who throve in England between the world wars was understood to be not apart from the real world, but quite a large part of it, where that "real" world was specifically understood to be under duress of the severest sort, and where qualities such as reticence, understatement, local attachment, self-control, and an irony bordering on cynicism were understood not as decorative graces but as constitutive elements of a national character, including national manhood, that had seen the worst and survived with a composure at once fragile and admirable.

4 Jane Austen's World War II

n October 1940, the *London New Statesman and Nation* published a letter to the editor from a gentleman who boasted being "the only man in London who has been bombed off a lavatory seat while reading Jane Austen" during the Blitz. "She went into the bath," he continues, "I went through the door."[1] Even if he may have been the only one to brag publicly about being knocked off the toilet while reading Austen, he was certainly not the only Englishman reading her books during the bombing raids of World War II. A year later, Georgette Heyer similarly declared that "if she were condemned to pass the rest of her days in an air raid shelter with the works of only one novelist available, she would undoubtedly choose Jane Austen."[2] In the previous chapter, we saw that Austen was critically if contrarily adored during World War I—on one hand (and somewhat counterintuitively) as an author whose clarity is born of alienation and disillusion and whose art is uniquely comforting under circumstances of shocking duress, and on the other hand as a gentle figure who signifies an equally therapeutic ideal of the graciousness of the English and England during the late Georgian period in periods of comparable loss and desolation. For many during World War II, Austen continues this latter move toward the center of English national identity. Because these wars were conducted and experienced in such different ways, however, the love of Jane Austen inevitably takes on a different cast. The Jane Austen we encountered in World War I is beloved in foreign parts, in strange lands, and in damp trenches by soldiers who are on their way to becoming, in Rupert Brooke's words, "dust whom England bore" ("The Soldier"). Part of the sublime and the ridiculous in the anecdote about the man bombed off a lavatory seat while reading Jane Austen is that the Blitz has thwarted the consolations of Austenian reading in private places. During World War II, Austen moves toward the center of a version of English identity felt to be coextensive with a cherished civilian home front under attack.

One London report in the *New York Times Book Review* in 1939 questions how Jane Austen could be relevant now, seeing that she was never "fitted with a gas mask by an A.R.P. warden."[3] This attitude may seem somewhat crude, but we find something of the same sentiment being articulated by no less than Virginia Woolf, whose "The Leaning Tower," delivered in May of 1940 to the Workers Educational Association Brighton, charges the entire English novelistic tradition, but especially Austen and Scott, with a class-bound remoteness from war that limits their pertinence to today's world. But Woolf's sense of the immanence and imminence of war may say more about the darkness of her inner life, despite the declared hope she expresses that the coming war will herald in a classless society. As Mary Favret has shown, Woolf undervalues the similarities many others found between the war of Austen's time and the war of their own.[4] In 1941 A. J. Hoppé, one of the directors of J. M. Dent, reported that sales of all "classic" English novels were up, but none more so than Jane Austen, whose *Pride and Prejudice* sold three times as many copies in 1940 as in 1939. And by 1942, a London bookseller reported that "Jane Austen was out of print for the first time since her death."[5] Because paper restrictions halted the republication of "classic" novels, and because storehouses, having been bombed in air raids, lost their stock, Austen's novels were hard to get. Evidently many English readers were turning to Austen despite her unfamiliarity with gas masks, finding her both to represent and to mobilize national feeling by being linked to the experience of peaceful privacy being rudely intruded on by war. Writing in 1939, writer and translator Laura Ragg, for example, judged the parallels between her own historical situation and Austen's to be glaring: Austen too lived through a long war and suffered the threat of invasion as well as anxiety for loved ones. Ragg readily concedes that Austen and her inland neighbors did not know the particular terror of the blitzkrieg: "Their nerves were not frayed by photographs and details from special correspondents, nor by the news bulletins of the B.B.C. No 'terror which flyeth in the darkness' roused them from their beds; and though for three or four years the menace of invasion haunted them, the danger seemed remote to those who dwelt inland."[6] Even though Ragg believes—rightly, of course—that the terror of the Blitz is distinctively modern, she insists on Austen's absorption in the everydayness of war, wondering pointedly and brilliantly, for example, whether Austen's income from *Sense and Sensibility* was taxed, as her mother's extra income would have been, given the war tax imposed from 1798 to 1815. Remarking further that other writers were as chary as Austen was of writing explicitly about the war—"Coleridge's Ancient Mariner shot a harmless bird, not a French sailor," she observes—Ragg finds that "far from being surprised that three out of Jane's completed novels contain no mention of the war, we should be astonished that it bulks so large in two of them" (*Persuasion* and *Pride and Prejudice*).[7] Ragg finds that the mood of war is everywhere in Austen's world and her novels: Austen knew the "stolid equanimity with which the English people supported twenty-one years of warfare with its attendant griefs and privations. . . . They suffered indeed from suspense, and from the heart-sickness of hope deferred to a degree which we can scarcely now imagine."[8] By this account, what looks like unperturbed placidity in Austen's novels is actually the "stolid equanimity" of a national community bearing up under the pressure of privation and grief, a heroic effort of mind and will—as when Elinor Dashwood in *Sense and Sensibility* chides her sister for assuming that self-control is possible only for those whose feelings are shallow to begin with: "The composure of mind with which I have brought myself at present . . . , the consolation that I have been willing to admit, have been the effect of constant and painful exertion;—they did not spring up of themselves; they did not occur to relieve my spirits at first" (*SS*, 299). Like earlier wartime readers of Jane Austen, Ragg reads Austen's silences as a full and positive presence, not as an absence, much as Elinor Dashwood's undemonstrativeness signifies the fullness of her feelings and the powers of her self-command, not the opposite.

For novelist Beatrice Kean Seymour, the mood of Austen's novels is even grimmer. Like Ragg, Seymour finds Austen's silence on war complex and symptomatic. Herself writing on the eve of World War II, Seymour thinks about Austen's conscious relationship to the national crises of her time, and she concludes that Austen's silence about the Napoleonic Wars results from her saturation by them, not from the oblivion imputed to her—"much as," she continues, "we to-day, in 'post-war England,' have got used to the various wars still being waged in the world . . . and this despite the continued threat of our own involvement. The human mind—especially in our own day, when news of fresh horrors reaches us so rapidly and continually—arrives at a point when, if existence is to be supported and sanity preserved, it has to shut itself up against the knowledge. . . . I suspect that for Jane the war did not bear thinking about. There was nothing to be done about it, yet all the time it was there, a cold horror at the back of the mind."[9] *A cold horror at the back of the mind.* This is probably not how the general public would describe the contents of Austen's consciousness, and Seymour is daring in saying this so boldly. To be sure, this view of Austen is rooted in the reception history prominent during World War I, but a wider, civilian public (as distinct from an exclusive club or sect) is now finding that horror adjacent to home, and on this account the heroism of enduring horror by recourse to the everyday is equally the province of men and women.

Although they are rarely quite as explicit about the grimness at the heart of Austen's novels, newspapers conjure this similar mixed image of Austen as both acutely vulnerable and quietly heroic. She is understood to be an important respite for a war-weary public, a precious resource in short supply. Taking up the question of war reading in *Time and Tide*, Lord David Cecil recommends Austen's novels because "it is surprisingly possible to imagine how Jane Austen's characters would behave in wartime," even though their lives seem to unfold in "quietness itself."[10] In April 1943, one London newspaper observes, "It is as pleasant to be told . . . that the young men and women in the Forces want to read MISS AUSTEN'S novels, as it is harrowing to learn that they cannot get them." So considered, shortages of Austen's novels seem punishing, for soldiers deserve reprieve: "If the best and most reviving literature for times such as these is that which gives a brief escape from thoughts of war," this writer continues, "then who should stand beside MISS AUSTEN? . . . The books are full of the drowsy humming of a summer garden which can deafen the ears even to the humming of the aeroplane overhead." This "brief escape" is clearly tenuous. Four years of war have made the writer momentarily wonder why the "idle young men" in Austen's novels have nothing better to do than go to London for haircuts, as Frank Churchill claimed to do: "No wonder Mr. Knightley, who would certainly have commanded the Donwell Platoon of the Home Guard, disapproved of such a trifler."[11] And even when tranquility resumes, we must find that it is so proximate to what is being escaped from that it cannot be separated from it: the humming of imagined gardens is said to be louder than the humming of airplanes overhead, but because Austen's novels do not represent any humming gardens, it is safe to conclude that the felt dangers of war are actually producing that drowsy, humming calm rather than being excluded by and from it.

The "humming" of airplanes was a threat not only to soldiers and civilians who read Jane Austen. Sometimes Austen's books—considered solely as physical objects—were the victims of the Blitz, and so themselves could represent both wartime vulnerability at the same time as their author's powers of comfort and inspiration: the *Pickering and Chatto [Sale] Catalogue #325* lists the first edition of *Northanger Abbey* and *Persuasion* as among books that have "withstood aggression in varying forms" for hundreds of years of English history and that shall continue to endure still despite "the honorable scars of war" they received during recent German air raids. Austen, we are informed, endured in her own day "in spite of Napoleonic Wars," and along with the other war-damaged volumes, it is "more than a match for the barbaric treatment that a nation of savages can inflict upon them."[12]

Books were not the only purveyors of such Austenian fellowship. Initially inspired by the success of Helen Jerome's stage production of *Pride and Prejudice*, the MGM adaptation of the novel went into preproduction in 1936 and was to star Clark Cable and Norma Shearer. After undergoing numerous casting changes, production began in February 1940, with a screenplay written primarily by Aldous Huxley, with Greer Garson and Laurence Olivier in the lead roles, and with a predominantly British cast. Despite a good deal of ludicrousness—antebellum costumes, Mr. Collins's metamorphosis into a librarian (the Hollywood production forbidding irreverent representations of the clergy), Lady Catherine's transformation into a swell old gal who pretends to be ornery only to test the lovers' devotion—the production was a critical as well as box office success, and not only to American audiences, whose judgment we might assume to be wanting. In November 1940, the MGM *Pride and Prejudice* afforded the reviewer in the *London Observer* "a deal of pleasure" that made him "forget for two blessed hours, that the world wasn't bounded by Longbourne, Rosings, Netherfield, and a wedding ring."[13] As Kenneth Turan has shown, having discovered a 1941 letter from an Englishwoman in Southampton to director Robert Z. Leonard, the film's reception in England could be even more heartfelt:

My husband is a Naval Officer and a few days ago he had one of his rare afternoons in port and a chance to visit the cinema. We went to see your film made from the book we know and love so well and to our delight were carried away for two whole hours of perfect enjoyment. Only once was I reminded of our war—when in a candle-lit room there was an uncurtained window and my husband whispered humorously, "Look—they're not blacked out." You may perhaps know that this city has suffered badly from air raids but we still have some cinemas left, and to see a packed audience enjoying *Pride and Prejudice* so much was most heartening.

I do thank you very much as well as all the actors and actresses for your share in what has given so much pleasure to us.[14]

Here too, as with humming gardens and humming airplanes, the film version of *Pride and Prejudice* works bidirectionally: it both helps viewers forget the war—"for two whole hours"—while at the same time invites them to remember it. The observation of the unconcealed candle points both to the fact that it was not necessary to curtain the windows during Austen's time and to the sense that someone ought to draw that curtain right away before the German bombers spot Longbourne!

Placing this adaptation in the context of Depression-era films, Diane F. Sadoff has insightfully argued that Greer Garson's Elizabeth Bennet is an update of the fast-talking gal of the screwball comedies of the 1930s, and Ellen Belton, placing it against the backdrop of the Battle of Britain, has argued that the movie, in idealizing English country life, creates a space for "Anglo-American solidarity in times of crisis."[15] These two explanations come together when we consider that American sympathy with Britain's plight during the early years of World War II was not a spontaneous outpouring, but was in many ways solicited by Britain's Foreign Office, calculated to encourage the United States' entry into the war and to counter the American public's stereotypes of Britain as imperial, aristocratic, and decadent, with a view of England as understated but robust and the war as the "people's war." Hollywood played its role in this process.[16] For isolationist US audiences in 1940, wary of entering a "European war," the MGM *Pride and Prejudice*—like the 1942 *Mrs. Miniver* later, if less dramatically—presented England as sensible, domestic, endearing, and spunky, an England worthy of our alliance. Once America entered the war, Henry Seidel Canby devoted a column of the

Saturday Review to war reading for American soldiers, and given his stature, in Gordon Hutner's words, as "one of the most influential arbiters of taste that mid-twentieth-century journalism ever produced," his recommendation is worth close consideration.[17]

Canby celebrated Austen and England alike with a rhapsodic intensity that is Trillingesque avant la lettre and that is extraordinary in its own right. "The greatest novels (in English at least) written in wartime," he writes, "are unquestionably Jane Austen's." Her relevance to the present war is obvious:

> Jane's stories are absolutely conditioned by the threats to the security of that marvelously integrated country life of England. In the lurid light coming from overseas, the character of the Englishman, the temperament of the English woman, took on a heightened importance. The English countryside, which they had built, seemed fairer, more desirable than ever before. The country life of parson, squire, and privileged neighborhood acquired an importance which it did not possess, because of its happy contrasts with confusion, loss, and breakdown abroad. In this provincial Utopia, bad temper, pomposity, servility, sentimentality, snobbishness, and greed were seen as especial dangers because they were the cracks which might topple down the magnificent stability of a society which had lost a new world in the West, and was standing fast when all of Europe fell.

At first Canby seems to be talking about the early nineteenth century, after England lost the "new world" of the American colonies, and the "lurid light" coming from overseas is produced by the French Revolution and the Napoleonic Wars. Once Canby talks about standing fast when all of Europe fell, however, our frame of reference changes abruptly to the present, and Austen becomes our contemporary once again. His tributes to English character, English gender, and English landscape endeared by danger remind American soldiers why England is worth fighting for and why novels of manners—novels about bad tempers, snobbishness, greed, and so forth—are not trivial stuff of interest only to silly women, but are deadly serious explorations of national character, which, during wartime especially, must be understood in urgently political ways for the insights they can provide into the foundational social and personal practices on which England's stability is built. Canby thus takes the long tradition of casting Austen as a supremely apolitical writer, a writer who passes over the momentous and world-shattering world at war around her and reformulates it in a different, positive way: she is a writer absolutely conditioned by the "lurid" light of war, which makes her value England and Englishness more than ever and which inclines her to explore them so closely. Canby concludes his peroration by coming very close to asserting that the United States entered the war in Europe to fight for Jane: The American war effort in Europe draws on a "reservoir" of "good will for England and the character and temperament moulded there through the centuries," Canby continues, and the English ought to "thank Jane Austen as much as anyone for that."[18]

𝕙𝕩 If Austen was as portable as the dust of English soldiers in Flanders or on the Somme during World War I, during World War II she is linked to the homeland assaulted by barbarity. Austenian places are the objects of attack. Take the Baedeker Blitz. Reportedly provoked by British bombing attacks on civilian targets in Lübeck in March 1942, the German air command executed retaliatory raids on Exeter, Norwich, York, Canterbury, and Bath, towns marked with stars in the *Baedeker Guide to Great Britain*. The *Baedeker Great Britain* of 1937 notes Austen's residence at 4 Sidney Place and mentions *Persuasion* prominently along with other works associated with Bath, such as *Humphry Clinker*, *The Rivals*, *Pickwick Papers*, and others, making it technically possible to imagine that Adolph Hitler (who was rumored to have ordered the raids personally) was aiming at Austen, among others Bath notables. The Baedecker bombings were understood as attacks not on sites of military importance but on English culture and history, calculated to demoralize the public. The bombings of Bath in particular were heavier and deadlier than those on other towns, consisting of three raids on the nights of 25 and 26 April and one raid on the night of 26–27 April 1942. Three hundred and twenty-nine houses were totally destroyed, 132 had to be demolished, and 19,147 suffered some damage, and the final death toll was estimated at more than four hundred.[19] In the feature on the Bath bombings that ran in the issue of *Picture Post* dated 4 July (fig. 4.1), Austen is a strong though purely intertextual presence that the reader brings to the article when gazing at photos of the Assembly Room or the Crescent in rubbles, as if the Nazis had taken aim at the England and Englishness she typified. As John Taylor has so persuasively shown, *Picture Post* includes no photos of the more extensive bombing damage done to houses, shelters,

THE HOUSE THAT DESERVED A LONG LIFE
Bath's climate is kind to old age. But in one night Nazi bombs destroy work that has lasted for centuries.

THE STREET THAT IS MORE FAMOUS THAN EVER
A strange disorder comes to the boldly sweeping Royal Crescent which Wood the younger started in 1767.

ALL THAT REMAINS OF A REGENCY VILLA
A great rent from roof to basement. Walls blackened by fire. A garden filled with masonry. But next door the walls stand.

IN THE ASSEMBLY ROOMS THE CHAIR SURVIVES
John Wood the younger built the historic Rooms in 1769-71. Just before the war they were restored. Now they are gutted.

BATH—WHAT THE NAZIS
MEAN BY A 'BAEDEKER RAID'

WALKING round Bath after the Nazi raid was like looking into an elegant drawing-room after a grimy, spiteful urchin out of the gutter has tried to do his worst in it. His spite does the gutter-snipe no good : it is beyond his power to destroy the walls and furniture of the room he has invaded. All he can achieve is trouble for his betters. But while the mess remains, people of taste shudder a little, less at the amount of damage done than at the evidence that there are still people in

Figure 4.1. *Bath after the Baedeker raid,* Picture Post *(4 July 1942).*

and people in poorer parts of Bath, and so in the process it suggests that it was "our heritage" that suffered during the Blitz and that this heritage is coextensive with sections of Bath that actually sustained relatively smaller damage: the Assembly Rooms, the Royal Crescent, the Regency villas, the "elegant drawing room[s]," and "the walls and furniture" of

Austen's time, which "people of taste" awoke to discover "we" were losing when the bombing began.[20]

The identification of Austen with the elegance and taste of Bath and Bath in turn with English heritage—which had been only implicit in *Picture Post*—becomes fully explicit in Lieutenant R. A. Lendon Smith's remarkable little book titled *Bath*, which was written in 1943 when he was twenty-eight and first published a year later, after his death in World War II. One in a long line of soldiers attached to Austen, Smith is described in the preface as a medievalist who had "a great devotion to all English things" and who "cherished and understood the high civilized traditions of his country," qualities typified by Bath.[21] Before the 1940s, accounts of Bath mention Austen as one among throngs of luminaries associated with that city: the *Baedecker Great Britain* of 1910, for example, names "Miss Austen" once, but does not mention *Persuasion*, and gives altogether more attention to Frances Burney's grave in Wolcott Cemetery, information omitted in the 1937 edition; and Edith Sitwell's *Bath* (London, 1932) celebrates the fashionable eighteenth-century Bath of Beau Nash and Sarah Siddons and mentions Austen in passing only on the last page.[22] During the war years, it appears that she is more strongly identified with Bath. Smith's penultimate chapter is devoted entirely to Austen, inviting us to see Bath through her eyes by presenting long passages from *Northanger Abbey* and *Persuasion*. A devout Catholic whose trip to Bath was part of a "pilgrimage," Smith saw Bath as a holy city, "a new Jerusalem built by some magic hand in England's green and pleasant land." As the rhapsodic, eschatological tone suggests, Bath occupies historical as well as transcendent temporalities: on one hand it is eternal, and on the other hand it is an embattled city below. Though comprehending Rome as well as the Middle Ages, Bath reaches its peak during Austen's time—just before giving its downward spiral from Regency elegance into dreary "great wastes of the Victorian Age," with its inferior development styles. No wonder Smith applauds a heritage-conscious decree that "all building in the city shall be of Bath stone and consonant to the architectural style of the eighteenth century," thus forever ensuring that the Georgian and Regency Bath that Austen knew would forever be Bath tout court.[23] Bath becomes Austen's city, then, just as the city itself becomes in some sense Austen at the same time. Forget that Austen hated Bath; forget that she found its yellow stone glaring and headache inducing, as Smith himself half acknowledges: the myth here is the point. The Bath Austen knew is seen as Bath perdurable, a feminine manifestation of national glory and endurance. In passages such as this, it is momentarily difficult to tell whether Smith is talking about Bath or Austen or both at the same time: "She remains to-day in her architecture, her history, and her tradition, a perfect epitome of our national past: a harbinger of an even greater future."[24]

Having consolidated English history and national character into the simultaneously ancient and Austenian site of Bath, Smith is in a position to have it both ways when he turns in his closing pages to the Baedeker raids, which were surely fresh in his mind. On the one hand, the bombing of the Assembly Rooms and the Royal Crescent are savage attacks on the feminine serenity of the city. Photos of rubble are adduced to testify to the monumental incivility of enemies who would pound targets of such grace, as Smith describes how "planes roared down in dive-bombing attacks to as low as 50 feet, and then mercilessly fired on streets and buildings with cannon and machine-gun." On the other hand, because Bath is eternal, it is beyond the possibility of real injury. And so the enemy is both atrocious and curiously ineffectual:

> In spite of the destruction of the Assembly Rooms . . . one is amazed at the smallness of the irreparable injury that the Luftwaffe has been able to inflict on the Queen City of the West. Two houses in the Royal Crescent were gutted by fire but their outer fabric still stands in all its majesty loveliness. . . . Bath bears her scars bravely. Her head is proud and erect, for in her two thousand years of recorded history she has seen much of pagan hatred and fury. In historical perspective the latest Teutonic assault cannot seem much more formidable than the onslaught of the Angles and Saxons on the peaceful undefended Aquae Sulis. Conscious of the greatness of her historic past, Bath can afford to endure the present and to contemplate the future with a lustrous calm born of ripe experience.[25]

Much as *Picture Post* had represented the Nazis as unmannerly "guttersnipes" vandalizing elegant drawing rooms, Smith's book portrays a city that is a woman of ostensibly Austenian poise whose dignity is so consummate that it cannot be violated, whose majesty so serene that it cannot be ruffled.

The foregoing confirms John Taylor's observation that "England was transformed between the wars from the masculine, heroic nation of the late Victorian and Edwardian periods into a 'feminized' country."[26] It also suggests that Austen is not merely *associated* with an elegiac ethos of Englishness but is *materially identified* with it. Elizabeth Jenkins's 1938 biography of Austen opens with a tribute to Georgian England inflected in feminine terms pointing to Austen. Weltering as we do "in a slough of habitual ugliness," we recognize spider's web fanlights, chintz fabric, and elegant lettering as remnants of an age whose exquisiteness contrasts with the "hideousness" of modern life: "The ghost of that vanished loveliness haunts us," she writes, "in every memorial that survives the age: a house in its park, a teacup, the type and binding of a book." Like Chapman a few decades earlier, Jenkins is attracted to the things of Austen's age that are fast being crowded out by the proliferating ugliness of modernity.[27]

The increasingly elegiac material identification of Austen with the "vanished loveliness" of Georgian England brings us to the founding of the Jane Austen Society. Compared to other literary societies, the Jane Austen Society (of the UK) is a latecomer. The Shakespeare Club was formed in 1824 and the Shakespeare Birthplace Trust in 1847; the Browning Society in 1881; the Brontë Society in 1893; the Dickens Fellowship in 1902; the Keats Shelley Memorial Association in 1906; and the George Eliot Fellowship in 1930. We have seen that Janeites appointed themselves a "sect" since the mid-nineteenth century, but they were never constituted as a formal club or society in the conventional sense of the term. The official Jane Austen Society was not formed until 1940, a year after England declared war. At its founding, its aim was not the appreciation of Austen's novels—officers of this society have boasted of never reading them at all!—but the preservation of Austenian property in the neighborhood. Even today, its stated goal is "to obtain possession of the house at Chawton (accomplished) and to make it available to the public as a show-place and museum."[28]

This was not the first attempt to memorialize Jane Austen at her residence in Chawton. In 1917, the centennial of Austen's death, a small band of Anglo-American Janeites gathered together to dedicate a plaque in her memory (fig. 4.2). The celebrants were anything but oblivious to the fact that World War I was not over. Clarence Graff, the only American present at the ceremony, observed that "it is perhaps a remarkable thing that, in these days of war, we can turn aside, even for a day, from the sterner demands of the moment to come together to pay this homage to the genius

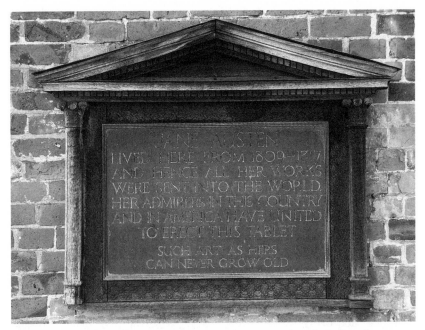

Figure 4.2. *Plaque dedicated to Jane Austen's memory (1917), designed in part by Ellen Hill. This wartime memorial did not draw a crowd. Courtesy of the Jane Austen Memorial Trust.*

of Jane Austen." At the same time the thought of Austen rededicated the assembled to a "new hope of the civilisation that we are fighting together to save."[29] We have already observed that Chawton Cottage was regarded as so unprepossessing that it was never before memorialized or recommended as a site for literary pilgrimage. In 1917 the lovers of Jane Austen seemed to share a certain wariness of the cottage itself. By design, the oak frame echoes the pediment and pilasters of a window from another place where Austen lived, 4 Sydney Place in Bath, from 1801 to 1804. The 1917 memorial effort did not consider the commemoration of place its only duty: the subscription raised money for a "schoolchildren's library" in the village and "a small scholarship, both to bear her name, in Steventon."[30]

Though memorialized as Austen's one-time home, the place where Austen lived was associated with Austen only by confirmed Janeites. Dorothy Darnell, an admirer of Austen who lived in nearby Alton, started the society after she happened to find its cast-iron fire grate along the side of the road.[31] Although she had evidently long had the general hope of reclaiming the cottage—then broken into three apartments and a village library—it was evidently war that transformed the recovery of this link to Austen's world into more momentous rescue work that involved the entire nation.

A 1952 article in the *Guardian* maintained that Austen "did not more beautifully ignore the possibility of [Napoleon's] conquering England than did Miss Dorothy Darnell, quietly beginning in 1940 to form a literary society, beautifully ignore the possibility of Hitler doing any better than Napoleon."[32] On the contrary, in 1940 the handful of founding members were aware that "the time for starting such a society could scarcely be worse," as Chairman High Curtis wrote, casting about for membership subscriptions from friends and descendants. Curtis adds, however, that it is "a good idea to-day to think of pleasant things like this though it may sound a little mad to you, amidst the general racket that is going on." That "racket," of course, was the Blitz. More than therapeutic diversion had to have been at stake in trying (as Curtis phrased it) "to put Jane's house in order"—the very phrase here denoting the act not merely of acquiring Austen's house and arranging it properly but also of regulating one's fiscal and domestic affairs in anticipation of death. Curtis opines that the Jane Austen Society will have a large membership "if & when things become more normal," and that "if" is important.[33] In 1940 it was by no means apparent that England would not end up in the same scrap heap in which Darnell found the fire grate. Putting Austen's house in order required marvelous hope. As elsewhere in England, where lovers of "heritage" hid national treasures from the depredations of the feared invader, the Jane Austen Society would attempt to preserve Jane's donkey cart, bacon roller, and wash house as relics and to record living recollections of Austen; in the next chapter we will turn to these specific items. In 1946, acquiring the property seemed a pipe dream. The Jane Austen Society appealed for contributions from "admirers of Jane Austen's works, who would like to see this house . . . preserved as a national monument."[34] And on December 7 of that same year, the *Times* reprinted and endorsed that appeal, observing that Chawton Cottage "deserves preservation, in an age of destruction and decay."[35]

Austen's status as a national treasure was not sufficient to raise a stunning £5,000 worth of purchase and repair costs at an annual subscription rate of a half-crown during or immediately after the war. Once again a soldier's Janeism came through. T. Edward Carpenter, a London solicitor, noticed the *Times* article. He visited the cottage in 1947 and in 1948, purchased Chawton, and funded its repairs in memory of his son, Philip John Carpenter, a lieutenant in the First Battalion of the East Surrey Regiment, who died in action in Italy in 1944. Carpenter said that "his son was deeply interested in Jane Austen's novels,"[36] and Chawton Cottage became his memorial as much as it is a museum devoted to Austen herself: a marble panel commemorating him is in the drawing room.[37] The monument and museum together suggest that Austen is what Philip John Carpenter fought and fell for.

⁊§ The *Luftwaffe* was not the only enemy. Another conflict was breaking out, this time over the authority to read Jane Austen properly, during World War II in particular and for all time in general. D.W. Harding's pathbreaking essay, "Regulated Hatred: An Aspect of the Work of Jane Austen" (1940), was widely reprinted in anthologies, proving incalculably important in academic criticism for the next half century. Its legacy is still very much with us, and it deserves close attention on account of its historic importance. First delivered as a lecture in March 1939 in Manchester, and published a year later in *Scrutiny*, "Regulated Hatred" invokes Austen's importance during wartime by calling her "a formidable ally" in our battle against "things and people which were to her, and still are, hateful" (*RH*, 25). When we come to examine the identity of these hateful enemies more precisely, it is with some shock that we discover them not to be the benighted folks who disregard or dislike Austen, but ones who adore her most extravagantly, who read her the wrong way and love her for the wrong reasons: "Her books are, as she meant them to be, read and enjoyed by precisely the sort of people whom she disliked" (*RH*, 6). Though Harding never cites his predecessors, he was certainly not the first reader to stress the sharp critical quality of Austen's laughter or even to notice that many Janeites were foolish—such claims are amply to be found in Alice Meynell, Reginald Farrer, or Virginia Woolf. Harding goes much further both in intensifying that critical quality to outright hatred and then in admiring her for this hatred, rather than pathologizing her for it as, say, Marvin Mudrick would later do in the 1950s, when he argued that Austenian irony was a personal defense against the terror of intimacy.

Who are these readers whom Austen was laughing at without their noticing? Among many others, R. W. Chapman, no doubt, though never mentioned, whose edition (as we have seen) memorialized the elegance of Austen's period—its dresses, dances, carriages, and language; probably Lord David Cecil, also unmentioned, who in 1935 had written, "There are those who do not like her, as there are those who do not like sunshine or unselfishness";[38] and certainly Elizabeth Jenkins, whose biography had appeared a few years earlier and who is mentioned in the essay. Such readers belong, in Harding's view, to an entire generation of readers deemed foolish because they believe that Austen typifies "the gentler virtues of a civilized social order" (*RH*, 5)—presumably the late Georgian period—and that "because she lived at a time when, as a sensitive person of culture, she could still feel that she had a place in society," she could confidently write as a "delicate satirist, revealing with inimitable lightness of touch the comic foibles and amiable weaknesses of the people she lived amongst and liked" (*RH*, 6). All of this, as Harding continues acidly, "was enough to make me quite sure that I did not want to read her." Although England had not yet declared war against Germany, war is clearly on Harding's mind, because he exemplifies the bad Janeite reader by reference to Eric Linklater's 1938 novel, *The Impregnable Women*, which imagines a second world war breaking out first between England and France.[39] This now obscure work features a doddering prime minister, Lord Pippin. This gentleman is given to *Country Life* pleasures, and his rank incapacity for leadership is signaled by the fact that, as Harding puts it, he "passes from surreptitious to abandoned reading of [Austen's] novels as a national crisis deepens"—first hiding volumes of *Emma* in chair cushions, reading them only in private and then later pulling them out brazenly during cabinet meetings, ignoring reports on military developments, and rejoicing when adjournments let him turn from war to "the pleasanter company of Jane Austen . . . Miss Woodhouse and Mr. Knightley" (*RH*, 5).

Harding extends Linklater's satire on Lord Pippin to an entire class of readers who regard Austen as "a refuge . . . when the contemporary world [grows] too much for them" (*RH*, 5). Whatever Linklater is up to, Harding's purpose in alluding to him is clear. Harding is anti-Janeite in order to be pro-Austen. His aim is to align Austen with his own side in that demanding, wartime "contemporary world" that Lord Pippin so disastrously fails. Harding's critique of Janeites is thus straightforward: first, it posits an opposition between the cozy domesticity of country life and the tough realities of the "real" world, especially as that world includes war; second, it claims that Janeites retreat to the former out of their irresponsible fear of the latter, completely misapprehending Austen along the way.

Harding's moves seem intuitively true but are demonstrably false. True, in Linklater's novel, Lord Pippin loves to talk about "fox-hounds and gundogs," "gardener's topics," and Austen's novels because he and his ilk do not want to discuss how "people in large numbers were being killed." As we have abundantly seen, actual Janeites regarded Austen as a way to endure war, not as a way out of it. Even Linklater's Lord Pippin himself has no distaste for war as such: he *loves* to make sonorous speeches about the "English character . . . especially as it revealed itself in times of peril or difficulty," and because he is *always* thinking about Jane Austen, it is a safe bet that she inspires such speeches.[40] Complicating the matter further, Harding omits saying that Linklater's novel is a modernization of *Lysistrata*. An antiwar strike by British women is what drives Lord Pippin to the pages of *Emma*. It is principally carnality rather than carnage that this Janeite cannot stomach. Whatever the justness of Harding's reading of *The Impregnable Women*, the real-life prototype for Lord Pippin was the Jane-loving Stanley Baldwin, prime minister of England from 1923 to 1924, 1924 to 1929, and 1935 to 1937 and the president of the English Association in 1927. Baldwin's opposition to rearmament in the 1930s and his perceived appeasement of Hitler's westward advances are the backstory of Harding's piece, and so hearing it as a lecture in March 1939 or reading it in 1940, one could not fail to recognize the stakes of Harding's characterizations. Having represented Lord Pippin/Stanley Baldwin as nerveless and etiolated, Harding is implying that his Janeism is a positive danger to the nation.

In his commitment to a new, hard Austen over and against an old, soft one, Harding also singles out Beatrice Kean Seymour as another culprit in feeble and enfeebling Janeism. He cites the closing words of *Jane Austen: Study for a Portrait* (1937) with stinging disdain: "In a society which has enthroned the machine-gun and carried it aloft even into the quiet heavens, there will always be men and women—Escapist or not, as you please—who will turn to her novels with an unending sense of relief and thankfulness" (quoted in *RH*, 5). Harding does not explain why this thought merits scorn. In the process of assuming the reason to be self-explanatory, he passes over the unusual, highly revisionist notion of escape Seymour proposed here. Seymour classes Austen with a range of socially engaged yet visionary writers most readers have never dreamt of associating with her with, writers such as D. H. Lawrence, William Blake, and Percy Shelley, figures Seymour calls "escapist" not because they withdraw from the world but because they posit "a vision of truth and beauty and a world that does not correspond to that vision."[41] Far from thinking of Austen as a delicate satirist of her neighbors' foibles, comfortable in her neighborhood, Seymour sees Austen as a visionary at odds with society as presently constituted. And far from conceiving of Austen as light and comic, Seymour posits, as we have seen earlier in this chapter, that "horror" dwelt at the back of her mind.

What accounts for Harding's animus against Janeites, his apparent determination to cast them as weak and foolish? Clues are to be found in Wendy Anne Lee's fascinating research into Harding's papers and into his work on the psychology of war, *The Impulse to Dominate* (1941), written at the same time that he was writing "Regulated Hatred."[42] Although Harding understands war as a form of large-scale regression, a dereliction from social ideals all sides agree are the norm, he also contends that war erupts both from the "hatred and fears" that are endemic within society and from the "techniques of domination and submission" that our civilization has developed to secure power without conflict. These techniques break down when war occurs, and yet at the same time actually produce the sort of contention that leads to belligerence. As Lee has explained, for Harding "the deep structure of domination and deference so pervades our lives that nearly all of our interactions take the form of war. . . . People or countries living together inevitably disagree, and war erupts in an understood commitment to winners or losers."[43] Although Harding endorses the ethical necessity of war at times, *The Impulse to Dominate* is devoted to thinking about what an alternative to the structure of domination and deference might look like, and he finds it in the psychological notion of "social integration," which "aims neither at leaving people as they are nor at making them like oneself, for it regards differences between two people as mutual invitations to development. Far from denying differences, it gives the closest attention to them, seeing them as an enrichment of human potentiality. Such an attitude does not imply a spineless or irresponsible abandoning of standards, nor a meek submissiveness. It does not exclude strong preferences and bitter dislikes. All that it does exclude is the itch to root out what we dislike."[44]

Understood in light of these theories about war—among nations, among individuals—the rationale for Harding's antipathy to gentle Janeites comes into focus. For Harding, Janeites continually airbrush out of Austen's novels precisely what makes them so interesting and valuable: her dramatization of the "eruption of fear and hatred into the relationships of everyday social life" (*RH*, 10).

Engaging in a tour de force of close reading, Harding inaugurates his discussion of Austen's "unexpected astringencies" by turning to a scene from *Northanger Abbey* (then a relatively unloved, unadmired novel) in which Henry Tilney reproaches Catherine Morland for harboring the suspicion that General Tilney murdered his mother:

> "Dear Miss Morland, consider the dreadful nature of these suspicions you have entertained. What have you been judging from? Remember the country and the age in which we live. Remember that we are English, that we are Christians. Consult your own understanding, your own sense of the probable, your own observation of what is passing around you. Does our education prepare us for such atrocities? Do our laws connive at them? Could they be perpetrated without being known, in a country like this, where social and literary intercourse is on such a footing, and where roads and newspapers lay everything open?" (quoted in *RH*, 6–7).

What Harding calls the "comfortable" reader will encounter this passage as a straightforward paean to Georgian civilization, to the religion, and nation, and the law, and the education, and the newspapers that make gothic suspicion foolish. In order to secure this complacent impression of "our" civilization, the comfortable reader must omit the penultimate clause, which Harding himself also withholds from his readers, the better to underscore his point. That unreadable, inassimilable passage is this: "where every man is surrounded by a neighbourhood of voluntary spies." Austen undercuts Henry's confidence in the mores of his age by referring to the wholesale invasiveness of the society Henry is actually idealizing, thus calling into question his rosy view of English institutions in general—and all in such a way as to "slip through [her readers'] minds without creating a disturbance" (*RH*, 8). Demonstrating not only his own impressive attentiveness as a reader but also Austen's wicked subtlety, her gift for lulling her unwary readers into accepting propositions they would refuse if they were ever actually to notice them, Harding shows how Austen becomes a "literary classic of the society which attitudes like hers, held widely enough, would undermine" (*RH*, 6).

Harding's close analysis of Austenian astringency continues with a fascinating discussion of the Coles's dinner party in *Emma*: "The rest of the dinner passed away; the dessert succeeded, the children came in, and were talked to and admired amid the usual rate of conversation; a few clever things said, a few downright silly, but by much the larger proportion neither the one nor the other—nothing worse than every day remarks, dull repetitions, old news, and heavy jokes" (*E*, 236). Nothing worse? For Harding, this phrase typifies the stealth of Austen's style and the plasticity of her social attitudes. Of course it is a sarcasm at the expense of the tedium of everyday converse in civilized society, wearying particularly to a mind as quick and inventive as Emma Woodhouse's and, we may assume, Jane Austen's. Harding insists that "nothing worse"—a phrase seldom noticed—is more than a mere sarcasm because indeed there are things worse than boring conversation: "'Nothing worse' is a positive tribute to the decency, the superficial friendliness, the absence of the grosser forms of insolence and self-display at the dinner party. At least Mrs. Elton wasn't there" (*RH*, 11). Harding's Austen values the politeness achieved by her civilization and respects the necessity "to keep on reasonably good terms with the associates of her everyday life." But Harding's Austen also knows that "real existence depended on resisting the values"—the crudeness and complacencies—of that same society. And so "nothing worse" manages both respect and penetrating critique: "The effect of the comment, if her readers took it seriously, would be that of a disintegrating attack upon the social intercourse they have established for themselves" (*RH*, 11).

Austenian commentary—up until this moment—had rarely been so closely focused on voice and interpretation in so sustained a way, and though Harding was a psychologist rather than a literary critic, it is easy to see why his essay became a classic for the generation of "close readers" to come. Yet the key word here is "disintegrating," given the status of "integration" in Harding's thoughts about building a peaceful rather than warlike society. Austen is a treasure at this particular moment because she declines to disintegrate the world with which she is in conflict, because she takes those conflicts and renders them into an art that keeps the peace. She is to be read and respected, then, not because she is delicately satirical or charming, and certainly not because she is the representative of a better, lovelier time. On the contrary, she is to be respected because (as Lee has so brilliantly observed) she understands and practices not hatred, but *regulated* hatred, a distinction we have tended to elide.[45] Harding's wartime claim here is to be distinguished from Farrer's earlier wartime claim, though they share common features. Farrer's Austen was a calm and merciless iconoclast, without commitments to anything but her art, and infinitely above the world she only seemed to occupy. Harding's Austen, like Farrer's, has no "missionary" zeal, no "didactic intention" to improve the world she lives in, but far from being cool and godlike, she is actually "desperate," and her novels are efforts to ensure her "spiritual survival, without open conflict with the friendly people around her," many of whom she needs and loves. Such desperation, Harding believes, has something to teach us now, during the war, of all times: if more readers understood Austen's regulated hatred, he wrote in the lecture version of this essay, they "would grasp her present-day significance more readily"—and that significance finally is that it is possible to hate productively, peaceably, even sociably.[46]

It would be tempting to argue that Harding's Austen is a hero of social integration, confident enough, as Lee has put it, "to be playful, malleable, and optimistic," to test "propositions against an opponent's out of a spirit of inquiry rather than competition," and to be "governed by the desire for conversation and not by a defensive impulse to leave the table when confronted with difference."[47] If we turn, as readers now rarely do, to part 2 of "Regulated Hatred," however, we discover that Austen's position is actually somewhat defensive and risk averse and more in the grip of artistically productive but nevertheless unconscious processes than in self-consciously playful self-mastery. In this section Harding attempts in some ways to "apply" the principal aperçu of regulated hatred to the novels as a group, and we might expect readings of comparable subtlety and nuance. Here, however, he shows his hand as a psychologist working with rather inflexible paradigms, arguing that all of Austen's novels take a revenge on the social group toward which she is so ambivalent (and vice versa) by employing the Cinderella theme, sans the intervention of a fairy godmother, which realistic fiction forbids. In this manner, the heroine achieves preeminence "above her reasonable social expectations by conventional standards, but corresponding to her natural worth" (*RH*, 16). Harding allows Austen's compensatory, consolatory treatment of the Cinderella theme to be complex—arguing, for example, that the later novels make more allowances for the possibility that the heroine, whose virtues and liveliness had previously owed virtually nothing to "the social group," comes to have a greater reliance on and respect for it. Still, after the incisive, detailed readings of short passages from the novels in part 1, the thematized summaries of plot that take up the lion's share of part 2 seem shallow by comparison, allowing no place for irony at the level of plot, and often somewhat crudely psychologized, as in the following description of Anne Elliot's relation to the wicked or (in this case) merely flawed stepmother figure, Lady Russell, who takes the place of the idealized mother-figure who can be unambivalently loved because she is dead. Because Anne Elliot refuses to regret her submission to Lady Russell's advice not to marry Wentworth (before the action of the novel begins), Austen "brings the idealised mother back to life and admits that she is no nearer to perfection than the mothers of acute and sensitive children generally are" (*RH*, 25).

Harding's reading of Austen is expansive, and he admires her precisely for her resistance to the mores of her society, and especially during wartime, but it is also worth noting that he regards the marriage plot (via the Cinderella story) as the principal significance-bearing element of her novels, the chief reward and consolation for the heroines. In this respect Austen becomes in his hands—and in those who come after him—emphatically resexed as feminine. During the postwar period, Marvin Mudrick takes Harding further, and in a different direction, far from the realm of social and political conflict, for he makes sex, as distinct from marriage, his touchstone of interpretation, maintaining that Austen converts "her own personal limitations"—emotional and sexual limitations stemming from her abnormal coldness—"into the very form of her novel." When Mudrick wrote that Austen "was interested in a person, an object, an event, only as she might observe and recreate them free of consequences, as performance, as tableau," he was complaining about the same divine detachment that earlier readers such as Wilde, Woolf, and Farrer so admired. For different reasons but to much the same effect, C. S. Lewis would take away from Austen the status of fabulous progenitor and redefine her instead as a dutiful daughter: "She is described by someone in Kipling's worst story as the mother of Henry James," he taunts in reference to "The Janeites," [but] "I feel much more sure that she is the daughter of Dr. Johnson." Engaging in a frontal assault on the ironized or gloriously impersonal Austen, herself a divinity of sorts, Lewis disciplines Austen by making her the teacher, the enforcer of discipline, finding in her comedy "hard core morality" and "a vein of religion."[48]

"Regulated Hatred" is thus a watershed, pivoting on vastly different views of Jane Austen. It also marks off an older belle-lettristic tradition of Austenian reception from the professional literary criticism that displaced it. To the extent that academics look down on Janeites—now seen as soft-minded, principally female readers of gentle Jane Austen's novels, readers we consider frivolous or wacky precisely because they read the novels so often and love them without knowing how (we would like to claim) to read—we have Harding to thank or blame. The specific wartime resonance of "Regulated Hatred," surely its most complex and compelling part, did not, in other words, become part of its legacy, and it must be said that Harding himself did not foreground it emphatically. What did become its legacy is actually a secondary element within the essay. "Regulated Hatred" created an absolute chasm between readerships, although there were certainly divisions before. Farrer's remorselessly iconoclastic Austen and Chapman's delicately civilized Austen would have been unrecognizable to each other, to be sure, but "Regulated Hatred" created an enduring enmity between them, making it impossible for these two camps to share any common ground. This was not Harding's fundamental intention. In fact, his penciled notes on his lecture version of this essay suggest that he was well aware that he exaggerated his position to underscore his purposes, which were largely corrective: "Simply tried to underline one or two aspects of her work that don't seem to have filtered down into the popular impression of J. A.," thus making her available at precisely a moment in history when we most need her.[49] This concession notwithstanding, having so provocatively, so contemptuously represented Janeites as committed to "the gentler virtues of a civilized social order," having trivialized "sensitive" and "cultured" "gentlemen of an older generation than mine" who disseminate gentle Janeism "through histories of literature, university courses, literary journalism and polite allusion" (*RH*, 5), his essay had the effect of wresting cultural authority away from largely upper-class men and women of letters and to legitimate a newer and middle-class professoriate who saw themselves and Austen alike as dissenters. This air of superiority annoyed William Empson, even though he allowed that "Regulated Hatred" was a "good essay." In an unpublished letter to *Scrutiny* responding to Harding's essay, Empson wrote: "This left-wing intellectual approach to the lady, the idea that Tories think she is praising the present system, but we pink boys know that her heart is with the rebels—it is equally grim whether Mr Harding is being absurd or the readers he considers normal are."[50] Empson is not fundamentally disagreeing with Harding, as it turns out, but claiming that any intelligent reader knows that Harding has merely stated the obvious.

The upshot shows that readers did indeed become polarized along the lines Empson suggests, while also showing that Austen's biting criticism (contrary to Empson's claim) was in fact not apparent to all intelligent readers. In his *Jane Austen: A Critical Bibliography*, R. W. Chapman returns Harding's scorn in spades. Grouping "Regulated Hatred" with Reuben Brower's "The Controlling Hand" (1945) and Marvin Mudrick's *Jane Austen: Irony as Defense and Discovery* (1952), Chapman declares that he is "so out of sympathy" with these "essays in iconoclasm" that "I do not trust myself to discriminate" among them.[51] Had Chapman been able to overcome his visceral antipathy, discrimination might have come quite readily, for these works are very different. Harding's article posited Austen's estrangement from her world, so it is no wonder that Chapman, who sought to memorialize the world of Georgian elegance and Austen's ostensibly contented relation to it, was riled by it. Brower, on the other hand, makes no such claims about Austen's alienation, but his interest in "incongruity" as the basis of Austenian wit is nevertheless enough to jar Chapman's nerves, given his commitment to thinking about Austen as balanced and serene. Mudrick regards Austen as hateful in a bad way (not in the good way Harding recommends), and his argument that Austen's mastery as a writer derives from her unnatural sexual coldness as a woman, an argument that implicitly endorses social norms, was no part of Brower's or Harding's discussion. No wonder it was beyond the pale of what Chapman could countenance.

During the late 1940s and 1950s, the fashion industry would run ads for a "Jane Austen dress,"[52] for gowns with "a Jane Austen air,"[53] and for white organdies having "a faint flavor of Jane Austen,"[54] both feminizing and mass marketing Austen for female consumers in an entirely unprecedented way. During the same period, an emerging postwar professoriate employed by English Departments needed to vindicate its specialized skills and seriousness as hard work. These factors produced the polarizing enmity between professorial literary critics of Jane Austen and amateur or belle-lettristic Janeites that became a prominent feature of

Austen culture during the postwar period and beyond, one often articulated in disparaging class- and sexuality-based terms. Jane Austen is at the very heart of F. R. Leavis's *The Great Tradition*, the starting point of the English novel. Accordingly, reading her properly, vigorously, manfully is signally important. Not accidentally, the opening chapter of *The Great Tradition* is a running diatribe against Janeite extraordinaire Lord David Cecil. For Leavis, Cecil's enjoyment of Austen's social comedy is an outrageous offense that links him to effete Bloomsbury aestheticism, effeminacy, and other failures of moral seriousness that make him unfit to understand not Jane Austen alone, but the "great tradition" of the English novel that she ushers in. David Daiches leaves class out of the picture, but he similarly zooms in on effeminacy when he witheringly describes Cecil's *Fine Art of Reading* as "superficial, imprecise, coy, positively schoolgirlish at times," suggesting that Cecil's girlish enthusiasm is undisciplined, whereas real reading and criticism was work, masculine work.[55] Elizabeth Jenkins responds with comparable disdain—and comparable misunderstanding—from the opposing camp when she characterized Mudrick's *Jane Austen: Irony as Defense and Discovery* as Marxist, out "to denigrate both [Austen] and her class in their relation to each other."[56] In this polarization between journalists who appoint themselves as Austen's guardians and literary critics who overturn received wisdom about her, we see mutatis mutandis the foundation of the "culture wars" over the figure of Jane Austen during the 1980s and 1990s. In this case, it was the linkage of Austen to sexuality rather than to social criticism that scandalized journalists. When distinguished critics and theorists such as Eve Sedgwick and Terry Castle discussed homo- or auto-eroticism in Austen's novels, they were decried as tenured radicals recklessly and gleefully flying in the face of the self-evident truth of Austen's primness and defiling her purity in the process.[57]

≈§ In December 1943, late in the war, when he was ill with pneumonia, Winston Churchill finally followed his doctors' advice and put aside the work of war to recuperate. In this manner, Churchill became one in a long line of readers to turn to Austen in order to get well. Having read only *Sense and Sensibility* before, Churchill (who, unlike Stanley Baldwin, we will readily infer, was not a Janeite) asked his daughter to read *Pride and Prejudice* to him while he convalesced: "What calm lives they had, those people!" he observed. "No worries about the French Revolution, or the crashing struggle of the Napoleonic Wars. Only manners controlling natural passion so far as they could, together with cultured explanations of any mischances."[58] Churchill found Austen as isolated from World War II as she was from the Napoleonic Wars and no doubt precious on these grounds: English soldiers fought to restore a peaceful world where "calm lives" can be lived and where manners are enough to control passions, making the unnatural and uncultured trials of war unnecessary.[59] Reading her novels is thus a restful respite because they are completely free of the world of war. As was the case for World War I readerships, World War II Janeites did not understand Austen as a site for restorative escape in the first place, however effectual that temporary, healing escape might be. Churchill's words are proudly displayed in "Jane Austen's House" in Chawton today, but they are a pretty equivocal tribute. The many readers I have discussed here saw Austen not simply as someone we fight *for* but also as someone we fight *with*. By consigning Austen to a landscape entirely outside of national conflict, a figure apart from rather than a part of catastrophic global conflict, Churchill put strict limits on the ability of her novels (along with M&B sulfa drugs) to help us endure anything more potent than pneumonia. This view of Austen has its upside, of course. The private, hermetically sealed Austen that readers of my generation grew up studying was an author whose very independence from or indifference to the world at war was the given that enabled her to turn with such intensity of moral discrimination to the manners of courtship and neighborhood tittle-tattle and to mine these sources for her penetrating art. This too is an Austen to be cherished, of course. However, if this intensifying diminution of scope comes at the cost of forgetting the broader and more urgent ways in which she could be, as Harding put it, a "formidable ally," it is a loss as well.

5 Jane Austen's House

O n the face of it, there is something disconcerting about the spectacle—something misleading, or at the very least something profoundly wishful (fig. 5.1). This squat brick dwelling wears its two commemorative plaques awkwardly. Topped with five ungainly chimneys and fronted with an implausibly short picket fence, which makes a somewhat futile feint at separating the house from the street, it is certainly not the kind of cottage Marianne Dashwood might rapturously envision. Not thatched, shuttered, or covered with honeysuckles, this house is (we might just as well admit it) strikingly charmless: it is a functional edifice, not a cozy one. Its many traces of windows and doors bricked over, moved, and modified disrupt the symmetries they still imply without evoking the quaintness that we associate with irregularity in its more idealized, picturesque forms. True, the brick wall along one side that encloses an English garden is more of a piece with the idyllic loveliness one expects from such a place, but the house itself stands aloof. A large white wooden sign cheerily informs us that we are looking at "Jane Austen's House." To the extent that this possessive lulls us into a sense that the house and its diverse effects and appurtenances were—and in some sense still are—*Jane Austen's* and that in entering the house we might be visiting Jane Austen herself, we will be charmed, but it is inevitable that we will be disappointed as well. The charm and disappointment aroused by this dwelling and the things gathered within it are what I will be pondering in this chapter.

It starts in the parlor. There, one is drawn to a square piano, dated promisingly circa 1810. Not so long ago a dog-eared note card once informed us, "Although this piano is not the one Jane Austen used . . . she bought a similar type." The Jane Austen House Museum is undergoing a complete refurbishment of late; the note cards are updated and lami-

Figure 5.1. *Jane Austen's House Museum (2001).*
Photograph courtesy of Allan Soedring.

nated now, but the current one reads in much the same way, giving us
with one hand what it so very conscientiously takes away with the other:
"Piano made by Clementi in London. This may be similar to the piano
that Jane bought after arriving here." In the next room, we encounter a
handsome dining room table. "This table," we read on the explanatory
note card, "is of early nineteenth-century design, probably after Jane
Austen's death in 1817. It was, however, in use at the Great House at
Chawton, in the lifetime of Edward Knight (Austen), Jane's third brother
(1768–1852)." Am I the only pilgrim flummoxed by this mixed message?
The inventory entry tells us that the table is dated later than Austen's
death in 1817, but the "family" (who exactly?) "still" (still?) refers to the
table as "Jane's"? What could the "family" think they are doing when they
"still" call it "Jane's" even though they know it isn't? Clearly, we are being invited knowingly to make believe that the things before us bring us
closer into Jane Austen's presence, just as we did with the piano, and as
we do with the handsome set of china on the table, which no sooner do
we notice than we learn that the set is *not* Jane Austen's either, but was

rather used at the manor house and was known to and described by her. The teakettle in the hearth, as it turns out, belonged to Kate Greenaway. Even the precious writing table poised by the window, at which we are asked to imagine Austen writing her novels, both is and is not Jane Austen's: "only the top," we read, "is original."

Of course, not all the things on display in "Jane Austen's House" bear a secondary, tertiary, or often altogether indirect relation to Austen. We find many genuine objects of Austen's here as well. For example, the music books were Jane Austen's, indeed, some copied out in her own hand; a framed lace collar once graced her throat; the topaz cross hung around her neck; the blue-bead bracelet encircled her wrist; the patchwork quilt that Austen's mother stitched, using material that Austen and Cassandra chose, covered her; the donkey cart bore her down the village lanes. We even find an ivory bilboquet that Austen is said to have played with at Chawton House or at Godmersham (J. E. Austen-Leigh wrote in the *Memoir* that Austen's "performance with cup and ball was marvellous"). And preeminent among all of these is the famous lock of her hair, important as what theologians would describe as a "primary" relic, a remnant of Austen's actual body (fig. 5.2). Alberta Hirschheimer Burke, the most important American collector of Austen's letters and Austeniana, bought this lock at a Sotheby's auction in 1948 as part of a lot also containing literary items, such as Austen's (last) verses on St. Swithin's Day, written three days before she died, and Cassandra's chronology of the composition of the novels. The locks came to "Jane Austen's House" in a dramatic way, as Burke's husband would later relate: "When we attended the [first] Jane Austen Society meeting on July 23, 1949, Mr. Edward Carpenter . . . complained bitterly that because of a shortage of funds valuable relics were leaving England and noted with particular sadness that a lock of Jane Austen's hair had been purchased at Sotheby's by an American. Alberta muttered under her breath, 'I will give them the damned hair.' She then rose and said very simply, 'I am the American who bought Jane's hair and if the Society would like to have it, I shall be glad to make a contribution of the hair.' At that point, the tent in which the meeting was being held almost collapsed."[1] Accounts of this event appearing in the reports of the Jane Austen Society present it as a happy coincidence. But Burke was irked to find herself reproached as a grasping American, purchasing what Britons themselves offered for sale, and she never forgot the ungraciousness that she shamed by her generosity.

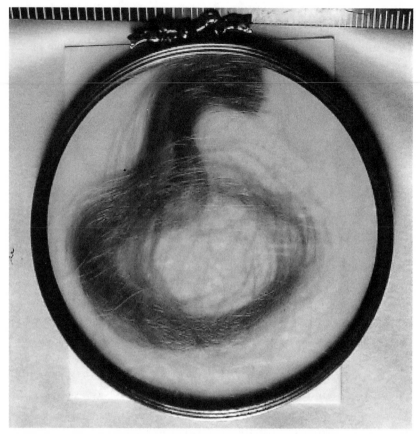

Figure 5.2. *Lock of Jane Austen's hair (1817). One of several of its kind, this lock was shorn by Cassandra after her sister's death and distributed as a remembrancer. Courtesy of the Jane Austen Memorial Trust.*

Several London newspapers reported on the incident—"Jane Austen's Locks Returned," one touted, implying perhaps that they had left the country under suspicious circumstances—and though one item errs in identifying Mrs. Burke's home as Baltimore, Ohio, they all attest, however briefly, to the national status of this event.[2]

These Austenian things notwithstanding, most of the objects in the house are remoter approximations of Jane Austen—such as the Regency period maple and marquetry writing table with leather panel inset, or the 1815 three-shilling coin, so we may better understand Mrs. Croft's pain in *Persuasion* when Admiral Croft says, "She, poor soul, is tied by the leg.

She has a blister on one of her heels, as large as a three-shilling piece" (*P*, 184). And some artifacts have nothing whatsoever to do with Austen. One display case contains (among other things) a hand plane mislaid on the premises by a seventeenth-century carpenter; spillikins, fish counters, and letters used in games with no connection to Austen other than the fact that she would have known what they were; and silver-tipped bottles that belonged to her niece Mary Jane and a box that was Fanny's. We can also find shards of cups, clay pipes, spoons, rusted spikes, pins, bottles, and a toy pistol. A while back, one could even find on display two bustle irons dated circa 1888—a fine retrojection of the Victorian Austen we have already discussed—household items belonging to the folks who occupied the house from Cassandra's death through the 1940s. These things call out for our attention and our respect either because they shared the same space Austen occupied, albeit at different times, or because they shared the same time with Jane Austen, albeit in different places. They may be efficacious in evoking Jane Austen by their virtual contiguity with her, but their charm is of a second order.

As we have previously seen, Dorothy Darnell, a woman from nearby Alton who had long admired Jane Austen and the places associated with her, decided to form a Jane Austen Society in 1940 when she happened to find the cast-iron fire grate from the drawing room in Chawton along the road on a heap of nettles, having been wrenched out to make way for gas fire and discarded as garbage.[3] Amid a general atmosphere of siege and loss, Austen's house at Chawton and any objects or memories connected with her were to be preserved from destruction. Between 1943 and 1946, before the Jane Austen Society was formally chartered and before the cottage came into its possession, members had gathered only a few items—a copy of the Steventon glebe plan (donated by R. W. Chapman), an old photo of Chawton village, a reproduction of Cassandra's sketch of her sister, and that cast-iron grate, the only item that was the real thing rather than reproduction of one. Once T. Edward Carpenter's purchase of Austen's house in February 1948 was announced, and later, when Jane Austen's House Museum was officially opened on July 23, 1949, an event widely covered by the English press, efforts began in earnest to find and purchase relics of Jane Austen, using proceeds from membership dues. In this manner, the Jane Austen Society acquired such items as the two Hepplewhite chairs and walnut escritoire that were in the Steventon rectory when Austen lived there and so remained when

Austen's brother James lived there. In the meantime, however, and just as often, descendants of Austen's family and lovers of her work across England and in the United States lent or gave all manner of smaller, humbler items that still evoked Jane Austen, however weak their status as relics or tenuous their relation to Austen. One Ruth C. Koch of Cambridge, Massachusetts, sent the museum a photograph of a green coat from her childhood during the 1890s, handmade by her mother and patterned after a coat supposedly owned by Jane Austen, by reference to Kate Greenaway, "who put the graceful dress of Jane Austen's time upon her children."[4] Surely, neither the dress nor the photo of it has the dignity of a relic, and to my knowledge was never displayed, but it was accepted and duly recorded as an Austenian thing nonetheless, one that obviously carried genuine meaning for the donor. Similar treatment was given to the gift of a handmade doll representing Jane Austen, presented by Dorothy Austen-Leigh and based on Cassandra's sketch, which had recently resurfaced from oblivion and been ensconced at the National Portrait Gallery (fig. 5.3). The inventory tells us that this effigy was made by "a Mrs. King, aged eighty years." Did Miss Dorothy Austen-Leigh and old Mrs. King imagine that Jane Austen's House Museum was so hard up for relics that it required proxies this remote to fill the gaps? I doubt it. The doll was accepted, as it was offered, with complete sincerity as an Austenian token: as the inventory puts it, the "modeling and needlework are exquisite, and the cap of real old lace." In this rather abject category we might also place photos of collateral descendants, claiming "strong family likeness" to Cassandra's sketch and dressed up as Jane Austen: great, great grand-niece Diana Shervington impersonating both the figure in Cassandra's sketch and Jane at her worktable, in period costume; and great, great, great grand-niece Sarah Jenkyns, in Jane's sole surviving pelisse, made of "bombazine, shot brown and yellow with raised yellow spots" with a "high collar and long sleeves."[5] She is pictured here striking what we have come to think of as an Austenian pose by the window, watching the world go by. The committee of the Jane Austen Society endorsed the commemorative project carried out not only by the wearing of these outfits by Austenian descendants but also by taking a photographic record of it, directing that the power of these particular people wearing these particular items of clothing be supplemented and recorded in photos specifically arranged "to include something personally connected with Jane Austen"—the pose from Cassandra's sketch, the

Figure 5.3. *Effigy doll of Jane Austen (1948). One of many "treasures" sent by the public to the Jane Austen House Museum after it opened its doors and announced its project to collect relics. Courtesy of the Jane Austen Memorial Trust.*

worktable, and the window cut into the wall of the building by Austen's brother when Austen moved there with her mother and sister in 1809.[6]

When I call attention to these numerous things that are not Jane Austen's and were never Jane Austen's, it is not at all to criticize the museum—nothing could be further from my purpose. From its very beginning, this museum was exemplary in its integrity: it made no effort to palm approximations off as the real thing, but always clearly differentiated genuine relics from other sorts of mementos or proxies. My intention, rather, is to call serious attention to the variety of things that lovers of Jane Austen contributed to fill a house devoted to invoking her, an impulse that is not always strictly curatorial. All these things I have mentioned so far were proffered and displayed not only on account of their capacity in some ways to authenticate Jane Austen, to show that she did indeed exist and has not altogether vanished, but also, and even more important, to impersonate and to embody her and in the process to make it possible for us to connect with her, even as they also scrupulously and candidly declare their insufficiency (e.g., this table is not Jane Austen's, though the family says it is; I am not Jane, but I am related). When I first visited Jane Austen's House Museum, my hunch was that all of these diverse things simply, inevitably, and sometimes ludicrously fail their allotted task to evoke Austen's presence, but this hunch was misguided as well as ungenerous: for the people who made this doll, posed for these photographs, or donated these "treasures," and for people who visit the museum, these things have indeed summoned forth Jane Austen in some form or fashion, though such things work their magic at a cost.

As it happens, Austen's own fiction can help us ponder the work performed by the relics at Jane Austen's House Museum. Domestic interiors are actually not very interesting to Austen, and in a period when more and more people encounter Austen's work first through movies rather than novels, this point is worth underscoring. By their very nature as a visual medium, of course, movies foreground things and physical details not present in the novels, and attention to decor and costumes carries us almost inevitably in a nostalgic direction, idealizing the specific elegancies of Regency England. With the notable exception of Patricia Rozema's *Mansfield Park* (1999), which refuses to glamorize the country, which is deliberately made to look cold, at times scarcely furnished, and in evident disrepair, most cinematic productions have inflated into sheer opulence the elegance rightly or wrongly associated with Jane Austen. Country houses have become grandiose and costumes more lavish, probably as a result of the success in England, as well as in the United States, of heritage movements during the 1970s, which identified historic buildings as precious national treasures, as monuments to a better time, and, as such, as places to be preserved from destruction. The preservation and renovation of country houses dating from the eighteenth century and earlier was a particular aim of these movements, and so Austen's novels lent themselves to particularly lush, idealized, and idealizing realizations from the 1980s onward —not that anyone really likes costume dramas. An honest curiosity about the texture of daily life in the past is just about the only honest pleasure the novels indulge. While we make a big thing out of furniture and dress in screen adaptations, Austen's novels are indifferent to this kind of specificity. Far from lingering over tea sets—which reviews of adaptations always seem to mention—Austen never mentions them, and we are very rarely told anything about the dress of her characters. Yes, characters inside Austen's novels inhabit a world rich with material objects, but taking note of them unduly, as we necessarily do when we watch the movies, marks us as outsiders to that world and thus makes us disconcertingly like that other outsider, Mrs. Elton herself.

The exception to this rule tells us a good deal, however. Fanny Price, for example, is distinctive among Austenian heroines in her attachment to—even fixation on—things. Fanny has a "favourite box in the East room, which held [we are told] all her smaller treasures" (*MP*, 303). Among these is a sheet of paper on which her cousin Edmund had begun a letter to her, only to have stopped when Fanny entered the room. Once he leaves the room, she

> seized the scrap of paper on which Edmund had begun writing to her, as a treasure beyond all her hopes, and reading with the tenderest emotion these words, "My very dear Fanny, you must do me the favour to accept"—locked it up with the chain, as the dearest part of the gift. It was the only thing approaching to a letter which she had ever received from him; she might never receive another; it was impossible that she ever should receive another so perfectly gratifying in the occasion and the style. Two lines more prized had never fallen from the pen of the most distinguished author—never more completely blessed the

researches of the fondest biographer. The enthusiasm of a woman's love is even beyond the biographer's. To her, the hand-writing itself, independent of anything it may convey, is a blessedness. Never were such characters cut by any other human being as Edmund's commonest hand-writing gave! This specimen, written in haste as it was, had not a fault; and there was a felicity in the flow of the first four words, in the arrangement of "My very dear Fanny," which she could have looked at for ever (*MP*, 307–8).

One of the many striking features of this passage—and passages like it elsewhere—is the sharpness with which the narrator disavows Fanny's attachment, affectionately but markedly calling attention to the difference between what that piece of paper actually is—a scrap, something Edmund left carelessly behind as something of no worth—and how it is seized and cherished by Fanny, as she proceeds not merely to value it but explicitly to *over*value it, as though the "characters" (i.e., the letters) cut by Edmund somehow conjured the character (i.e., person) cut by Edmund himself. Neither is, in reality, prepossessing. The handwriting—which the narrator tells us is unremarkable ("the commonest")—to Fanny's loving eyes is felicitously flowing; and its first words, "My very dear Fanny"—a no doubt affectionate but nevertheless entirely conventional salutation—are read again and again as if they conveyed a world of import: "Two lines more prized had never fallen from the pen of the most distinguished author," the narrator interjects, indulging Fanny's "love" but also marking it unmistakably as an excess, and a risible one, our affection for Fanny's youthful ardor notwithstanding.

It is the narrator who makes the comparison I am exploring here, the comparison between Fanny's attachment to Edmund's scrap and the biographer's emotional investment even in the fragmentary remnants of a historical subject. So far as Jane Austen's House Museum is concerned, we are the "biographers," and as such we are to Jane Austen, perhaps, as Fanny Price is to Edmund, treasuring up the tiniest remainders or reminders of Austenian presence under circumstances of remoteness and loss. Thinking about Fanny's relation to things she deems precious might help us understand our relation to Austenian things; and conversely, our own love of and simultaneous disappointment with Austenian things can help us understand Fanny Price, Austen's most complicated and controversial heroine.

If ever a novelist knew the worth of things, Jane Austen is that novelist, the one, as W. H. Auden observed, who is more deeply shocking than the merely racy James Joyce because she "reveal[s] so frankly and with such sobriety / The economic basis of society."[7] People's property, their homes, their carriages, their dress—all such things carry values openly appraised and canvassed in Austen's novels, and a vigorous subset of literary criticism is now emerging given over to the discussion of the material culture of Jane Austen's time and to her absorption in it. To assess the worth of things, which Austen does do, is very different from describing things, which she does very rarely. No realistic novelist is less interested than Austen in the minutiae of physical description. This might seem counterintuitive. Didn't Austen herself describe her artistic method as attention to small things—as that "little bit (two Inches wide) of Ivory on which I work with so fine a Brush" (*L*, 323, 16 December 1816)? Yet Austen spends remarkably little time describing small things, and in fact she explicitly recommended that her niece Anna avoid doing so in her attempts at novel writing: "You describe a sweet place, but your descriptions are often more minute than will be liked. You give too many particulars of right hand & left" (*L*, 275, 9 September 1814). Austen's lack of interest in representing particular things in the visual world was so striking to George Henry Lewes, as we have already seen, that he postulated the weakness of her eyesight: "The absence of all sense of outward world—either scenery or personal appearance—is more remarkable in her than in any writer we remember" (*CH1*, 159).

Accordingly, I lay it down as axiomatic that whenever objects are made to stand out with any sort of specificity in Austen's novels, something is wrong. In rare cases, of course, such attention is spared the lash—as when Mr. Knightley shows Mr. Woodhouse "books of engravings, drawers of medals, cameos, corals, shells, and every other family collection within his cabinets"—but this is only because we understand that Mr. Woodhouse is like a child, who is to be amused with small things, and we do not expect anything more strenuous from him. In most cases, though, particular things become prominent because they are noticed by a character who is a snob, a bore, or worse. In *Northanger Abbey*, for example, we learn about the hothouse pineapples, Rumford stoves, and a set of Staffordshire china manufactured two years earlier because General Tilney, that great and nasty social climber, brags about them. He calls that set of Staffordshire "old" because he has a passion for new and newfangled things, and two years makes them pitifully out of date. Similarly, when we learn in the final chapter of *Persuasion* that Anne Elliot Wentworth is now the "mistress of a very pretty landaulette" (*P*, 272), it is not because the possession registers on Anne's superb consciousness—we never see it doing so—but rather because Anne's envious, small-minded sister Mary notices it as a status object that threatens her sense of precedence, much as a silver knife is specified at Fanny's home in Portsmouth only as the occasion for two of her sisters to fight. Mr. Collins in *Pride and Prejudice*, we are told, *examines* and *praises* the "hall, the dining-room, and all its furniture" at Longbourn so vigorously that even Mrs. Bennet cannot suppress the "mortifying supposition of his viewing it all as his own future property" (*PP*, 73). And Mr. Collins directs his attention to these things with apparently more care than he spends choosing a wife among the Bennet daughters, who seem themselves to be interchangeable acquisitions. In *Mansfield Park*, the mean Mrs. Norris is always on the lookout for things—like the "green baize" (*MP*, 228) she filches when the theatrical is disrupted by Sir Thomas's return, or the "few pheasants' eggs and a cream cheese" she "spunges" from Mrs. Whitaker at Sotherton (*MP*, 123), or the "Moor Park apricots" (*MP*, 64) she brags about to Dr. Grant, who is very unimpressed.

To eye things particularly, then, to single them out for notice, is to show oneself shallow or grasping, and Austen takes her revenge in a proto-Dickensian way by virtually subsuming that person's character to the objects so inappropriately adored. It is impossible to think about Mrs. Elton without recalling her iterations about her brother-in-law's barouche-landau; impossible to think about Robert Dashwood without recollecting his attachment to the silver toothpick case; about Mrs. Allen without linking her to muslins; or about Sir Walter without his bottles of Gowland's lotion. I allow a few apparent exceptions, but they actually prove the rule. In rare instances where excess is coded positively, attention to them is entirely appropriate. In *Pride and Prejudice*, for example, "beautiful pyramids of grapes, nectarines, and peaches" (*PP*, 296) are described with uncommon particularity as instances of the *profuse* hospitality to which Elizabeth is treated as a guest at Pemberley, and as such they are attentively noted by Elizabeth and approved by the narrator in much the same way that the generous Emma Woodhouse urges her guests to enjoy "minced chicken and scalloped oysters" while Mr. Woodhouse (torn between hospitality and hypochondria) recommends with good conscience nothing more than a "small basin of thin gruel" or "an egg boiled very soft" (*E*, 24) by Serle. For the most part, dwelling on specific things spells trouble, even when they are not obviously derogated. Edmund Bertram's attention to the "glossy spots" on Fanny's white gown, for example, turns out to be symptomatic of his obsessive enchantment with Mary Crawford. "Has not Miss Crawford a gown something the same?" (*MP*, 259) he says, in words that surely sting Fanny's tender heart, for she would wish him to notice those glossy spots for herself alone, rather than for Miss Crawford, of whom she is intensely though covertly jealous.

Needless to say, Fanny Price is not a shallow or silly character. Like Edmund, she cathects onto things not because she is enchanted by their material value, and not because of the prestige they may signify, but rather by virtue of their association with people, and this is part of the deeper and more complicated problem. As we have already seen, this penchant for linking things to people is comical at times, and it is no credit to Fanny that it allies her with Harriet Smith. Harriet, we recollect, presents to Emma a box marked with the words *most precious treasures*: "I cannot call them gifts," she says, "but they are things that I have valued very much" (*MP*, 366). Like Fanny's scrap of paper, Harriet's treasures have neither use nor exchange value; their worth to her is entirely singular. Indeed, the strip of court plaister that Mr. Elton had touched when bandaging a cut to his finger and a pencil stub ("without any lead") that he "left upon the table as good for nothing" (*E*, 368) qualify as trash in the larger economy of things (even though Emma points out that the plaister, unlike the pencil stub, might be preserved from the flames as still having the value of usefulness).

Having encouraged Harriet's adoration of Elton, Emma feels guilty about what she calls these "relicks" (*E*, 367), and she experiences it in explicitly religious terms—"Oh! my sins, my sins!" (*E*, 367). Her feelings are divided between *wonder*ment over their influence on Harriet ("have you actually found happiness in treasuring up these things?" [*E*, 368]), and *amuse*ment over the infatuated quality of Harriet's devotion ("Lord bless me! when should I ever have thought of putting by in cotton a piece of court plaister that Frank Churchill had been pulling about!" [*E*, 367]). As usual, the joke is in part on Emma herself, however, for the "relicks" prove more powerful than mere aids to memory. If we read closely, we find that they possess an almost talismanic power. For Harriet, of course, they both commemorate and evoke Mr. Elton, but for Emma they call forth not Frank Churchill, but someone Emma really does love, however ignorant of the fact she may yet be, someone who, not coincidentally, is also connected to what the relic summons. Confronted with the pencil stub, Emma is momentarily taken outside herself, as she exclaims with fantastic excitement: "'I do remember it,' cried Emma; 'I perfectly remember it.—Talking about spruce beer.—Oh! yes. Mr. Knightley and I both saying we liked it, and Mr. Elton's seeming resolved to learn to like it too. I perfectly remember it. Stop; Mr. Knightley was standing just here, was not he? I have an idea he was standing just here'" (*E*, 368). In this passage, Knightley is not merely recollected, but momentarily called up, made present, "standing just here." Having an attachment to particular things may be ridiculous in some senses, but that is not because such things have no power—just a scrap of paper, merely a pencil stub, only a strip of cotton—but on the contrary because they *can* have a certain efficacy, their apparently abject status notwithstanding.

The mysterious power things really can have over people attached to them is made disturbingly clear in Fanny's case. No heroine's room is described with the detail of Fanny's East Room. Austen never asks us to think about the rooms of Emma Woodhouse, or Elizabeth Bennet, or Anne Elliot. True, when the Dashwood womenfolk move to Barton Cottage we are very briefly told they are at first busy arranging their "particular concerns" and "endeavouring, by placing around them books and other possessions, to form themselves a home. Marianne's pianoforte was unpacked and properly disposed of; and Elinor's drawings were affixed to the walls of their sitting room" (*SS*, 35), but this is a one-time deal, and Austen's description remains general. The East Room is a little world of objects that Austen particularizes with entirely unwonted detail, and Fanny bears a very close and continuous relationship to them: "She could scarcely see an object in that room which had not an interesting remembrance connected with it.—Every thing was a friend, or bore her thoughts to a friend." Here things are not simply conduits to people (Every thing "bore her thoughts to a friend"), but they actually become loved in and of themselves ("Every thing was a friend"). What are these things bearing the extraordinarily personal property of friendship? The narrator itemizes them carefully as household leftovers deemed worthless or shoddy: "a faded footstool of Julia's work, too ill done for the drawing-room"; "three transparencies, made in a rage for transparencies," one of "Tint-

ern Abbey," one of "a cave in Italy," and the last of "a moonlight lake in
Cumberland"; a "collection of family profiles thought unworthy of being
anywhere else"; and an evidently amateurish, ill-proportioned but treasured sketch of William's ship, where the letters H.M.S. Antwerp are as
tall as the mainmast (*MP*, 177–79).

Such, the narrator observes with an irony not in the least devoid of
sympathy, are the furnishings of Fanny's "nest of comforts," such are
the things that are not merely *reminders* of friends but *friends* themselves to Fanny. The process by which people become things or things
become people is generally seen by critics and theorists as a matter of
great alarm, reification being a special case of alienation and violence.
Here, the process seems reversed. Things seem to become people, and
so the phenomenon—Every thing was a friend—seems initially at least
to wear a gentler face. Outside the East Room, the real Julia and Tom
are hardly the boons of Fanny's existence, but apprehended through the
things they have given to Fanny, they create what Lewis Hyde has described as "feeling bonds" that firmly attach them to her.[8] Situated in the
East Room, they take on discrete and idealized forms as benevolent and
attentive companions gathered cozily around our otherwise bereft heroine to make her world feel both warm and full. This is a novel where all of
the heroine's friends turn on her, and the "friends" in Fanny's East Room
are no exception. After being urged against her will to act in *Lovers' Vows*,
Fanny retreats to her East Room to seek comfort from them, "to see if
by looking at Edmund's profile she could catch any of his counsel, or by
giving air to her geraniums she might inhale a breeze of mental strength
herself." Things here, as it turns out, are far from inert, but actively and
powerfully impinge on gentle Fanny's determination not to act in the
theatrical: "As she looked around her, the claims of her cousins to being
obliged were strengthened by the sight of present upon present that she
had received from them. The table between the windows was covered
with work-boxes and netting-boxes, which had been given her at different times, principally by Tom; and she grew bewildered as to the amount
of the debt which all these kind remembrances produced" (*MP*, 179–80).

Bewilderment is a strong, intensely charged word in the lexicon of
Mansfield Park. Throughout the novel, bewilderment denotes a loss of
moral compass. As such, the term brings the *wilderness* (that other, even
more conspicuously charged term) at Sotherton to mind: "It was a hot
day, and we were all walking after each other, and bewildered" (*MP*, 285),

Henry Crawford explains to Fanny when her eyes reproach him for his behavior there, and it is somehow typical that Henry would describe being bewildered in a wilderness as an excuse for his moral failings rather than as grounds for concern to begin with. Well might Fanny marvel that the "memory is sometimes so retentive, so serviceable, so obedient; at others, so bewildered and so weak" (*MP*, 243), for the supposedly good guys in *Mansfield Park* are subject to a sort of forgetfulness akin to moral confusion as well—as when Sir Thomas "finds himself bewildered in his own house" (*MP*, 214) on returning unannounced from Antigua, later destroying all evidence of the theatricals and talking himself into believing that the marriage between Maria and Mr. Rushworth will be a happy one, or when Edmund says that it would not really be inconsistent of him to act in *Lovers' Vows* after all. Even the placid and apparently vacuous Lady Bertram has her moment of moral confusion when she consents to the semipunitive scheme to send Fanny to Portsmouth against her own better judgment: in the privacy of her dressing room and "unbiassed by [Sir Thomas's] bewildering statements" (*MP*, 427), she does not see why Fanny should leave Mansfield Park, nor can she agree that she would not miss Fanny very much. The narrator is describing Mary Crawford when saying that her "mind [is] led astray and *bewildered*, and without any suspicion of being so; darkened, yet fancying itself light" (*MP*, 423), but the description suits everyone's understanding in this dark and dense novel, where everyone is benighted without suspecting themselves so, where no one can stand for the reader as a repository for truth or good sense—as, say, the Gardiners can in *Pride or Prejudice* or Mr. Knightley in *Emma*—and where manifestly sympathetic and earnest characters such as Fanny are as fallible at times as manifestly irreverent ones such as Mary Crawford.

It is an ominous fact that the treasures of the East Room are instrumental in bringing Fanny herself to a state of bewilderment. Fanny is bewildered because she misrecognizes as *friends* (i.e., persons who wish her welfare in a disinterested way) things that are actually *gifts* that, as Marcel Mauss put it, carry the stringently exacting obligation to accept, and the equally exacting obligation to reciprocate, and that as such are not "free" but are inexorably stern taskmasters, even if they may at first (as they do for Fanny) have a gentler-seeming face.[9] The things in Fanny's East Room are thus not tokens of esteem but active enforcers of social facts, of relations that are dangerously awry at Mansfield Park.

The principal relation her things impress on her is *debt*, for every thing she sees is a gift that calls for her compliance in return and that therefore makes her refusal to act in *Lovers' Vows* seem selfish and wrong. As this passage shows, Fanny is keenly aware that gifts entangle her in a network of compromising obligations—consider not merely Tom's presents, mentioned here, but also the chain Mary Crawford (acting as Henry's proxy) proposes that Fanny accept for her amber cross, which (like her brother's promotion to lieutenant) she cannot refuse even though she knows it is calculated to bind her affectively to Henry and thus to trammel her freedom to act or not to act as she chooses. Fanny is slow to grasp that her very presence at Mansfield Park is a gift and that a return is compulsory: "She had hoped that, to a man like her uncle, so discerning, so honourable, so good, the simple acknowledgment of settled *dislike* on her side would have been sufficient. To her infinite grief she found it was not." In other words, Fanny has ("to her infinite grief") mistaken Sir Thomas (like the objects in her room) for a friend at precisely the moment when he calls in her debt: "You do not owe me the duty of a child. But, Fanny, if your heart can acquit you of *ingratitude*—" (*MP*, 368).

Fanny is bewildered to discover that her simple "no" is not to the material purpose. To change her mind, Sir Thomas decides to take Fanny's *things* away—or, rather, to take Fanny away from her things, concluding that "a little abstinence from the *elegancies and luxuries* of Mansfield Park would bring her mind into a sober state" (*MP*, 425). Sir Thomas's "medicinal project upon his niece's understanding" (*MP*, 425) is a success: the squalor and coarseness of her parents' abode drive her to "bewildered, broken, sorrowful contemplation" (*MP*, 442). Fanny's privation at Portsmouth—the "incessant noise" (*MP*, 453), the "thinness of the walls" (*MP*, 441), the "confined and scantily-furnished chamber that she was to share with Susan" (*MP*, 448)—prompts her to misrecognize the comforts of Mansfield Park for moral authority and social harmony and to pine for the treasures of her East Room, which seems capacious by comparison to her quarters in her parental abode:

> The elegance, propriety, regularity, harmony—and perhaps, above all, the peace and tranquillity of Mansfield, were brought to her remembrance every hour of the day, by the prevalence of every thing opposite to them *here*. . . . At Mansfield, no sounds of contention, no

raised voice, no abrupt bursts, no tread of violence, was ever heard; all proceeded in a regular course of cheerful orderliness; every body had their due importance; every body's feelings were consulted (*MP*, 453).

Not long ago, this passage was read as the truth about Mansfield Park, rather than as Fanny's poignant apprehension of it, and I am contending that Fanny's thing-friends are in no small part responsible for the mystification in evidence here. True, no sounds of contention, no raised voice, no abrupt bursts, no tread of violence *was ever heard* at the Park, and that is the trouble: resentments, animosities, and conflicts are roiling turbulently, but silently. Mansfield Park (regardless of what it ought to be) is not the abode of harmony and propriety. It is not any more contented, cheerful, or well regulated than Fanny's cramped and raucous home in Portsmouth—in one place sisters quarrel over a silver knife, in another over a double-dealing gentleman—nor, arguably, is it less violent. And at neither place are Fanny's feelings consulted. To think otherwise is to be bewildered, indeed, and "without any suspicion of being so; darkened, yet fancying itself light" (*MP*, 423). Fanny's sister Susan journeys to Mansfield Park with her mind full of the things she expects to find there, "meditating much upon silver forks, napkins, and finger-glasses" (*MP*, 517), all of which for her mean upward social mobility. For Fanny, particularly amid her sense of loss and deprivation, her "dear, dear friends" at Mansfield Park—friends that are things as well as people—are overfreighted with intensely idealized moral and social meanings that they actually do not bear, and if Fanny seems more admirable than Susan to us, it is not because her understanding of things is more clear-sighted.

We have seen something like this *almost* happen in *Pride and Prejudice*, when Elizabeth Bennet beholds Pemberley and exclaims "to be mistress of Pemberley might be something." When she actually enters the house and beholds the paintings, the furniture, and the miniatures within, Elizabeth indulges a moment's fantasy of personal possession that very much calls Mr. Collins to mind: "'And of this place,' thought she, 'I might have been mistress! With these rooms I might now have been familiarly acquainted!'" (*PP*, 272). Starting with Sir Walter Scott, many readers have believed that Pemberley as a collection of objects brings Elizabeth to her senses at last: she "does not perceive that she has done a foolish thing [in refusing Darcy's hand] until she accidentally visits a very handsome seat and grounds belonging to her admirer" (*CH1*, 65).

Yet it is not the seat and grounds that Elizabeth most powerfully esteems, but rather the harmonious, well-regulated state of relations they signify, ordered as they are by a man whose virtues are conceived relationally: "As a brother, a landlord, a master, she considered how many people's happiness were in his guardianship!" (*PP*, 277)—and Elizabeth does not mistake the tastefulness of the furniture for the owners whose good polity in the regulation of relations (in contradistinction to Sir Thomas's) is what makes it desirable in the first place. Nor do beloved things bewilder Anne Elliot, particularly that one big thing, Kellynch Hall itself: dearly as she might wish to be the mistress of Kellynch Hall for her mother's sake, she (unlike Fanny) realizes with astonishingly little fuss or fret that the estate would be a cipher of the great and good once the base Sir William is in charge. These counterexamples show, I think, that though Jane Austen took in the enjoyments of consumer culture during the Regency period, and though she understands the material props of wealth and status with unsurpassed acuteness, finally it is relations rather than things—whether they are commodities or relics—that compel and that carry her moral and artistic allegiance.

So where does this leave "Jane Austen's House?" When pondering the comparison Austen draws between the researches of "the fondest biographer" and "the enthusiasm of [Fanny's] love," we must recollect that *enthusiasm* and *fondness* still carry some of that pejorative weight they did for Austen's favorite moralist in prose, Dr. Johnson, who defined one as "a vain belief of private revelation; a vain confidence of divine favour or communication"—in short, a delusive religious fervor that has always been at the heart of Janeism, after all —and the other as "foolishly tender; injudiciously indulgent." Fanny's enthusiasm and her fondness are never reprobated, but they are not exactly recommended either: we can see, as Fanny cannot, Edmund's dereliction. And we might contrast Fanny's fond kind of loving with that of the more grown-up Anne Elliot, who knows a thing or two about privation, about "loving longest, when existence or when hope is gone" (*P*, 256). Loving longest "when existence or when hope is gone" precisely describes our relation of hopelessly perpetual loss with respect to Austen. It is our sense of loss and deprivation, after all, that prompts us to memorialize her at Jane Austen's House Museum. Yet we never see Anne stanching her pain by recourse to a box of most precious Wentworthian treasures during her many years of grief, we are never told that she fingers (Harriet-like) tokens of his remembrance or reads and rereads his letters. If such things existed beyond the experience Austen represents for Anne Elliot, they have no sway over or attraction to Anne. Through her, I think we see Austen's sense—call it stoical, call it intensely Protestant—that loss and loneliness and absence cannot be overcome or anaesthetized by the equivocal magic of relics, but are to be endured with patience and lucidity.

Does this mean by analogy, then, that the Jane Austen Society—founded first and foremost for the purposes of preservation, with the expressed mission to preserve the cottage at Chawton, along with any "most precious treasures" related to Austen that could be gathered—is a "fond" and thus somehow an un-Austenian project at base? No, but Austen's novels do teach us to consider the costs of treasured things, including proxies of Austen herself. Dorothy Darnell preserved that cast-iron fire grate from the drawing room in Chawton with the same alacrity that Fanny seized the scrap bearing her beloved Edmund's handwriting. It is because we love Jane Austen fondly that we seek to memorialize her by gathering her extant scraps into this collection at the Chawton museum, where they bear witness to her life and worth for us and where they also seem to promise our intimacy with her here, in her own domestic space. Even while the things at Chawton function as souvenirs authenticating and calling up the absent, they also function, as Susan Stewart has put it, to discredit the present, as "either too impersonal, too looming, or too alienating compared to the intimate and direct experience of contact which the souvenir has as its referent."[10] The treasures we contemplate are calculated to create a space of presence and authenticity so that the absent beloved—Jane Austen—lives again before us in a particularly idealized form, while everything between these things and Austen seems to vanish, as if by magic. This amazing legerdemain can be seen in the 1946 notice in the *Times*, which decries the historical present as an "age of destruction and decay" and which presents Chawton Cottage in glowingly utopian terms when it solicits funds for the house at Chawton so that we can "preserve for posterity more than a vestige: a solid monument of Georgian comfort and Georgian elegance."[11] Unless we are under the same spell of nostalgia, we must register the enormous force of idealization at play that could misrecognize this sturdy but decidedly unglamorous building erected in the second half of the seventeenth century (not the Georgian period) as a *monument* to *Georgian comfort* and *elegance*.

I cite this not to expose the author as careless or ignorant, but rather to show how that longing we lovers of Jane Austen invest in this particular, material place—the cottage at Chawton where Austen lived—(much like the longing Fanny invests in her precious things at Mansfield Park) makes this kind of intensely idealized illusion possible. The things that magically make Austen visible to us, albeit in a spectral or attenuated form, also turn on us in a sense by magically making other things invisible as well. Making the world we do not wish to see invisible, in fact, is the precise object for the reporter for the *Times Literary Supplement* who described being in Austen's drawing room for the first time when the Jane Austen House Museum opened in July of 1949: "In that quiet low room, the visitor, forgetful of the stream of traffic on the Portsmouth road outside, can recapture something of the calm atmosphere in which the finest miniature painter in English literature did her work."[12]

The exterior to Chawton itself lays bare the untidiness of its history and (if we are paying any attention) tells us that (no matter what the sign says) it never really was *Jane Austen's house* any more than Fanny Price's East Room is hers. We call it so as a manner of speaking because she lived there from July 1809 until May 1817 on the largesse of her wealthy brother, Edward Austen Knight. Enchanted by Austen's presence in the cottage, we tend to forget what this photograph (fig. 5.4), taken about 1940 of one of the laborer's apartments in the cottage, so dramatically shows: many people—many very poor people—lived in what we now call "Jane Austen's House" at Chawton. Once called Petty Johns and only very recently Chawton Cottage, the place where Austen lived was also home to many. First the home of farmers, during its brief incarnation (1781–87) as The New Inn, it was the site of not one but two murders that took place evidently in drunken rages, and after the second Edward Austen Knight let the cottage to Bailiff Bridger Seward.[13] Cassandra Austen lived at Chawton until her death in 1845, after which time the house was divided into small apartments for laborers. At the outset of the twentieth century, it was more remarkable as a workman's club rather than the home of England's great novelist.[14] It only became "Jane Austen's House" in 1948 when Edward Knight sold the house to Thomas Edward Carpenter for £3,000, an enormous sum during those postwar years, on the condition that the poor folks living there be permitted to stay on so long as they wished or until they found suitable lodging elsewhere. The tenants and Knight alike regarded the Jane Austen Society as a newcomer

Figure 5.4. *Laborer's apartment in the Chawton Cottage (1940). Occupants of "Jane Austen's House" were eventually relocated so that the museum could use the entire building. Courtesy of the Jane Austen Memorial Trust.*

muscling in on an established neighborhood, and Knight wrote Carpenter quite sharply, telling him to back off: "I have been told by all three cottage tenants, that they have been worried by the Jane Austen Society to give up certain rooms, people come and demand to be shown round the house, all rather disturbing for them. They are all good Chawton people and I feel until other accommodation in Chawton can be found for them, it is not right to disturb them under present conditions. . . . I do hope you will not think I am being stupidly stubborn about this, but I am sure that Jane Austen . . . would rather her house be lived in by Chawton people, than have them turned out."[15] Edward Knight conjures Jane Austen to enforce the same principles of social responsibility Elizabeth esteemed in Darcy "as a landlord," and he was probably right about what the real, historical Jane Austen would have preferred. The idealizing nostalgia that now permeates the place and makes "Jane Austen" seem so real obscures the "good Chawton people" who lived there too, people who were relocated so that the museum could open and eventually occupy the entire building.

And finally, if our nostalgia for Austen's presence makes us filter out as unreal or unimportant the history, indeed the very character, of her dwelling, as we stroll through the house now filled with things Austenian (or not, as in the case of "Jane's table," we recall), the power of their charm can hoodwink us into a sense of its plenitude. Deidre Lynch has brilliantly demonstrated the connections among inscriptions of Austen as a domestic, "homely" novelist, the emergence of English literary studies in which the canon would be a sort of home, and a developing notion of "rural England—more specifically, the landscape of the 'Home Counties' (to the exclusion of the Midlands and North England)" as the "site of that all but lost traditional national essence."[16] The project to establish Jane Austen's own home is no coincidental part of this project. As we have seen, however, furnishing that home and thus making it possible to fantasize being at home with Jane Austen was not inevitable and was anything but easy. The fact that the museum proudly displays fragments of wallpaper contemporaneous with Austen still visible beneath the layers of plaster painstakingly peeled away (fig. 5.5) demonstrates how desperate we are for any material shreds that can connect us with her, and we go to these lengths to materialize her—even, as we have seen, to impersonate her—in part because there is so remarkably little of her left. Being "at home with Jane Austen" has led us to wish to share her domestic

Figure 5.5.
*Wallpaper
contemporaneous
with Jane Austen.
This poignant image
show how few shreds
of "Austen" remain.
Courtesy of the Jane
Austen Memorial
Trust.*

space, to fill it with homey things that were hers, and while the fact that such things are very hard to come by might seem to puncture the wish for familiarity we indulge, in fact it underscores the power of that wish, which can subsist on so lean a diet. And so when we wonder why, of all beloved writers, Austen is so haunting, why we continually grapple with her invisibility and resort to magic to evoke her, we must not overlook the obvious, which the things in the house sometimes conceals. So little of Jane Austen has been preserved in large part because she was not rich and appears to have owned so few things in the first place, things that might have substantiated her more fully for the future.

If Jane Austen herself was for Victorians a kind of fetish that magically makes labor and its attendant anxieties and alienations disappear, the Jane Austen House Museum is home to fetishes of a different sort, things that stand for the Jane Austen who is not there and that distract us from the soreness of that absence. When the Jane Austen Society was founded, it sought not only to find extant relics—remnants of Austen that, being touched in some way by her, still bore traces of her real presence—but also to find and preserve still living, local memories of her. One such memory was recorded in the *Jane Austen Society Report* for the years 1943–46, the first report issued since the society's founding in 1940. It comes from Mrs. Luff, a village woman who was over eighty years old in 1942, when she related this story to Dorothy Darnell: "Mrs. Luff's grandmother, Mrs. Eliza Andrews, lived as a child in the cottage on the high road. . . . The family in Mrs. Andrews' cottage used to see Jane Austen walking from the back of her garden across the field to call on Mr. Prowting's family. Mrs. Andrews used to say, 'We called her the poor young lady, and now she's gone.' As Jane Austen cannot have been much under forty at the time, the phrase is an interesting comment on her appearance."[17] Mrs. Andrews's recollection has a bit of the ghost story to it. If we place it alongside Constance Hill's descriptions or Oscar Faye Adams's, we might imagine Jane Austen to be almost transparently traversing the field. This is not how the Jane Austen Society receives the narrative. Somewhat like the *Times* report that calls Chawton Cottage a monument to Georgian elegance, this account is bewildered by the preciousness of Mrs. Luff's memory into misapprehending it in a curiously blinkered way. The report dwells on only one of the two adjectives Mrs. Andrews uses to describe Austen, as though the only remarkable feature of this story was the fact that Jane Austen seemed to be a "young lady" even though she was around forty years old at the time. Is this really a recollection about Austen's preternaturally youthful appearance? Mrs. Andrews says that "we" called Austen "the poor young lady," not "the young lady." The report passes over without comment—indeed, without apparent notice—Mrs. Andrews's allusion to what looked in some sense pitiable about Jane Austen, as if Mrs. Andrews were saying that "Jane Austen is youthful" and not "Jane Austen is unfortunate." Mrs. Andrews—perhaps anyone who saw Austen pass by in the village of Chawton—knew something we do not know: that the sight of Jane Austen inspired not terror at her wit or awe at her accomplishment, of which they were in all probability ignorant, but compassion for some reversal or distress that has since been expunged or simply forgotten. In her 1980 address to the annual meeting of the Jane Austen Society in Chawton, Elizabeth Jenkins further reinvents Mrs. Luff's 1942 recollection of her grandmother's recollection of Jane Austen, walking to the Prowtings', between 1809 and 1817: "They used to see Jane Austen running across the field to call on her friends, the three Misses Prowting. The vision of this light-footed being, with the energy that is inseparable from genius, was preserved for us by Dorothy Darnell . . . but may we not feel that it is also evoked for us by one of Blake's sayings: 'Everything that lives is holy; Life delights in Life.'"[18] Jenkins had, moments earlier in her lecture, referred to the Jane Austen House Museum as "enchanted ground," and the sway of that enchantment is visible in her transformation of the "poor young lady" Mrs. Andrews saw into a fleet-footed genius with vitality and vitalizing power as well as an ecstatically mystical delight in the holiness of life. In this manner, Mrs. Luff's story is a gospel indeed, and the "poor young lady" becomes none other than the Divine Jane.

The entire contents of Chawton Cottage were sold and dispersed without fuss in 1845, after Cassandra's death, and some things were given away earlier. That famous tripod writing desk now *called* Jane's, for example, was so little treasured, so evidently unregarded as personally touched by her, that old Mrs. Austen gave it to her footman, William Littleworth, when he grew too old to work and moved into a nearby cottage that needed some furniture. Jane Austen herself willed "every thing of which I may die possessed, or which may be hereafter due to me" to her sister (excepting £100 in legacies and her own funeral expenses), but the *possessions* (and *most precious treasures* they were) she had in mind were her extant literary productions and the income they had and would in the future produce. With the exception of a few personal effects (items of jewelry and clothing, which Cassandra distributed as keepsakes, along with locks of hair shorn from her sister's head), the diverse and often endeared paraphernalia of daily life that fill the domestic spaces of homes, such as drawers, bookcases, cabinets, and shelves, along with ephemeral instruments of Austen's particular genius, her pens and inks and blotters, for example—all of this, no one appears to have saved for posterity to venerate. Thinking of Fanny's attachments to things, I might ask what wouldn't anyone give for a scrap of paper bearing Austen's handwriting? Wouldn't we, as Fanny does with Edmund's note, cherish it fondly, "independent of anything it may convey" as "a blessedness"? The answer is a resounding "yes." The case of Fanny Price also shows us, however, that the *treasures* we might cherish for their power to conjure Austen's presence can also *bewilder* us into a false sense of the fullness of her being, which, if we are to feel it at all, we will find only in reading her novels.

Afterword
Jane Austen's Ubiquity

My previous chapter explored how a sense of lack and loss animates a particular stage of Janeism, making us long not merely to memorialize her but to recover her by gathering her things. By contrast, today's "Jane Austen" is a bonanza of presence, to all appearances the answer to every Janeite's dream for more and more. She seems to be everywhere, reaching well beyond the English-speaking world. Once considered the most quintessentially English, the most irreducibly local—even parochial—novelist, she is now among the most global, enjoying wide and informed readerships in Korea, Japan, and Argentina, among other places far from Highbury, and as Katie Trumpener has so brilliantly demonstrated, her literary influence is detectable across much of South Asia, in writers as diverse as Vikram Seth, Upamanyu Chatterjee, and Shyam Selvadurai, whether signifying the "colonial cringe" or possibilities for ideological resistance and personal fulfillment.[1] Clearly, "Jane Austen" is more widely pervasive today than ever before as a legendary figure, and membership in her cults shows no sign of abating.

This ubiquity also extends beyond the literary. We encounter her in dazzling movies from Hollywood, Great Britain, and Bollywood, often featuring our favorite stars; in TV adaptations produced with seeming-historical authenticity; and in other cinematic spin-offs and homages. And Jane Austen is always good for a news story or editorial. In newspapers and now on the web, there is always some brouhaha brewing. For better or worse, fans of Trollope or Fielding or Dickens or even Shakespeare and Wordsworth do not find it common to encounter the headlines that we come across so often: the torrent of articles appearing in response to the *London Review of Books'* publication in August of 2003 of "Was Jane Austen Gay?"; the floods of notices, reviews, and interviews about her screen productions from the mid-1990s forward; the flurry over her spelling and punctuation; the steady stream of articles about the cause of her death; the identity of the real Mr. Darcy; the moral weightiness of her work; and, self-reflexively, her celebrity status itself, to which every new item contributes.

If James was revolted by the commercialization of literature and scorned the mass production of *printed* Austeniana, how he would recoil today, when the marketplace is hawking not merely her novels or coffee-table volumes about her world but also "Jane Austen" book bags, paperweights, key chains, and T-shirts sporting versions of Cassandra's portrait. We see her on coffee mugs averring, via Kipling, that there is no one to beat Jane when you are in a tight place; on action figures (where she sports a deadly quill); on bumper stickers announcing, "I'd rather be reading Jane Austen"; and on pseudo-Regency kitsch—note cards, soaps, thimbles, tea strainers, and chocolates. It is both Jane Austen's popularity we notice here and her power to sell—and to sell not merely her novels but also knickknacks—that prove how right James was when he observed that "our dear, everybody's dear Jane" served a very "material purpose" (*CH2*, 30). So well did Hollywood understand the selling power of Austen's name that in 1998, Touchstone Pictures distributed a spoof on mobster movies titled *Jane Austen's Mafia!*—a movie in which she is never mentioned, even indirectly—in part to satirize and in part to capitalize on the slew of movies based on Austen's novels in the mid-90s.[2]

If one of the missions of Janeites, according to Kipling's story at least, is to be fruitful and bring forth more Janeites, disseminating Jane's words far and wide, then Austen's ubiquity today must surely be a triumph for Janeism and as such a perfect way for me to conclude this book. For one thing, the conditions of Austen's current celebrity seem to rescue Austen from the disembodiment that has been a steady theme in this book, which began, after all, with a ghost story, for disembodiment is in fact the precondition of her uncanny ability to haunt. This is probably the single most important reason Austen portraits, while desired on one hand, have also been discomfiting on the other, for that feeling of being haunted by Jane Austen is in fact an immensely satisfying and desirable one. But hauntings are no longer necessary, perhaps no longer even possible, now that Austen is everywhere before us. If George Henry Lewes was right in thinking that Austen was so indifferent to visual description that her characters live "in a purblind world, wherein nobody ever saw anybody" and where we are made to "know" characters rather than "see" them, then it seems that television and movie adaptations have compensated for this singular "defect" in Austen's art by representing the physical world of characters' bodies, miens, and environs implied but rarely depicted in the novels.[3] And there is more: two recent productions (eager no doubt to have more narratives to adapt than the six novels) have audaciously gone on to give us the person of Jane Austen herself.

This very surfeit poses some important questions that seems at once obvious and almost impious to ask: Is there such a thing as having too much Jane Austen? Is there anyone willing to admit to being a little bored with her, a little sick of her? Has Austen's celebrity produced that concomitant of celebrity, exhaustion? Has any Janeite ever wanted to say aloud, "Enough already!"? These are trick questions, of course. The Janeites I have discussed here would never admit to them because their Divine Jane is by definition limitless, and their pleasure is by definition equally so. They might well be bored with themselves and with each other, to be sure, but never with her. If they were bored, that would only prove that they were not really one of the elect to begin with. And that is the trick, for the Janeites discussed here would not regard a screen adaptation, whatever other aesthetic or social pleasures it might provide, whatever other kinds of significance it might bear, as the real thing, which always remains the words of Jane Austen. I think they would also be skeptical about the possibility that screen adaptations, however smart or sublime some may be on their own terms, have to conjure Austen's novels or her body. The object-laden opulence of screen productions, as we have seen in the previous chapter, could just as likely feel like a distraction rather than an enhancement to or a realization of the novels, where inwardness and voice are what we crave. And even granting the fact that screen representations are by most accounts in their very nature spectral, and thus in some sense compatible with the Austenian ghostliness I have traced here, they still, however momentarily, endow "Jane Austen" a visible, local habitation and a name. Casting Austen herself as a character can seem, until the lights turn on, temporarily to demystify Austen at last, to give Austen to us for a while, and thus overcome the problem of her absence. But I find that movies depicting Jane Austen in some ways have merely restated and confirmed the problem of Jane Austen's body by absorbing her into the marriage plot and imagining that plot as the sole resource for passionate satisfaction. "Jane Austen" is in deep body trouble throughout most of *Miss Austen Regrets* (2008), for example—passionate, frustrated, regretting her missed chances for love and compensating for them through make-believe: "The only way to get a man like Mr. Darcy is to make him up," she is made to say, as if "getting" Mr. Darcy had been the motive for creating him, the mainspring of her artistry. *Becoming Jane Austen* (2007) is even grimmer, concluding as it does with a scene of heady sublimation, beneath a domed roof in Bath, where a prim, wizened Jane Austen, having foregone passion, reads the opening of *Pride and Prejudice* to a roomful of listeners who nod sagely, but utterly joylessly, as though she were reading a sermon aloud, and not one of the funniest chapters in the one of the funniest novels ever written. Placing art and passion in opposition, these narratives cannot imagine what is so obvious to the Janeites discussed throughout this book: that *writing* was Jane Austen's passion, not a regrettable substitute for it. In these productions, we may well wonder if Austen has not been evacuated of any specificity at all, beyond an empire-styled gown, which sells movies wondrously.

Despite many similarities, then, Jane Austen's celebrity today is categorically different from the sorts of renown I have traced here in that it is so commonly mediated through screen adaptations. And if this remains the case, Janeism in the future will be a different thing. From the beginning of the twentieth century until around the 1990s or so, when relatively modest television adaptations gave way to the big screen, Janeites shunned the visual in favor of the textual, and the Victorian practice of illustrating the novels fell into disrepute. For one thing, they usurped the prerogatives of our own imaginations as they engaged variously with Austen's prose. In 1916, we might recall, Reginald Farrer described a centenary "Dream Edition" of Austen's novels, insisting first and foremost that it contain "no illustrations of episodes or characters, for everyone who knows and loves them must make his own presentment of their mortal shape, and cannot away with anybody else's."[4] And almost every reviewer of Chapman's 1923 edition of the novels applauded his decision to (as Forster put it) "purge the mind" of such illustrations, on the grounds that they are fatuous in themselves (never again, Forster writes, will readers "tolerate 'illustrations' which illustrate nothing") or on the grounds that they were perniciously distracting and predominating (approving Chapman's decision, Desmond McCarthy wonders "how many of Dickens' fine strokes of portraiture I have missed, owing to pictures of Mr. Dick or Micawber superseding his own descriptions in my memory").[5]

To the extent that Austen is known first and sometimes primarily or solely as a creature of visual culture, then, her modern-day cult is a breakaway sect that has eliminated her fundamental aspects of her mystery rather than reveled in it. Some present-day fans are frankly impatient with the slow pace of the novels but, in support of their professed Janeism, still boast about watching entire cycles of television and movie adaptations of Austen's novels annually, often with their mothers or friends. This practice seems to carry over the older Janeite practice of reading all the novels every year: the same ritual element, the same braggadocio, the same quest for a totality of absorption, and the same drive to share their pleasure. In comparison to Janeite readers, however, their absorption is very easy to come by if you can spare a few hours—pop in a DVD—and something fundamentally game-changing in Austen has been lost in that ease. For even the most elegiac of Janeites I have discussed throughout this book, by contrast, Jane Austen was rare, wonderful, elusive, and difficult. She was invisible in one sense, as we have seen, but she was accessible, albeit in one way alone. Only by reading and rereading her novels could her acolytes begin to fathom her secrets and marvel at her glory. Only then would the Divine Jane return the favor of readerly devotion by gradually unfolding her splendor and bestowing on them the vividness of her companionship through all kinds of ennui, duress, and loss.

Jane Austen is not commonly an author associated with difficulty. She might (or might not) be enjoyed on first readings, but she is understood best only after repeated ones. "I cannot speak well enough to be unintelligible," Catherine Morland says in *Northanger Abbey* when she is baffled by Henry Tilney's archness. Those who believe that Austen is a transparent writer, easy to access, understand that she is siding here with clarity over obscurity and that Henry Tilney's retort—"Bravo! An excellent satire on modern language"—represents her own judgment as well; that her ideal of novelistic art is as reassuringly pellucid as the clear glass panes that General Tilney has installed in the windows of Northanger Abbey itself; and that she banishes stylistic opacity just as surely as she eschews gothic veils and shadows. But rereaders of Jane Austen tread softly, duly recognizing that Austen knows exactly what Catherine Morland does not yet know: how to speak well enough to be unintelligible and accordingly to proceed cautiously through her novels. And these novels turn

often quite severely on characters—and readers who—like Emma, preeminently—stop paying attention because they think they understand
everything perfectly already. When Mr. Weston, flattering Emma's vanity, observes that M and A are the two letters that spell perfection, Mr.
Knightley objects to the weakness of this wit: "*Perfection* should not have
come quite so soon," he complains (*E*, 404). Perfect understanding of and
in Austen's novels never comes quickly and probably never comes at all,
and certainly not easily, and the challenge of teaching her novels today
consists of obliging screen-oriented, plot-hungry readers to slow down
and read. Janeites of yore boasted about reading her novels hundreds
and hundreds of times not because they loved to reiterate their pleasure
but because their pleasures were different and deeper each time. And
claiming a familiarity with "Jane"—the privilege, perhaps, of using her
Christian name—entailed an intimacy with her texts earned slowly, over
a lifetime of rereading.

Hunting for plants high in the Himalayas, Reginald Farrer is reported
to have ordered a servant to scramble "thousands of feet down a Hima-
layan pass to fetch *Northanger Abbey* and when this man, who couldn't
read in any language, struggled back with *Emma*, showed little clem-
ency."[6] This anecdote is surely not a credit to Farrer's temper, but it is an
indication of how intemperately important it was to him to read Austen's
novels, complete sets of which he carried with him on all his expedi-
tions—to China, Korea, Japan, Ceylon, and Burma, to name only a few.
In his tribute to Austen written on the centenary of her death, Farrer
explains how he and all of Austen's "faithful" sustain Austen's vitality,
her immortality. Normally, he writes, "from the first sentence, [Austen]
submerges herself in the single thought of the story's development, with
that wholeheartedness of delight in creation for its own sake which is the
prerogative of the highest genius alone, alone awakening in the reader
an answering rapture of conviction and absorption. Thus it is that, to her
faithful, Jane Austen has become flesh and blood of their mind's inmost
fabric. Who commonly quotes Charlotte Brontë or George Eliot? But every turn and corner of life is illuminated or defined for us in our 'dusty
mortal days' by some sentence of Jane Austen's" (RF, 10–11). According
to Farrer, in the "answering rapture" of Austen's readers we find the best
answer to the problem of her (dis) embodiment and to the question of her
progeny that so interested Kipling's Janeites as well as modern viewers
who imagine that spinsterhood left her without issue. Farrer holds that

Austen is incarnate within us. Constance Hill, as we have seen, wanted to "commune" with Jane Austen by visiting her homes and haunts. The Janeites explored here want, with that communion, a yet closer union, so that Austen is everywhere within them, rather than ubiquitous and visible without. And what Farrer so astonishingly proposes in his sacramental celebration of the "the divine Jane" is that the DNA of Austen via the textuality of her novels becomes absorbed into our own bodies. By reading, rereading, and quoting her, we have transformed her novels into our own "flesh and blood," into our imaginations' "inmost fabric," and eventually, as Farrer says, into "the very texture of humanity's mind" from "generation to generation" (RF, 11). World without end.

Appendix
Austen Family Folk Tales

I n chapter 3 of this book, I mention that Jane Austen's nephews and nieces recollect Austen as a narrator of fairy tales, and though no tales known for sure to be invented or told by Jane Austen survive, three tales known to be told by Edward Austen Knight live on. But as the foregoing shows, these same tales were also told by Francis Austen to his daughter and, in turn, to Francis's grandson, John Hubback, author of *Jane Austen's Sailor Brothers* (1906). Clearly, then, the tales were narrated in Jane Austen's household when she was a child, and if Edward and Francis Austen heard and told the tales, passing them on to their children, it is a pretty sure thing that Austen heard them too.

The following transcriptions of these stories were given to me by the late Henry Rice, who in turn was given them by Marcia Rice (1868–1958). Marcia Rice transcribed them with scrupulous exactitude from versions narrated by her aunt Cam (Caroline Cassandra Rice), who was the granddaughter of Edward Austen Knight.

Marcia Rice printed these tales in a leaflet published by St. Mary and St. Anne School in Abbots Bromley, where she was headmistress from 1900 to 1931. John Hubback in some manner read them, and he wrote Marcia Rice about his recollections of the tales. Clearly, the scattered offspring enjoyed comparing the different versions. I print them here because they contribute in however small a way to our sense of the Austen family culture in Austen's time and after.

Three Dane Court Stories as Told by Grandmama[1]

I

Once upon a time there was an old woodman named Gaffer Clinch. One day he was working in the wood, cutting down trees—chop—chop—chop—chop. At last he knew by the sun it was time to go home, so he picked up his axe, hung his faggot over his shoulder and set off home. Trudge, trudge, trudge, trudge. Suddenly he heard somebody calling out "Gaffer Clinch! Gaffer Clinch!" So he looked around but couldn't see anybody, and went on—Trudge—trudge—trudge—trudge. But[2] he heard again "Gaffer Clinch! Gaffer Clinch!" And looking up he saw a large black cat (sitting in oak tree) and it said: "Tell thy cat when thou goest home that Housey Rousey Barton's bairn's dead."

So he said "Very well Puss so I will."

Then he went on Trudge—trudge—trudge—trudge till he got home.

Then he put his faggot down and came in to have his supper. His wife put a little table by the fire and a (white) cloth on it. Then she plunged her fork into the pot over the fire and [*sic*] out a large piece of bacon. Then she plunged it in again and brought out some green cabbage and put them on the table. Then she got a piece of cheese and put it on the table. Then they sat down to have their supper. While they were having their supper their cat came and rubbed itself against Gaffer Clinch's knee and he gave her a piece of rind of cheese. When she had done it came again "Miaw Miaw Miaw" and he gave her another piece and she took it away and she eat it. Then she came back and begged again "Miaw Miaw." But he said "No, No Puss! You have had quite enough you must not have any more." Then he called her back and said, "Oh Puss. I forgot, I have got a message for you. Housey Rousey Barton's bairn's dead."

[At that the cat stood on her hind legs and said "Then I am the King of the Cats!"] Then she crossed her two front paws in front of her, made a low curtsey to Gaffer Clinch and said: "Goodbye to ye master." Then she made a curtsey to his wife, "Goodbye to ye Dame." She took a brand out of the fire and put it on her tail and ran [flew?] up the chimney, and was never heard of before or since.

II

Once upon a time there were two men ploughing in a field. They went up and down the field from one end to another. When they got to one end they heard a voice saying "I've broken my peel—I've broke my peel."

They looked about and saw no one, and then they heard the voice saying again "I've broke my peel—I've broke my peel—I've broke my peel."

So one of the men said, "Have ye? Leave your peel here, and I'll mend it for you."

Then they went back: plough, plough, plough, plough.

When they got to the end they saw a broken peel lying on the ground and a hammer and nails by it. So the man sat down and mended it. Then they set off again plough—plough—plough—plough, to the other end of the field and then turned their horses and came back to the other end, plough, plough, plough, plough, and when they got to the end they found the peel taken away and in its place a smoking hot plum pudding (and so they sat down and eat it and then set off again—plough—plough—plough—plough).

III

Once upon a time there was a workman at work in the wood chopping down trees—chop—chop—chop—chop. When he heard a voice calling out "Ri-car-do! Ri-car-do! Ri-car-do!" So he looked about and couldn't see anybody when suddenly under a tree close by where he had left his jacket and his dinner he saw a little bundle. He went and looked close at it and he found there was a baby inside wrapped up in a scarlet cloak.

So he picked it up and carried it home. Now he and his wife hadn't got any children, so gave the baby to his wife, and she was delighted with it. But she said "but we have no cradle. I don't know where to put it." Then she said "Oh! I know what I'll do." So she drew out one of the empty drawers from her chest of drawers, made up a comfortable bed, and laid the baby in it.

So they kept the baby, and it grew into a little boy till it was about twelve years old. They were immensely fond of it as if it was their own; but it never could speak.

When it was about twelve years old the man was working in the same part of the wood where he found it, when he heard the same voice calling out, "Ricardo! Ricardo!" He didn't see anybody and when he got back in the evening he said to his wife, "Do you know Dame when I was working today I heard the same voice that I heard when our little boy[3] found calling Ricardo!"

So the little boy who was listening directly he heard [*sic*] that he spoke for the first time and said, "That's my Daddy."

So the next morning the old woman was miserable and cried. She put on him as many of the clothes as she could that he was found in which were very fine. She kissed him and wished him Goodbye and was miserable.

Then he went off with the woodman and he told him to sit down under the tree where he had found him. He was working near and kept looking round to see if the little boy was always right.

He was always there. He was there at dinner time. All the afternoon the man kept looking round. Still he was sitting under the tree. Just before it was time to go home he looked round and the little boy wasn't there.

So he took up his things and walked home. When he came in he said, "So wife! [It is no use.] He has gone [to his Daddy]." So they were very unhappy and miserable and missed him dreadfully.

They heard nothing more of him, but the next year on the same day they were sitting on the evening outside their door when they heard the sound of a pony cantering up the land clackity clackity, clackity, clack, and a little pony stopped at the door and their little boy beautifully dressed jumped off and ran up to them and threw his arms round them.

So he couldn't tell them anything about himself. But he gave them a bag with twenty pounds in it and said, "No, I can't tell you anything about myself, but I shall come again every year and bring you this, but you mustn't ever ask me who I am."

Note from Marcia A. Rice

"These stories were told by Mr. Knight of Godmersham to his children and so handed down word for word to each generation. Aunt Cam dictated them to me in Jan 1922 when she was nearly 87. Where I have put a bracket is where she and I question a word or a phrase. My father always said 'Then I am the King of the Cats.' Aunt Cam exclaimed at this and said 'Grandmama *never* did.' But Father could hardly have invented this, and I think Gaffer Clinch is a very old folk story and that I have seen it in some folk lore book (which certainly Father never read!) with this phrase. Alice at once exclaimed when I read her Aunt Cam's version 'But she has forgotten "Then I am the King of the Cats."' Helen, who was told these stories *(not* Ricardo!) by My Aunt Adi had Aunt Cam's version."

Note from John Hubback[4]

"My mother,[5] a niece of Jane Austen, was very clever with all sorts of stories for her three boys, a faculty which she cultivated diligently; she traced the aptitude to her aunt Cassandra, who spent which time in Portsdown Lodge in her later days, with her brother Sir Frances Austen and his daughter.

"Many of her tales were her own inventions made up as she talked, but others she would say had been told to her in childhood.

"Of the three stories told in the Annual Leaflet of the school, I have a vivid recollection of that as to the finding of a hot plum pudding in the field, which I also believed to be the 'DownField' close by Portsdown Lodge, but I cannot recall anything but 'I've broke my Peel.'

"Of the Gaffer Clinch narrative I remember more, the fact of the woodland and message to the fireside cat for instance, but certainly the climax of the story was the announcement Then I am the King of the Cats with the disappearance up the chimney.

"Of Ricardo, I have the clearest memory as it was a favorite of my mothers. It survives in an album of hers still in my possession though the details of the versified narrative in her handwriting are not quite identical with those in the Leaflet. I do not know whether these verses are her own but possible they were copies from some unknown source. The story is illustrated by her own pen and ink sketches."

Notes

Introduction

1. The "bit (two Inches wide) of Ivory" phrase has become everyone's watchword for Austenian style. Just as striking in this letter, and possibly more accurate, is Austen's metaphor for "twigs" for chapters and "Nest" for novel.

2. Kathryn Sutherland has argued that what we now consider to be Austen's style was actually a creation of William Gifford, the famously scrupulous editor who worked for John Murray, the publisher of the second edition of *Mansfield Park*. Sutherland has most recently made this argument in connection with the online publication of *Jane Austen's Fiction Manuscripts Digital Edition* (see, for example, "Pride, Prejudice and Poor Punctuation," *Guardian*, 23 October 2010, 7), but her superb *Jane Austen's Textual Lives from Aeschylus to Bollywood* (Oxford: Oxford University Press, 2005) makes similar arguments about the way Austen's style has been tamed by editors such as Gifford and R. W. Chapman. While I disagree with most of her conclusions, Sutherland's powerful claim obliges us to think more closely about how editors—and, I would add, typesetters—produce what we have come to expect from an Austenian page.

3. This letter is written just as *Pride and Prejudice* is appearing for the first time, and while Austen acknowledges that a "'said he' or a 'said she' would sometimes make the Dialogue more immediately clear," she resolves not to fret but rather to trust her readership.

4. "Personal Appearance," in *More Talk of Jane Austen*, Sheila Kaye-Smith and G. B. Stern (London: Cassell, 1950), 208–16.

5. Francis Darwin, *Rustic Sounds and Other Studies in Literature and Natural History* (Freeport, NY: Books for Libraries Press, 1969), 66–67, 76–77. Darwin's essay, "Jane Austen," was first published in 1917.

6. Henry Woodd Nevinson, "A Letter from a Ghost" in *Between the Wars* (London: Hutchinson, 1936), 48–49.

7. "Editor's Easy Chair," *Harper's Magazine*, November 1913, 958, 961.

8. Constance Hill, *Jane Austen: Her Homes and Her Friends* (London: John Lane, 1902), 14, 54, 72.

9. Oscar Fay Adams, "In the Footsteps of Jane Austen," *New England Magazine*, n.s., 8 (1893): 598–99.

10. G. B. Stern, *A Name to Conjure With* (New York: Macmillan, 1953), 157.

11. E. M. Forster, review of Chapman's 1923 edition of the novels: "Jane, How Shall We Ever Recollect . . . ," appearing in *Nation and Athenaeum*, 5 January 1924, 512–14, and later reprinted in *Abinger Harvest* (1936).

12. Stern, *A Name to Conjure With*, 157.

13. Deirdre Le Faye, *Jane Austen: A Family Record* (Cambridge: Cambridge

University Press, 1989), 275. For a superb account of Janeite visitors to Winchester, see Brian Southam, "Jane Austen and Winchester Cathedral," *Persuasions* 24 (1 January 2002): 226–40.

14. Montague Summers, "Jane Austen: An Appreciation," *Transactions of the Royal Society of Literature* 36 (1918): 8.

15. Virginia Woolf, "Jane Austen at 60," *Nation*, 10 November 1923, 433–34.

16. "What *Is* It about Jane Austen," in *More Talk of Jane Austen*, 1–2.

17. For a splendid discussion of friendship with Austen and friendship in her novels, see Mary Ann O'Farrell's "Jane Austen's Friendship," in *Janeites: Austen's Disciples and Devotees*, ed. Deidre Lynch (Princeton, NJ: Princeton University Press, 2000), 45–62.

18. Clara Tuite, "Period Rush: Queer Austen, Anachronism and Critical Practice," in *Re-Drawing Austen: Picturesque Travels in Austenland*, ed. Beatrice Battalgia and Diego Saglia (Naples: Liguori, 2004), 305–22.

19. Stephen Greenblatt, "What Is the History of Literature?" *Critical Inquiry* 23 (1997): 479.

20. Lionel Trilling, "*Emma* and the Legend of Jane Austen," first published as the introduction to the Riverside Edition of *Emma* (Boston: Houghton Mifflin, 1957). Reprinted as "*Emma*," *Encounter* (June 1957); also in Trilling, *Beyond Culture* (New York: Viking Press, 1965) as "*Emma* and the Legend of Jane Austen."

21. See my "The Divine Miss Jane: Jane Austen, Janeites, and the Discipline of Novel Studies," *boundary 2* 23, no. 3 (Autumn 1996): 143–63, and "Austen Cults and Cultures" in *The Cambridge Companion to Jane Austen*, ed. Edward Copeland and Juliet McMaster (Cambridge: Cambridge University Press, 1997), 211–26.

22. See especially Deidre Lynch, "At Home with Jane Austen," in *Cultural Institutions of the Novel*, ed. Deidre Lynch and William Warner (Durham, NC: Duke University Press, 1996), 159–92. See comparable efforts in Johnsonian criticism in Kevin Hart's *Samuel Johnson and the Culture of Property* (Cambridge: Cambridge University Press, 1999) and Helen Deutsch's splendid *Loving Dr. Johnson* (Chicago: University of Chicago Press, 2005), which has been particularly inspiring for me.

23. See John Wiltshire, *Recreating Jane Austen* (Cambridge: Cambridge University Press, 2001); Sutherland, *Jane Austen's Textual Lives from Aeschylus to Bollywood*; and Claire Harman, *Jane's Fame: How Jane Austen Conquered the World* (Edinburgh: Canongate Books, 2009).

24. In this respect I followed a time-honored though not universally acknowledged principle of textual editing, *Lectio difficilior potior*, the more difficult reading is the stronger, as did R. W. Chapman in his *Oxford Edition of the Novels of Jane Austen* (Oxford: Clarendon Press, 1923) and John Wiltshire in the now authoritative edition of *Mansfield Park* (Cambridge: Cambridge University Press, 2005), both of whom take the 1816 text as their copy text. Using the 1814 text as the copy text in her 2003 edition of *Mansfield Park* for Penguin, Kathryn

Sutherland, by contrast, places the comma after *civility*. For a discussion of the contrasting editorial principles of Sutherland and myself, see B. C. Southam, *"Mansfield Park*—What Did Jane Austen Really Write: The Texts of 1814 and 1816," in *Re-Drawing Austen*, 247–60.

Chapter One

1. From "The Lady of the Lights" by Lesley Drew in *Winchester Cathedral Record* 68 (1999): 9. I am grateful to Mr. John Hardacre, former curator of the Cathedral Library, for calling this article to my attention.

2. For a full study of the forms taken by the love of Samuel Johnson, see Helen Deutsch's fabulous *Loving Dr. Johnson* (Chicago: University of Chicago Press, 2005).

3. Susan J. Wolfson, *Romantic Interactions, Social Being and the Turns of Literary Actions* (Baltimore: Johns Hopkins University Press, 2010), 212; Lauren Berlant and Michael Warner, "Sex in Public," *Critical Inquiry* 24, no. 2 (Winter 1998): 547–66.

4. For a discussion of Charlotte Smith's management of her image as a wronged mother writing to support her family, see Sarah Zimmerman, "Charlotte Smith's Letters and the Practice of Self-Representation," *Princeton University Library Chronicle* 53 (1991): 50–77, and Jacqueline Labbé, *Charlotte Smith: Romanticism, Poetry and the Culture of Gender* (Manchester, UK: Manchester University Press, 2003). Catherine Gallagher makes something like the opposite argument about the invisibility of women writers, in part on generic grounds, in *Nobody's Story: The Vanishing Acts of Women Writers in the Marketplace, 1670–1820* (Berkeley: University of California Press, 1994), to which I am much indebted.

5. Lewes's unsigned review originally appeared in *Blackwood's Edinburgh Magazine* 86 (July 1859): 99–113.

6. "Literary Women: Jane Austen," *Athenaeum* 200 (27 August 1831): 553.

7. Henry Austen, "Memoir," in *Memoir*, 151. Here Bentley himself inserts a note: "No likeness ever was taken of Miss Austen; which the editor much laments, as he is thereby precluded from the gratification of prefixing her portrait to this edition." In her note on this note, Kathryn Sutherland writes that Bentley here means to say that no likeness was ever taken by a professional artist, but I can see no reason to delimit his meaning in this way.

8. I am much indebted to Susan J. Wolfson's fine chapter on Jewsbury in *Borderlines: The Shiftings of Gender in British Romanticism* (Stanford, CA: Stanford University Press, 2006).

9. Austen's fancied self-description here—particularly the tilted head—bears some resemblance to figure 1.20 below, the watercolor portrait said to be of Jane Austen by James Stanier Clarke. That sketch was taken in 1815, two years after Austen's letter.

10. See David Nokes's review article of Deirdre Le Faye's edition of Austen's *Letters* in *Times Literary Supplement*, 15 September 1995, 14. John Wiltshire

briefly reviews and then thoroughly refutes claims that Jane Austen's characters have no bodies in *Jane Austen and the Body* (Cambridge: Cambridge University Press, 1992).

11. Claire Tomalin reviews theories regarding Austen's cause of death in *Jane Austen: A Life* (London: Viking, 1997), 289–90.

12. For a penetrating discussion of this phrase, see David Nokes, *Jane Austen: A Life* (London: Fourth Estate, 1997), 254–55, 397–404.

13. I am grateful to B. C. Southam's "Jane Austen and Winchester Cathedral," *Persuasions* 24 (2002): 226–40 for observing that seven of the eleven notices refer to Austen's novels: the *Salisbury and Winchester Journal,* the *Hampshire Telegraph and Sussex Chronicle,* the *Kentish Gazette,* the *Courier,* the *Gentleman's Magazine,* the *Monthly Magazine,* and the *New Monthly Magazine.*

14. B. C. Southam spells these connections out in "Jane Austen and Winchester Cathedral," 233–34. Southam suggests that the plan to bury Austen at Winchester evolved gradually and that Austen herself may have known of it. I incline to agree with others that Henry Austen pushed this plan and that Cassandra would have preferred her sister to rest in the churchyard at Chawton.

15. In addition to noting that memorial slabs of a certain size were required in order to ensure the evenness of the floor, the archives at Winchester Cathedral mention that there was a fee charged for burial within the cathedral during the first two decades of the nineteenth century, but do not specify what that fee was. An audience member at a lecture I once delivered assured me that this fee was discovered to have been £18, but none of the research I conducted before or after confirmed this figure, nor has the past curator, John Hardacre, or present archivist, Gill Rushton.

16. Austen left her entire estate to Cassandra, with the exception of two provisions of £50 each, one to Henry Austen and one to Mme Bigeon, the retainer of Eliza and Henry, who had lost money in Henry's bank failure. Once deductions were made for probate, legacy duty, and small debts, Cassandra's legacy amounted to £653.2s, of which a whopping £92 went for funeral expenses, leaving her at last with £561.2s.

17. John Britton, *The History and Antiquities of the See Cathedral Church of Winchester* (London: Longman, Hurst, Rees, Orme, and Brown, 1817), 109.

18. This letter refers to Henry Austen's proud announcement of his sister's authorship of *Pride and Prejudice* to Lady Robert Kerr, who had praised the novel: "A Thing once set going in that way—one knows how it spreads!—and he, dear Creature, has set it going so much more than once. I know that it is all done from Affection and Partiality." Interestingly, this same letter plays with the idea of greater fame: "The Secret has spread so far as to be scarcely the Shadow of a secret now—and I beleive [*sic*] that whenever the 3rd [novel] appears, I shall not even attempt to tell lies about it.—I shall rather try to make all the Money than all the Mystery I can of it.—People shall pay for their Knowledge if I can make them" (*L,* 231).

19. Virginia Woolf, "Jane Austen at Sixty, *Athenaeum,* 15 December 1923, and

New Republic, 30 January 1924; reprint in *CH2*, 301; D. A. Miller, "The Late Jane Austen," *Raritan* 10, no. 1 (1990): 55–79.

20. See John H. Hubback, *Jane Austen's Sailor Brothers* (London: Ballantyne, 1905), 226.

21. Middleton's description is quoted by Deirdre Le Faye's "Recollection of Chawton," *Times Literary Supplement*, 3 May 1985, 495.

22. Anna Lefroy to James Edward Austen-Leigh, 20 July 1879; Cassandra Esten Austen to James Edward Austen-Leigh, 18 December 1869; Elizabeth Rice to James Edward Austen Leigh, January [1870]. R.W. Chapman collected and transcribed this material, which became the basis of his section on Cassandra's sketch in *JAFP*, 212–13.

23. *Winchester Cathedral: Its Monuments and Memorials* (London: Selwyn and Blount, 1919), 11. The text reads:

JANE AUSTEN
known to many by her
writings, endeared to
her family by the
varied charms of her
Character and ennobled
by Christian faith
and piety, was born
at Steventon in the
County of Hants Dec.
XVI MDCCLXXV, and buried
in this Cathedral
July XXIV MDCCCXVII.
"She opened her
mouth with wisdom
and in her tongue is
the law of kindness."
—Prov. XXXI v. XXVI.

24. With characteristic fervor, Oscar Fay Adams (who coordinated contributions from the United States, totaling £65), strongly favored placing the memorial in the Lady's Chapel: "The great seven-light windows in the chapel offer much better opportunities for the stained-glass treatment than do the narrow three-light windows in the nave aisles. Should the east window of the chapel be selected for the Austen memorial, the effect when seen from the retro-choir across the long space intervening, is likely to be especially fine." See *Critic*, n.s., 29 (January–June 1898), 218.

25. "*October 13*. The window over the grave of Jane Austen in the north aisle of the Nave has been filled with stained glass in her memory, designed by Mr. C. E. Kempe." *Winchester Cathedral Chronicle*, 1900, 72.

26. *Winchester Diocesan Chronicle*, May 1901, 71.

27. In all probability Augustine of Canterbury—the English Augustine—not Augustine of Hippo.

28. Evert A. Duyckinck, *Portrait Gallery of Eminent Men and Women of Europe and America* (New York: H. J. Johnson, 1873).

29. Letter from Caroline Manning Austen (Colonel Thomas Austen's second wife) to Morland Rice, September 1884, belonging Rice Family Papers, located at the Kent Record Office in Maidstone, UK. This letter includes an extract from Elizabeth Fitzhugh (1820–96), niece of Colonel Thomas Austen, which cited Cholmeley Austen-Leigh's belief that the portrait represented Jane Austen, but goes on to say that she and her brother contend that the sitter is Jane Campion. This view is considered and dismissed by William Austen-Leigh and Richard Arthur Austen-Leigh in *Jane Austen: Her Life and Letters: A Family Record* (London: J. Murray, 1913).

30. Memorandum of 6 October 1932. This memorandum, along with other correspondence about the Rice Portrait, in the Closed File No. 1 on Jane Austen in the Heinz Archive and Library at the National Portrait Gallery, London.

31. This postscript was omitted from the second edition of the *Memoir*.

32. These descriptions of Austen are quoted from David Cecil, *A Portrait of Jane Austen* (London: Constable, 1978), 67.

33. Caroline Austen, *My Aunt Jane Austen: A Memoir* (Winchester, UK: Jane Austen Society, 1952), 5.

34. Sir Egerton Brydges's description is in *The Autobiography, Times, Opinions, and Contemporaries of Sir Egerton Brydges* (London, 1834), 11, 39–41. Fulwar-William Fowle's description is recorded by Kathleen Tillotson in a letter to *Times Literary Supplement*, September 17, 1934.

35. Margaret Anne Doody and Douglas Murray, *A Portrait of Jane Austen* (privately published, 1995), 14.

36. Arthur Quiller-Couch, "Our Incomparable Jane," *Speaker*, 8 April 1893, 401.

37. The trail of documentary evidence regarding portraits of Austen may not be stone cold. The story of Bentley's attempt to find a frontispiece in 1832 is more complicated than we have assumed, for Henry was not completely unforthcoming. He affirms in a letter of 4 October 1832 that "a sketch of [Austen] had been taken," though when he researched it further he could only find something that did not meet the purpose because "it was merely the figure and attitude—The countenance was concealed by a veil—nor was there any resemblance of features intended—It was a 'Study'" (Henry Austen to Richard Bentley, British Library, add. ms 46611, f 311–12). Almost everyone who has written on this subject has assumed that this "Study" refers to the watercolor Cassandra drew of Jane Austen seated outdoors wearing a large bonnet, her back facing the beholder (see fig. 1.23 below). But Henry's words hardly describe the back of the seated figure here. Henry may be referring to a "study" for the "figure and attitude" represented in the Rice Portrait, for "studies" were customarily taken in preparation of for-

mal portraits, particularly when (as here) the face and the dress were probably painted by different persons working at the same studio. If this is so, his remark may be a tantalizing if fragmentary piece of contemporary documentary evidence as yet unrecovered.

38. Agnes Repplier, "Jane Austen," *Critic* 37 (1900): 514–15.

39. *Times* (London), 27 April 1912.

40. Percy Fitzgerald, *Jane Austen: A Criticism and Appreciation* (London: Jarrold and Sons, 1912), 9–10.

41. Kevin Hart, *Samuel Johnson and the Culture of Property* (Cambridge: Cambridge University Press, 1999), 16.

42. Designed by S. E. Dykes Bower, surveyor of the fabric, the tablet in Westminster Abbey was dedicated 17 December 1967 at the suggestion of Miss P. K. M. Sweeting. See *Collected Reports of the Jane Austen Society, 1966–1976* (Alton, UK: Jane Austen Society, 1999), 30–32.

43. See the Burke Collection, Goucher Library, http://meyerhoff.goucher.edu/library/Web_folder_Jane_Austen_Books/Composition_book_10/phcb10a01.htm.

44. Joan Austen-Leigh, "The Many Faces of Jane Austen," *Hampshire* (February 1978): 43.

45. Ibid.

46. See Richard James Wheeler, *James Stanier Clarke: His Watercolour Portrait of Jane Austen Painted 13th November 1815 in His Friendship Book* (Sevenoaks, Kent, UK: Codex Publications, 1998).

47. *Christies Catalogue: Godmersham Park, Canterbury, Kent, The Property of the Late Mrs. Robert Tritton*, vol. 1, *Objects of Art, Furniture, Porcelain, Pictures, Silver and Linen, 6–9 June 1983* (London: Christie, Manson and Woods, 1983). For a critical review of some of the images discussed here, see Deirdre Le Faye, "Imaginary Portraits of Jane Austen," *Jane Austen Society Report* (2007), 42–52.

48. This watercolor is now in the private collection of descendants of Francis Austen.

Chapter Two

1. James's remarks, originally appearing in "The Lesson of Balzac" (1905) and reprinted in *The House of Fiction*, are included in B. C. Southam's *CH2*, 230.

2. Ibid.

3. For the publication history of Austen's novels, I am vastly indebted to Southam's invaluable introduction to *CH2*, especially 58–70; David Gilson, *A Bibliography of Jane Austen* (Oxford: Clarendon Press, 1982), 211–34; Geoffrey Keynes, *Jane Austen: A Bibliography* (London: Nonesuch Press, 1929); and Jan Fergus's invaluable *Jane Austen: A Literary Life* (Houndmills, UK: Macmillan, 1991).

4. For a discussion of Austen's reputation in the United States during this period, see Southam, *CH2*, 49–58, and Mary Favret's splendid "Free and Happy:

Jane Austen in America," in *Janeites: Austen's Disciples and Devotees,* ed. Deidre Lynch (Princeton, NJ: Princeton University Press, 2000), 166–87.

5. James, "Lesson of Balzac," in *CH2,* 230.

6. For the discovery of the earlier appearance of the term than the one attested to by the *OED,* I am grateful to Lorraine Hanaway's brief but informative "'Janeite' at 100," *Persuasions* 16 (1994): 28–29. Saintsbury's own usage attests to the fact that the zeal for Jane Austen predates his printed reference to it. Although I cannot concur in his tendency to minimize the cultural importance of Janeites and anti-Janeites as an amusing controversy, I am very much indebted to B. C. Southam for having uncovered so much fascinating material in his *Critical Heritage* volumes and in "Janeite/Anti-Janeites," in *A Jane Austen Handbook,* ed. J. David Grey (London: Athelone, 1986), 237–43.

7. See D. A. Miller, "The Late Jane Austen," *Raritan* 10, no. 1 (1990): 55–79.

8. Constance Hill, *Jane Austen: Her Home and Her Friends* (London: John Lane, 1902), v.

9. Ibid., v, viii, 1.

10. Thomas Edward Kebbel, "Jane Austen at Home," *Fortnightly Review* 43 (1885): 270.

11. I am much indebted to Deidre Lynch, "Homes and Haunts: Austen's and Mitford's English Idylls," *PMLA* 115, no. 5 (October 2000): 1103–8; the essays in Nicola Watson, ed., *Literary Tourism and Nineteenth-Century Culture* (Houndmills, UK: Palgrave/Macmillan, 2009); Harald Henrix, ed., *Writers' Houses and the Making of Memory* (New York: Routledge, 2008); and Nicola Watson, *The Literary Tourist: Readers and Places in Romantic and Victorian Britain* (Basingstoke, UK: Palgrave/Macmillan, 2006).

12. See chapter 2 ("Shakespeare Land") in John Taylor, *A Dream of England: Landscape, Photography and the Tourist's Imagination* (Manchester, UK: Manchester University Press, 1994), 64–89.

13. Hill, *Jane Austen,* 8, 10, 10–11.

14. Ibid., 4, 14, 54, 72, 258.

15. Oscar Fay Adams, "In the Footsteps of Jane Austen," *New England Magazine,* n.s., 8 (1893): 594, 597 (italics added).

16. Ibid., 598–99 (first and third quotations), 602 (second and fourth quotations).

17. Walter Stafford [Second Earl of Iddesleigh], "The Legend of St. Jane," *Monthly Review* 7 (1902): 159.

18. Claudia Johnson, "The Divine Miss Jane: Jane Austen, Janeites, and the Discipline of Novel Studies," *boundary* 2, 23, no. 3 (Autumn 1996): 143–63.

19. Meynell's article first appeared (unsigned) in "The Classic Novelist," *Pall Mall Gazette,* 16 February 1894, reprinted in *CH2,* 221–22.

20. I am grateful to Henry Rice for showing me Marsha Rice's typescript of "Three Dane Court Stories as Told by Grandmama," dated 1922. In a note appended to the stories, Rice explains that her grandmother clearly remembered

Edward Austen Knight to have narrated the stories. Marsha Rice published these stories in the 1931 *Annual Leaflet* published at St. Mary's Girls School in Abbot's Bromley, Staffordshire. John Hubback read them there and wrote Rice on 5 May 1931 to tell her that his grandfather narrated almost identically the same stories.

21. *Argosy* 34 (1882): 387, cited in *CH2*, 38; George Saintsbury, preface to *Pride and Prejudice*, reprinted in *CH2*, 218.

22. Oscar Fay Adams, *The Story of Jane Austen's Life* (Chicago: A. C. McClurg, 1891), 120–21; 233

23. Fanny (Knight) Knatchbull wrote this in an undated letter of 23 August 1869, when Austen-Leigh was soliciting recollections for his *Memoir*. Needless to say, Austen-Leigh does not air opinions such as these. Lady Knatchbull's letter was belatedly published in *Cornhill Magazine* 163 (1947–49): 72–73.

24. For a discussion of Victorian treatments of the fairy-bride motif particularly as it pertains to Victorian anxieties about women's rights, see Carole Silver, *Strange and Secret Peoples: Fairies and Victorian Consciousness* (New York: Oxford University Press, 1999), 89–116.

25. Anne Thackeray Ritchie, *A Book of Sibyls* (London: Smith, Elder, 1883), 197–229.

26. G. Barnett Smith, "More Views of Jane Austen," *Gentleman's Magazine* (1885): 26; *Spectator* 64 (March 22, 1890): 403.

27. Francis Darwin, *Rustic Sounds and Other Studies in Literature and Natural History* (Freeport, NY: Books for Libraries Press, 1969), 66–67, 76–77. Darwin's essay "Jane Austen" (first published in 1917) is on pp. 61–77.

28. See C. S. Lewis, "A Note on Jane Austen," *Essays in Criticism* 4 (1954): 359–71; D. W. Harding, "Regulated Hatred: An Aspect of the Work of Jane Austen," *Scrutiny* 8 (1940): 346–47. I shall discuss these essays at greater length in chapter 4 below.

29. Ritchie, from *Book of Sibyls*, 208, reprinted in *CH2*, 164.

30. *Spectator*; E. S. Dallas, *Times* (London), 26 June 1866, 6; *Athenaeum* 2976 (November 8, 1884): 585; "A Glimpse at a British Classic," *Chamber's Journal*, March 5, 1879, 160; *Temple Bar* 64 (1882): 356, 357.

31. Catherine Gallagher and Stephen Greenblatt, *Practicing New Historicism* (Chicago: University of Chicago Press, 2000), 169, 168.

32. Ibid., 170.

33. *Chamber's Journal*, 158.

34. Walter Stafford [Second Earl of Iddesleigh], "A Chat about Jane Austen's Novels," *Nineteenth Century* 47 (1900): 811.

35. Margaret Oliphant, "Miss Austen and Miss Mitford," *Blackwood's* (1870): 294–305, reprinted in *CH1*, 215–25.

36. Thomas Kebbel, "Jane Austen," *Fortnightly Review* (January–June 1870): 190.

37. Sarah Chauncey Woolsey, *Letters of Jane Austen* (Boston: Little, Brown, 1894), iii, iv.

38. Janet Harper, "The Renascence of Jane Austen," *Westminster Review* 153 (1900): 442–44.

39. Smith, "More Views of Jane Austen," 26.

40. *Nation*, 24 February 1870, 124–26. This unsigned review was penned by Goldwin Smith and reprinted in his *Lectures and Essays* (New York: Macmillan, 1881), 311–19.

41. Kebbel, "Jane Austen at Home," 265.

42. See Kebbel's *A History of Toryism: From the Accession of Mr. Pitt to Power in 1783 to the Death of Lord Beaconsfield in 1881* (London: W. H. Allen, 1886).

43. *Nation*, 124. It bears stressing that Goldwin Smith's awareness that Austen writes about ordinary and real things does not essentially contradict his sense of her magic as an artist memorializing a charmed, preindustrial world.

44. Kebbel, "Jane Austen at Home"; Stafford [Lord Iddesleigh], "Chat about Jane Austen's Novels," 819; *Spectator*, 404.

45. Kebbel, "Jane Austen at Home," 262.

46. Review in *Academy* 655 (22 November 1884): 333.

47. Southam is quoting Ruskin's "The Effect of Modern Entertainments on the Mind of Youth" (c. 1867), in The *Works of John Ruskin*, ed. E. T. Cook and Alexander Wedderburn (London: George Allen, 1903–12), 17:xvii, 468.

48. *St. Paul's Magazine*, 632; Andrew Lang, *Letters to Dead Authors* (New York: Scribner's, 1886), 82–83; *Temple Bar* 64 (1882): 355.

49. Anna Thackeray's famous rhapsody on Jane Austen was originally published as "Jane Austen," *Cornhill Magazine* 34 (1871): 158–74, and later became a part of her *Book of Sibyls* (cited and discussed in Brian Southam's *CH2*, 22–26). Although Southam is far more dismissive of "twaddle" than I am, his account of Anne Thackeray Ritchie acknowledges that Ritchie is a sensitive reader of Austen.

50. Oscar Wilde, "Four Letters from Reading Prison," Letter 4, in *De Profundis* (London: Methuen, 1908), 21.

51. Woolsey, *Letters of Jane Austen*, v.

52. Ibid., iii.

53. *Athenaeum* 2202 (1870): 54.

54. Rowland Grey, "The Bores of Jane Austen," *Fortnightly Review* 70 (1901): 38, 39; Darwin, *Rustic Sounds*, 65–66.

55. Stafford [Lord Iddesleigh], "Chat about Jane Austen's Novels," 811.

56. Ibid., 820.

Chapter Three

1. Harrison's letter to Thomas Hardy is dated 10 November 1913 and is quoted in *CH2*, 87–88.

2. *Choice of Books* (1900), *Memories and Thoughts* (1906), and *Studies in Early Victorian Literature* (1895). In attempting to level the pretentious term "escritoire" against Austen, Harrison has, of course, been cut off at the pass by

Jane Austen herself in *Love and Freindship*: Laura writes, "They had been married but a few months when our visit to them commenced during which time they had been amply supported by a considerable Sum of Money which Augustus had gracefully purloined from his Unworthy Father's Escritoire, a few days before his union with Sophia" (*J*, 116).

3. Leo Bersani, *A Future for Astyanax: Character and Desire in Literature* (Boston: Little, Brown, 1977).

4. D. W. Harding, "Regulated Hatred: An Aspect of the Work of Jane Austen," in *Regulated Hatred and Other Essays on Jane Austen*, ed. Monica Lawlor (London: Athlone, 1998).

5. Virginia Woolf, *Mrs. Dalloway* (New York: Harcourt, Brace and World, 1953), 283. For an exceptionally fine account of literature about living in wartime, see Mary Favret, *War at a Distance: Romanticism and the Making of Modern Wartime* (Princeton, NJ: Princeton University Press, 2009).

6. Arthur Quiller-Couch, "Patriotism in English Literature 2," in *Studies in Literature* (New York: G. P. Putnam's Sons; Cambridge: Cambridge University Press, 1918), 289–305.

7. Arthur Quiller-Couch, "Patriotism in English Literature 1," in *Studies in Literature* (New York: G. P. Putnam's Sons; Cambridge: Cambridge University Press, 1918), 288.

8. My discussion here has been much influenced by Alun Howkins's "The Discovery of Rural England" in *Englishness: Politics and Culture, 1880–1920*, ed. Robert Colls and Philip Dodd (London: Croom Helm, 1986), 62–88.

9. Declan Kiberd, "Romantic Ireland," *Times Literary Supplement*, 31 July 1998, 25. This article reviews Richard English's *Ernie O'Malley: IRA Intellectual* (Oxford: Clarendon Press, 1998). I am very grateful to Jonathan Arac for calling this fascinating material to my attention.

10. Hugh Walpole, *Reading: An Essay* (New York: Harper and Brothers, 1927), 78–79. He had singled out Victorians such as Tennyson, Carlyle, and Eliot.

11. Virginia Woolf, "Jane Austen," in *Common Reader: First Series* (New York: Harcourt, 1925; Port Washington, PA: Harvest Books, 1984), 137. Citation refers to the Harvest edition.

12. In *Bookman* 59 (December 1920): 24.

13. Katherine Mansfield, review originally in *Athenaeum*, 3 December 1920, reprinted in *Novels and Novelists*, ed. J. Middleton Murray (New York: Knopf, 1930), 314.

14. For a still authoritative study of World War I, in which war's tedium figures as prominently as war's clamor, see Paul Fussell, *The Great War and Modern Memory* (Oxford: Oxford University Press, 1975).

15. George Sampson, "Jane Austen," *Bookman*, 65, no. 388 (January 1924): 191, 193. Fitzgerald's report about Cowell is cited in B. C. Southam, *CH2*, 9. David Gilson, *A Bibliography of Jane Austen: New Introduction and Corrections by the*

Author (Winchester, UK: St. Paul's Bibliographies; New Castle, DE: Oak Knoll Press, 1997), 296–300.

16. See Kathryn Sutherland, *Jane Austen's Textual Lives: From Aeschylus to Bollywood* (Oxford: Oxford University Press, 2005), 43–44. Although our readings are certainly compatible, our emphases are very different.

17. R. W. Chapman, *Jane Austen: A Critical Bibliography* (Oxford: Clarendon Press, 1955), 6.

18. Reginald Farrer, "A Jane Austen Celebration," *Times Literary Supplement*, 7 January 1916, 9.

19. Ibid.

20. *The Novels of Jane Austen: The Text Based on Collation of the Early Editions*, ed. R. W. Chapman (Oxford: Clarendon Press, 1923), 1:389.

21. Ibid.

22. *Sense and Sensibility*, in *Novels of Jane Austen*, 1:xii.

23. Sutherland, *Jane Austen's Textual Lives*, 36.

24. *Emma*, in *Novels of Jane Austen*, 4:491.

25. Sutherland, *Jane Austen's Textual Lives*, 46.

26. See my "Divine Miss Jane: Jane Austen, Janeites, and the Discipline of Novel Studies," *boundary 2* 23, no. 3 (Autumn 1996): 143–63.

27. A. B. Walkley, *Edinburgh Review*, 32. This rewords his essay "Jane Austen" in *Nineteenth Century and After* 91, pt. 2 (1922): 634–47.

28. Desmond MacCarthy, *New Statesman*, 10 November 1923, 145.

29. Virginia Woolf, "Jane Austen at 60," *Nation*, 15 December 1923, 433.

30. Caroline Spurgeon, "Jane Austen," in *Essays by Divers Hands: Being the Transactions of the Royal Society of Literature of the United Kingdom* (London: Oxford University Press, 1927), 7:81.

31. Benedict Anderson, *Imagined Communities*, rev. ed. (London: Verso, 1991), 6.

32. Stanley Baldwin, introduction to *English Humour*, by J. B. Priestley, in English Heritage Series, ed. Viscount Lee of Fareham and J. C. Squire (London: Longmans, Green, 1929), vi.

Chapter Four

1. Reproduced in the *Baltimore Evening Sun*, 31 October 1940, under the heading "A London Diary," with a credit to the *London New Statesman and Nation*.

2. Reported in the *New York Times Book Review*, 20 April 1941. This article is part of the Alberta Herschiser Burke Collection at Goucher College in Baltimore and can be found online. See http://meyerhoff.goucher.edu/library/Web _folder_Jane_Austen_Books/Composition_book_1/cb1ja18.htm.

3. *New York Times Book Review*, 28 May 1939.

4. See Mary Favret, *War at a Distance: Romanticism and the Making of Modern Wartime* (Princeton, NJ: Princeton University Press, 2010), 46–47.

5. *Baltimore Sunday Sun*, 2 August 1942, http://meyerhoff.goucher.edu/library/Web_folder_Jane_Austen_Books/Composition_book_1/cb1ja28.htm. The *New York Times Book Review*, 27 June 1941, includes this report from London by Herbert Horwill about the increased sales of *Pride and Prejudice*, and the *Baltimore Sun*, 2 April 1947, has the story about reprinting demands after the war. See http://meyerhoff.goucher.edu/library/Web_folder_Jane_Austen_Books/Composition_book_3/cb3ja28.htm.

6. Laura M. Ragg, "Jane Austen and the War of Her Time," *Contemporary Review* 158 (1940): 546–47.

7. Ibid., 548.

8. Ibid., 546.

9. Beatrice Kean Seymour, *Jane Austen: Study for a Portrait* (London: Michael Joseph, 1937), 246–48.

10. In *Time and Tide*, quoted in *New York Times Book Review*, 28 May 1939, Burke Collection, http://meyerhoff.goucher.edu/library/Web_folder_Jane_Austen_Books/Composition_book_1/cb1ja16.htm.

11. London Paper (*Times*), April 1943, part of the Burke Collection, http://www.goucher.edu/documents/Library/MS0020BurkeResearchCollection.pdf.

12. *Pickering and Chatto [Sale] Catalogue #325* (1940), 64, Burke Collection, http://www.goucher.edu/documents/Library/MS0020BurkeResearch Collection.pdf.

13. C. A. Lejeune, "Pride and Prejudice," *London Observer*, 3 November 1940, Burke Collection, http://meyerhoff.goucher.edu/library/Web_folder_Jane_Austen_Books/Composition_book_2/ppcb2a58.htm.

14. Kenneth Turan, "*Pride and Prejudice*: An Informal History of the Garson-Olivier Motion Picture," *Persuasions* 11 (1989): 140–43. This letter is dated 10 February 1941 and is written by a woman named Betty Howard.

15. Dianne F. Sadoff, *Victorian Vogue: British Novels on Screen* (Minneapolis: University of Minnesota Press, 2010), 27; Ellen Belton, "Reimagining Jane Austen: The 1940 and 1995 Film Versions of *Pride and Prejudice*," in *Jane Austen on Screen*, ed. Gina Macdonald and Andrew F. Macdonald (Cambridge: Cambridge University Press, 2003), 186.

16. Susan A Brewer, *To Win the Peace: British Propaganda in the United States during World War II* (Ithaca, NY: Cornell University Press, 1997), esp. chap. 89 ("The Story of Comrade in Arms"); and Nicholas John Cull, *Selling War: The British Propaganda Campaign against American "Neutrality" in World War II* (New York: Oxford University Press, 1995).

17. Gordon Hutner, *What America Read: Taste, Class, and the Novel* (Chapel Hill: University of North Carolina Press, 2009), 15.

18. Henry Seidel Canby, *Saturday Review*, 5 December 1942, 26.

19. Nial Rothnie, *The Baedeker Blitz: Hitler's Attack on Britain's Historic Cities* (Shepperton, UK: Ian Allen, 1992), 141. For comparison purposes: Canterbury was bombed on three different nights, but reportedly suffered forty-nine

deaths, one by accident. Exeter was raided on four nights, but two of those raids are described as "minor" or as "nuisance," and 246 deaths are recorded. What seems to set Bath apart is the fact that it was bombed three times as heavily on the first night and with high explosives. Bombing the second night was also heavy, though more incendiaries rather than explosives were used.

20. John Taylor, *A Dream of England: Landscape, Photography, and the Tourist's Imagination* (Manchester, UK: Manchester University Press, 1994), 195–97. I am particularly indebted to Taylor's book.

21. R. A. L. Smith, *Bath* (London: B. T. Batsford, 1944), vi.

22. In *The Book of Bath* (Bath, UK: Ballantyne Press, 1925), edited by F. G. Thomson, George Saintsbury comes out as a "devotee" of "Jane" and singles out scenes in *Northanger Abbey* and *Persuasion* as contributions to the "great literature" of Bath in his chapter "Bath in Literature," and Christopher Hussey's chapter titled "Bath and the Eighteenth-Century" features Austen along with discussions of gaming, assembly rooms, manners, etiquette, and literary figures.

23. Smith, *Bath*, 110.

24. Ibid., 10.

25. Ibid., 112–13.

26. Taylor, *Dream of England*, 112, 124.

27. Elizabeth Jenkins, *Jane Austen: A Biography* (London: Victor Gollancz, 1938), 5. For a splendid discussion of Austen's function in defining domestic national literature during this period, see Deidre Lynch, "At Home with Jane Austen," in *Cultural Institutions of the Novel*, ed. Deidre Lynch and William Warner (Durham, NC: Duke University Press, 1996), 159–92, to which I am much indebted.

28. *The English Association Handbook of Societies and Collections,* ed. Alicia C. Percival (London: Library Association, 1977), 5.

29. Frederick Pollack, *Jane Austen Centenary Memorial* (London: Jane Loan Co., 1917), 13. In 1917 a similar centenary memorial to Jane Austen was erected in Southampton, but it has been lost. Though that city now has a Jane Austen trail, featuring many plaques, the city has not in general been associated with Austen despite her residence there, so it is not surprising that the 1917 memorial went unregarded and has now dropped out of view.

30. Ibid., 11.

31. Elizabeth Jenkins, introduction to *Jane Austen Society: Collected Reports, 1949–1965* (London: William Dawson and Sons, 1967), ix, 43. In one place, Jenkins says the grate was in a heap of scrap metal at the local forge; in another, she says that it was in a heap of nettles.

32. *Guardian,* 19 July 1952, 30.

33. Private letter, dated 17 July 1940, from Hugh Curtis [F.S.A.] to Gwen Rice, given to me by Henry Rice.

34. *An Appeal for Jane Austen's House at Chawton New Alton, Hampshire* (1946), published by the Jane Austen Society. Copy in possession of the author.

35. *Times* (London), 7 December 1946.

36. Printed in the *Baltimore Sun* (Thursday, 21 July 1949), 17, and carefully transcribed and typed by Alberta Hirsheimer Burke and placed in her notebook of cuttings.

37. T. Edward Carpenter, *The Story of Jane Austen's Chawton Home* (Chawton, UK: Jane Austen Memorial Trust, 1976).

38. David Cecil, *Jane Austen* (Cambridge: Cambridge University Press, 1935), 6. Note that Cecil does not regard other lovers of Austen as the problem, but rather those readers who do not like her. Although Cecil regarded Austen as a good-tempered writer rather than a good hater, he himself appears to have absorbed some of Harding's claims, as in the following passage from *The Fine Art of Reading* (London: Constable, 1957): "Even more entertaining than any single character . . . is the manner of the telling, that characteristic Austenian irony, so exquisite, so good-tempered, so ruthless. . . . No aspect of the story, however solemn, is protected from it. We find it pressed beneath each page like some delicious *astringent* herb and the whole book is sharp with its scent" (155, emphasis added).

39. Eric Linklater, *The Impregnable Women* (London: J. Cape, 1938), 190, 201.

40. Ibid., 170.

41. Beatrice Kean Seymour, *Jane Austen: Study for a Portrait* (London: Michael Joseph, 1937), 255.

42. In his preface to *The Impulse to Dominate* (London: Allen and Unwin, 1941), Harding notes that he finished this book in 1940 but that the war delayed its publication by a year.

43. Wendy Anne Lee, "Resituating 'Regulated Hatred': D. W. Harding's Jane Austen," *ELH* 77 (2010): 1001.

44. Harding, *Impulse to Dominate*, 208.

45. Lee, "Resituating 'Regulated Hatred,'" 1001.

46. From Harding's unpublished draft of *Regulated Hatred*, 28, quoted in Lee, "Resituating 'Regulated Hatred,'" 1012n5.

47. Lee, "Resituating 'Regulated Hatred,'" 1002.

48. Marvin Mudrick, *Jane Austen: Irony as Defense and Discovery* (Princeton, NJ: Princeton University Press, 1952), 194, 3; C. S. Lewis, "A Note on Jane Austen," originally published in *Essays in Criticism* 4 (1954): 359–71.

49. See Lee, "Resituating 'Regulated Hatred,'" 1012n5.

50. *Selected Letters of William Empson*, ed. John Haffenden (Oxford: Oxford University Press, 2006), 123. I am grateful to Susan J. Wolfson for calling this letter to my attention.

51. R. W. Chapman, *Jane Austen: A Critical Bibliography*, 2nd ed. (Oxford: Clarendon Press, 1955), 52, entry no. 162. Brower's essay was revised and published under the chapter title "Light and Bright and Sparkling: Irony and Fiction in *Pride and Prejudice*," in *The Fields of Light: An Experiment in Critical Reading* (New York: Oxford University Press, 1951), 164–81.

52. *New York Herald Tribune*, 15 September 1946.

53. Ibid., 7 April 1949 and 17 April 1949.

54. *Vogue*, 1 March 1955.

55. See Claudia Johnson, "The Divine Miss Jane: Jane Austen, Janeites, and the Discipline of Novel Studies," *boundary 2* 23, no. 3 (Autumn 1996): 156; *New York Herald Tribune Book Review*, 21 July 1957, 4.

56. Elizabeth Jenkins, "A Marxist and Jane," *Manchester Guardian*, 22 October 1952, 4.

57. For a splendid account of this controversy, see Fiona Brideoake's essay "Sexuality" in *A Companion to Jane Austen*, ed. Claudia L. Johnson and Clara Tuite (Chichester, UK: Wiley-Blackwell, 2009), 456–66.

58. Winston Churchill, *Closing the Ring*, vol. 5 of *The Second World War* (Boston: Houghton Mifflin, 1951), 377.

59. For a discussion of Jane Austen and healing, see D. A. Miller's "The Late Jane Austen," *Raritan* 10, no. 1 (1990): 55–79.

Chapter Five

1. Private letter from Henry Burke to Charles Ryskamp, then director of the Pierpont Morgan Library, dated 1 July 1975. Henry Burke gave their collection of Jane Austen's letters to the Pierpont Morgan Library in New York.

2. "Jane Austen Relics," *Dispatch* (London), 24 July 1949; "Jane Austen's Locks Return," *Express* (London), 24 July 1949; "Relics for Jane Austen Museum," *Times* (London), 24 July 1949.

3. Elizabeth Jenkins, introduction to *Jane Austen Society: Collected Reports, 1949–1965* (London: William Dawson and Sons, 1967), ix, 43.

4. In a letter from Ruth Koch to Mr. and Mrs. T. Edward Carpenter, dated 24 March 1948. This letter is in the archives at the Jane Austen House Museum in Chawton.

5. *Jane Austen Society: Collected Reports, 1949–1965* (Chippenham, UK: Anthony Rowe, 1967), 173. This is from the report for 1960.

6. Ibid.

7. W. H. Auden, "Letter to Lord Byron," in *Letters from Iceland* (New York: Random House, 1937), reprinted in *CH2*, 299.

8. Lewis Hyde, *The Gift: Imagination and the Erotic Life of Property* (New York: Vintage, 1983), 56.

9. Marcel Mauss, *The Gift: Forms and Functions of Exchange in Archaic Societies* (London: Routledge, 1990), 31. See also p. xv.

10. Susan Stewart, *On Longing: Narratives of the Miniature, the Gigantic, the Souvenir, the Collection* (Durham, NC: Duke University Press, 1993), 139.

11. *Times* (London), 7 December 1946.

12. "Jane Austen and Chawton," *Times Literary Supplement*, 29 July 1949, 489.

13. See David Nokes, *Jane Austen: A Life* (London: Fourth Estate, 1997), 358–59.

14. See Gordon Home, *What to See in England: A Guide to Places of Historic Interest, Natural Beauty, or Literary Association* (London: Adam and Charles Black, 1908). For a history of Chawton Cottage, see Robin Vick, "Jane Austen's House at Chawton," *Jane Austen Society: Collected Reports, 1968–1995* (Alton, Hampshire, UK: Jane Austen Society, 1995), 388–91.

15. Letter 407, from Edward Knight to T. Edward Carpenter, dated 20 January 1949, in the archive of the Jane Austen House Museum.

16. Deidre Lynch, "At Home with Jane Austen," in *Cultural Institutions of the Novel*, ed. Deidre Lynch and William B. Warner (Durham, NC: Duke University Press, 1996), 160.

17. *The Jane Austen Society Report for the Period December, 1943–October, 1946* (n.p., n.d.), 5, in Jane Austen Collection, Goucher College, Baltimore.

18. Elizabeth Jenkins, "Address to Annual Meeting of the Jane Austen Society" (1980), in *Jane Austen Society: Collected Reports, 1976–1985* (Chippenham, UK: Anthony Rowe, 1989), 168.

Afterword

1. Katie Trumpener, "Jane Austen in the World: New Women, Imperial Vistas," *Blackwell Companion to Jane Austen*, ed. Claudia L. Johnson and Clara Tuite (Chichester, UK: Wiley-Blackwell, 2009), 444–55.

2. This movie was also distributed under the title *Mafia!* I have considered the possibility that *Jane Austen's Mafia!* is not merely joking about Austen popularity on film but also truly taking a lesson from her parodic impulses, spoofing Mafia films as she spoofed gothic and sentimental fiction. It was a nice thought, but probably too generous.

3. George Henry Lewes, *Blackwood's Edinburgh Magazine* 86 (July 1859): 106.

4. Reginald Farrer, "A Jane Austen Celebration," *Times Literary Supplement*, 6 January 1916, 9.

5. E. M. Forster, "Jane How Shall We Ever Recollect, *New Republic* 37 (30 January 1924): 478; Desmond McCarthy ("Affable Hawk"), *New Statesman* 22 (10 November 1923): 145.

6. Nicola Shulman, *Rage for Rock Gardening: The Story of Reginald Farrer: Gardener, Writer, and Plant Collector* (Boston: David Godine, 2004), 102.

Appendix

1. Grandmama would have been Elizabeth Knight, Edward Austen Knight's wife.

2. May read *And* instead.

3. The word *is* missing here.

4. Note from John Hubback as transcribed by Marsha Rice, 5 May 1931.

5. Caroline Austen, the daughter of Jane Austen's brother Francis.

Index